GLC - THE INSIDE STORY

WES WHITEHOUSE

GLC - The Inside Story

JAMES LESTER PUBLISHERS

Published by
James Lester Publishers
Almond House
Saxonbury Avenue
Sunbury-on-Thames
Middlesex TW16 5HA

ISBN
0-9538171-3-X

Typeset in Times by
James Lester Publishers
Sunbury-on-Thames, Middx
Printed and bound in Great Britain

Artwork by Peter W. Edmonds, E.A.C.
new headquarters
of the Greater London Assembly
courtesy of Richard Davies

ESME

For her understanding
-and her smile

MY THANKS...

Many people helped in the compilation of this book.
I would like to offer my special thanks to
Jack Barker, Norman Barnes, David Bayliss OBE, Bernard Bligh
Mick Brown JP, Brian Buckle, Delia Buckle, Charles Corcoran
Beryl Evans, Dick Fedorcio, Sir Alan Greengross, Tony Hosier
Norman Howard, John Howes, Maurice Hudson, Henri Jaume
Doreen King, Mike King, Geoff Lewis, Mary MacKenzie
Malcolm Mitchell, Maurice Stonefrost, Sir James Swaffield
Len Vigars, Ivor Watkins
the library staff at the London Archives, Clerkenwell
staff at the Government Office for London
and particularly to Mary Matthews who read the proofs with her
customary diligence and corrected my errors.

GLC - The Inside Story

1. ANOTHER ERA, ANOTHER VOICE

Farce. Chaos. Shambles. It's difficult to find a word which adequately describes the astonishing mess the two main political parties got themselves into when choosing their candidates for Mayor of London. The whole sorry process, deeply insulting to the capital's voters, forces an observer to question whether the government still considers the new office of mayor to be the useful, high-prestige appointment it originally foresaw. Or has Tony Blair's enthusiasm cooled on consideration that the incumbent could become a thorn in his side like that which aggravated the Tories and Margaret Thatcher when London last had a strongman?

As every good politician should know, it is often more important to be first than best.

For the mayoral race, it seemed at one time that Londoners voting for candidates of the two main parties would be asked to choose a candidate who had virtually selected himself. Labour's Ken Livingstone and the Conservatives' Jeffrey Archer had thrown their hats in the ring early and were campaigning vigorously for 18 months before their parties deigned to consider a nomination seriously. By that time both candidates were firmly entrenched.

A return to local democracy for London and the election of the country's first all-powerful, American-type mayor was news. It was predictable that the media would wish to examine it and discuss its implications, and include the views of contenders. With just two nominations to choose from - two men of boundless energy, imagination and charisma - these individuals were certain to get all the media exposure until the lumbering party machines and been kick-started into action. By that time it was too late. So far as the ordinary voter was concerned, they already knew who the candidates were.

It was no surprise, therefore, that Jeffrey Archer won the Conservative nomination by a mile, and Tony Blair was saddled with a candidate he did not want and whom he tried quite shamelessly to stitch-up thereafter. Only the Liberal Democrats came out of the nomination stages with any credit and even they were late in the field and with the little-known Susan Kramer.

As it transpired, Jeffrey Archer had one too many skeletons in the cupboard and stood down. But the Conservatives' ultimate choice, Steven Norris, was so far behind Archer in the first ballot that he was removed from the list for the re-run, only to be reinstated because his was the only well-known name among the Tory hopefuls.

Whatever Tony Blair's original intention of how Labour's vote should be organised, it was certain that his ultimate choice of the electoral college system would give Ken Livingstone the least chance of success. Especially since the electoral college system for MPs, in which one of their votes is worth one thousand of the party's ordinary mortals, is not a secret ballot; Members vote with the PM looking over their shoulder. In that situation, it would take a brave MP to vote against the Prime Minister's choice. Clearly Tony Blair thinks London's mayor should be appointed by him, not chosen by the electorate.

An early public opinion poll predicted that Livingstone would walk it if he were the Labour nominee, and would win by an even greater margin if he stood as an independent. If Labour were to stop him, clearly an election on the democratic basis of one person one vote was a non-starter.

Frank Dobson, Tony Blair's favoured son, publicly stated that the 'dirty tricks' aimed at stopping Ken Livingstone had done him (Dobson) no favours.

He's probably right. Britain traditionally favours the underdog. A candidate thought to have been given a raw deal is likely to get a sympathy vote. Ken Livingstone knows all about that. He has been the nation's folk hero before in a not dissimilar situation.

Ken Livingstone paddles his own canoe and cannot be relied on to toe the party line. Eighteen months ago he took out a large advert in *The Guardian* to stress that, if elected, he would work with the government and not against it. Clearly the Labour hierarchy was not convinced.

They wanted a pedigree lapdog not an independently-minded mongrel. They insisted that their nominee should toe the party line and abide by its manifesto - which negates the whole purpose of a direct election in which electors are reckoned to vote for the individual, not the party.

One of the main issues in Labour's final selection of its candidate was whether or not that candidate would agree to a particular system of funding the Underground. Leaving aside the merits of how the money should be raised, it is illuminating that the Prime Minister considered this the key question in picking the mayor. It is important, though only a side issue. It speaks volumes for the way in which the role is perceived, if how to fund the Underground is seen to be absolutely crucial to being acceptable as the person to run London.

It is the mayor's task to speak up for London. Voters expect him to fight London's corner. He's not concerned with the rest of the country. A strategic authority for London means what it says, whether it be the new Greater London Assembly system of mayor and assembly, or the old Greater London Council set-up of leader and council.

With a London-wide assembly and a high profile mayor, the new strategic authority seems destined to tread the road of its predecessor, the GLC. Indeed, representatives of some Tory boroughs see little difference and are already labelling it 'GLC Mark 2.' Comparisons with its predecessor become increasingly relevant if the new body is to avoid the mistakes of the past. Now, as then, the key to success is money. How much will be made available to the mayor and will he be given tax-raising powers? These decisions seem certain to be varied in the light of experience - even, dare one suggest, in the light of who wins the ballot. As London prepares for this new strategic body, it is interesting to look back at its predecessor and ask: What went wrong last time?

In the wide-ranging preliminary debate on what London needs to meet the challenges of the 21st century, no exciting, imaginative proposals have yet emerged. Little has been done - and nothing could be done on a London-wide scale - in the 14 years since the GLC was shut down, and the problems which beset the capital during the GLC's reign persist to this day, more acute than ever.

In many cases the possible solutions now being urged were either tried and abandoned by the GLC, or were examined by it and found wanting. Maybe the climate has changed with the passing years and now is the time to re-evaluate ideas once discarded as unacceptable. Perhaps some of the solutions tried and rejected yesterday will prove right for today.

In so many cases the necessary groundwork has already been done. The mayor and assembly are lucky to inherit a vast store of data, of tests and experiments, of studies and pilot schemes. Name it, the GLC probably tried it. Somewhere in the archives are all the facts relating to so many of the problems the mayor will face - the fallacies of perceptions, the successes and failures, a priceless cornucopia of ideas.

So how was it that the Greater London Council became such a thorn in the side of the Government that Margaret Thatcher's Conservative administration finally abolished it on April Fools' Day 1986? On the other hand, how did the last GLC, whose administration was ridiculed as being of the 'Loony Left,' finally become so popular that many of the most prestigious and traditional institutions in the land ended up urging its retention? And why did its leader, Ken Livingstone, of whom the *Sun* newspaper once asked: 'Is he the most odious man in Britain?' end his days in charge on a tidal wave of popularity and with a massive cult following?

Was the old council abolished simply out of political spite? Or was it a total failure which had outlived any possible usefulness? If it was a failure, did it fail because it lacked the powers to succeed? If that were the case, it is imperative that the new mayor and London Assembly do not find their hands similarly tied. Whatever the reason for the GLC's demise, its departure left a strategic vacuum which is now being filled.

It is illuminating to discover what happened last time with regard to that most pressing of all London's problems - traffic congestion.

Today, many voices are raised in support of free public transport as being the solution to both congestion and pollution. Free public transport was the dream of two GLC administrations and was council policy for London as far back as 1973. The principal stumbling-block then, one which persists to this day, was: Who shall pay for it? The sums are astronomical. Free travel for senior citizens alone now costs more than £100 million a year. Such highly desirable public transport improvements as a tunnel to link the capital's principal surface rail termini, has been costed at £300,000 a metre!

London-wide free travel, based on evidence from cheap fares policies pursued by two GLC administrations, would make a colossal difference to road congestion. But it is not a panacea without disagreeable repercussions for some, not least in its adverse effect on jobs. In the past, London Transport staff foresaw free travel causing mass redundancies and were largely opposed to it; the taxi trade feared for its own future; motor manufacturers and car components makers pondered the possible effect on sales, particularly of company cars; many petrol filling stations in London could face bankruptcy. And the government - if they permitted such a project to go ahead - could lose a fortune in fuel tax.

Another conundrum of free travel was: Who shall benefit? If the beneficiaries include commuters living outside Greater London, it is not fair to saddle London residents with stumping up the entire cost of it. On the previous occasions when the GLC attempted to introduce low fares leading to free travel, it resulted in monumental increases in rates.

The introduction of a tourist tax, (another old chestnut being roasted once more) could ensure that the 25 million overseas visitors who arrive in London each year made a contribution, but what of the tens of thousands of daily commuters from the Home Counties and beyond, and the millions who make occasional visits from elsewhere in the country? They would be getting a free ride in every sense of the term. Government money seems to be the only solution. Yet hitherto, Parliament has refused to contribute directly to hold down fares. Why should it change now - and not offer similar assistance to other cities?

No doubt the mayor will aggressively point out, as every GLC administration before him has pointed out, that the government unfairly punishes Londoners by taking from them billions of pounds more in rates and taxes than it gives back. Some of this money could and should be used for the capital's transport. If the mayor makes progress on that argument, he will be the first.

Charging motorists to drive into central London - now seen as another cure for chronic road congestion - was investigated by Conservative and Labour GLC administrations in the seventies and eighties. Political will has changed and advanced technology has reduced some earlier objections to it on technical and policing grounds. In the past, however, the system was always disliked by the Tories and dumped by Labour in the seventies on moral considerations which have not changed: it unfairly favours the wealthy and the company car driver. Now known as road pricing (the GLC called it 'supplementary licensing'), the name may have changed but not much else has.

David Bayliss, formerly the GLC's chief transport planner, said: 'The area for core pricing now being talked about is the same as the GLC suggested; the sorts of charges being talked about, adjusted for inflation, are pretty well the same; the other issues about re-timing traffic signals, having to provide a positive aspect to the scheme, having to improve bus services - they all feature. Twenty-five years on, son of supplementary licensing looks very much like its parent.'

Another recently revived suggestion, of express, limited-stop buses, was investigated more than 20 years ago and dropped. The idea, radical for its time, included a system to change traffic lights as a bus approached. It failed for three reasons:

Families objected to the displaced traffic being routed through residential streets; traders objected to casual custom being whizzed past their shops on high-speed buses, and there was a fear that taxi drivers would clog up the bus lane. All the problems persist today.

Keep London lorry-free during the day and make shop deliveries at night. That idea, now doing the rounds once more, was tried by the GLC, too, nearly 30 years ago. Operation Moondrop, as the council called its experiment, failed because only the largest traders could afford to have staff on duty at night to accept deliveries.

Travelling on empty roads at night had advantages for the big supermarkets but today, many supermarkets are compelled to accept a curfew on night deliveries as a condition of planning permission.

Yet another proposal currently finding much public support, that of taking pressure off roads by making greater use of the Thames for passengers and freight, was policy for all six GLC administrations going back to 1965. Precious little was achieved by any, for reasons which we consider later.

Deputy Prime Minister John Prescott entered the London debate, suggesting that traffic should be removed from Trafalgar Square and Parliament Square and those areas turned over to pedestrian use. This is one of the specific duties entrusted to the new mayor. The GLC sweated blood trying to achieve just such a solution, but failed to find alternative traffic routes to satisfy the police. Now that the police, too, come under mayoral auspices, this problem may be less intractable.

On another plane, Nick Raynsford, formerly Minister for London and the man originally charged with seeing through the local government changes, suggested that the new mayor could work to try to bring the Olympic Games to London. Even that was attempted by the GLC.

The government's claim that Londoners showed an 'overwhelming' desire for a mayor contains more than a little political licence. Three-quarters of the electorate didn't bother to vote and of those who did, a quarter voted No. Bromley council officially set itself against the idea and many Londoners felt that the only certainty from another layer of bureaucracy was that the rates would go up.

Today, two years after that vote, although the government's desire for a truly strong voice for London seems to have been diluted, the principal requirement being that the mayor should not rock the political boat, a voice to speak for London on the international stage remains one of the prime reasons for the new authority.

The capital has had powerful voices before, but what they said was not always music to government ears. For instance, no sooner had Ken Livingstone become leader of London's last strategic authority in May 1981, than he announced his intention of using the council's County Hall headquarters as a campaigning base to attack the Thatcher government. Although voters gave him no such mandate, history records that his activities so angered the Prime Minister that she abolished the entire strategic local democratic process in London, against the wishes of the vast majority of Londoners and many members of her own party. What is to prevent a similar confrontation in the future?

As a safety valve and to oversee what the mayor does, there is an assembly of 25 members, 14 representing 14 voting areas created from the existing electoral wards, the remaining 11, known as London-wide members, chosen by proportional representation. This system is designed to ensure a wide political spectrum and is so loaded to exclude extreme minority parties.

The assembly will act as a balance, with a duty 'to scrutinise the mayor's activities.' Last time there was a not dissimilar council of 96 elected members - and a majority agreed with what Livingstone did. It is no safeguard that three or even more political parties may be represented on the assembly. Usually three political parties had seats on the GLC, but in confrontation with Westminster, they tended to band together for what they regarded as the good of London. All of which suggests that the assembly is unlikely to be a stumbling-block to a determined mayor set on a collision course with Westminster.

Historically the relationship between Parliament and London local government has always been uneasy. From time to time, governments have tried to create a friendly, working liaison by appointing a Minister for

London, with limited success. There was a long history of confrontation between the GLC and the government, whichever party was in power.

There were always rows over finance and the amount of money London local government was to be given by the Exchequer. There were disputes over bus and train fares, planning powers, housing. London accused the government of meddling in its affairs. There seems no reason why these angry confrontations should not continue with London's mayor and a GLC Mark 2.

In spite of Ken Livingstone's newspaper advertisement promising that, if elected, he would work with the government and not in confrontation, if London's new leader is able to adopt that attitude, he will be the first.

When the London County Council, the capital's first overall local authority, was set up in 1889, Parliament had second thoughts about which powers it would devolve. A similar thing happened in 1963, when amendments were made to the recommendations of the Herbert Committee which set up the GLC. Intended powers were taken away, others watered down. Similarly, the functions of the mayor and London Assembly have been hugely amended since the White Paper setting it up was published.

Successive governments have seen London's size as a threat and been determined to contain its authority and keep a tight hold on the purse strings. Always Westminster has had one eye over its shoulder, lest it should sire an embarrassing competitor and not an obedient servant.

Therein lies the kernel of the latest attempt to promote a London-wide authority. Will the mayor and assembly be given sufficient powers and enough money to do its work properly? The government has promised 'sufficient resources to do the job,' though no-one yet knows what the job is or what tasks the mayor may choose to set himself. Many London-watchers have publicly expressed doubts that sufficient cash or powers will ever be handed over.

What of the 'Voice for London' which the government now sees as being so vital? Time will tell if a strong voice speaking for the capital proves as popular with the government in reality as in theory.

The strategic title of mayor may be new, but the old GLC - and the London County Council before it - threw up a succession of powerful leaders who spoke up for London and whose names, in their time, were known throughout capital. What's going to be different?

London certainly had a voice during the last Labour administration of

1981-86. Had anybody in the country not heard of Ken Livingstone? He was in the news almost daily. When he spoke, he spoke for London. Londoners may not always have agreed with what he said, but he spoke with the authority of the leader of the capital's democratically elected authority.

Is it likely that any other London official, no matter what title, will achieve more media exposure than he did? And if so, how would the government react to that? It was widely known that ministers of the Thatcher government were spitting blood because their speeches were often ignored while Ken Livingstone could guarantee a full house and headlines wherever he went.

Yet Livingstone was by no means the first politician to speak for London. After Herbert Morrison and Ike Hayward, the strongmen of the London County Council, the earliest attempt by the GLC to personalise London's strategic authority was in the mid sixties. Then Bill Fiske, later to earn a peerage and a niche in history as the man who decimalised Britain's currency, appeared nervously before the cameras to publicise Carnaby Street, the centre of the pop culture of the day. Reporters who attended recall Fiske being ill at ease in this publicity role and the experiment was not repeated during his administration.

The need to identify a face and a voice with London became firmly established during the Conservative administration of 1967-73, led by Sir Desmond Plummer, now Lord Plummer of Marylebone. Under advice, principally from Basil Andrew, the GLC's chief press officer, Sir Desmond saw all press releases of importance and reserved the right to take them over - meaning, to pen his name to the written words and make any TV appearances relating to them. Sir Desmond understood the value of publicity and took to the part like a duck to water. It was during his reign that the GLC set up a professional press office, staffed by experienced journalists from national newspapers.

Sir Desmond's media briefings became legendary. Before every TV appearance, even a two-minute slot on local news, his aide would call a massive meeting of top officers. Present would be chiefs and their minions covering every conceivable aspect of the subject and many more whose attendance was totally irrelevant. Sometimes there were two dozen highly paid officers present, ready with the facts, prepared to answer any criticism and nip any foreseeable problem in the bud. Overkill it may have been but the result was that, on screen, Sir Desmond knew every answer and every angle. There was never a gaffe, never an error or mis-statement to be cleared up by explanations next day.

Press-watchers knew Sir Desmond had the publicity bit firmly between his teeth when a building at Thamesmead was to be demolished and a photo-call was arranged with Sir Desmond pressing the detonator button. Instead of watching what he was doing, he smiled expansively into the press cameras while the structure disintegrated behind him.

There had been a behind-the-scenes dispute with this photo-call. The council had located a woman of 100 whom they wanted to press the button, but such was the desire to promote London's voice that Sir Desmond took it over. At least he possessed all the required expertise: he served during the war with a bomb disposal unit.

Gradually, Sir Desmond's name became known to an ever widening circle as the GLC press office set out to 'sell' him to the news media as 'Mister London.' People became used to watching him on TV and seeing his picture in the two London evening newspapers. When he spoke, people took notice. Eventually his name superseded that of the GLC in newspaper headlines. Whereas they formerly reported 'GLC acts to cut rush-hour jams,' it became 'Sir Desmond acts to cut rush-hour jams.' London's voice had arrived.

His personal standing was left in no doubt when he visited Tokio, principally to tell the Japanese how London was coping with its traffic. (By comparison, Tokio regarded London as a success story). On the same jumbo jet as the GLC leader was the late rock legend Marc Bolan and T-Rex, who were then among the biggest names in show business. At Tokio airport, a battery of cameras and newsmen waited on the tarmac, presumably for T-Rex. Then over the intercom came the captain's voice: 'Would Sir Desmond Plummer please make his way to the exit.'

GLC elections usually coincided with the traditional mid-term unpopularity of the national Government, hence there was a strong element of national protest in the London vote. The government of the day usually lost the GLC, so conflict was a foregone conclusion. It seems the lesson has not been learned. The four-yearly election to choose London's mayor and assembly, again coincides with mid term for the government.

So it was that the Plummer regime was voted out and in came Labour under the late Sir Reg Goodwin, a very different personality from his predecessor. Whereas Sir Desmond courted publicity, Sir Reg shied from it. He admitted to 'hating' television. His party colleagues, and the County Hall publicity machine which hoped to build on its Voice for London, despaired of his public inactivity. A religious man who would spend quiet moments in the County Hall chapel and who prayed before council meetings, Sir Reg was a strange mixture for a politician - a brilliant speaker but a poor communicator.

Frustrated members of his party complained bitterly that they never knew what was happening. They needed someone to lead from the front, to give London the type of public face that the government is now proposing. But when the news was breaking and the cameras were rolling, he was usually alone behind closed doors in his office on the first floor at County Hall.

On other occasions, when he needed to escape the rigours of London government to recharge his mental and physical batteries, Sir Reg would fly to his caravan in Ireland where peace was assured - because the caravan had no telephone! Should an emergency have arisen, the leader of the Greater London Council was totally incommunicado.

Often he would suggest that major GLC news be announced by his deputy, Illtyd Harrington, a warm, rich-toned, eloquent Welshman with a ready wit, who once told me that he would 'do anything' to get his picture in the paper. Many local government commentators knew Illtyd personally and his words and his company were always welcomed. But he was not the leader. London suddenly had two faces and two voices, each diluting the other.

Illtyd's Christian name, not the commonest in the clubs and pubs of the East End, also led to the occasional howler. Some people could not get their tongue round it, not least Bing Crosby, who came to County Hall to be honoured for services to London, and referred throughout to 'Iliad.'

Labour's lack of an identifiable face and voice to personalise the leadership was exacerbated by another problem. Sir Reg felt that the chairmen of his senior committees should themselves reap public approbation for their hard work. It was they, he thought, who should make major press announcements in their sphere. So when the GLC introduced its landmark scheme of free travel for pensioners, the single most important element of its manifesto and certainly the most popular, Sir Reg threw it away.

The occasion was of such monumental importance that even he, a pensioner himself, could not avoid launching it. However, instead of inviting the news media to a ceremony aboard a bus, say, in Islington on a weekday morning, he would agree to appear only at a low-key photo-call near his Bermondsey home - and on a Sunday. With most of the media enjoying the day off, publicity was minimal. Subsequently he left transport committee chairman Evelyn Denington (later Lady Denington) to make most of the announcements and take the glory.

When the Goodwin administration's four-year term expired, back came the Conservatives, this time under Sir Horace Cutler, a millionaire builder who boasted that he 'served six years in the navy and had had everything except leprosy.' Here was a barnstorming showman who saw the advantage of giving London one voice and who relished that it should be his.

Sometimes feisty, Sir Horace nevertheless mixed easily and was equally at home exchanging banter with market traders, horse-trading with government ministers or, as happened in Munich, doing the conga with girls in Hawaiian skirts and not much else.

When housing chairman in the Plummer administration, his luxurious home at Gerrards Cross was invaded one Sunday by about 100 rent rebels who also brought their children. Where lesser mortals might have called the police, Sir Horace invited them all in, served tea on the lawn and brought in an entertainer to amuse the youngsters.

On another occasion, GLC tenants staged a noisy demonstration outside County Hall at the time guests in evening dress were arriving for the social highlight of the GLC year, the chairman's annual reception. They brought with them a coffin stuffed with notices of rent increases which angry tenants had been encouraged to return to rent-strike leaders.

At the time Sir Horace was in one of the dining rooms supping on champagne and strawberries. As soon as he learned of the protest, he went out and defused a potentially ugly situation by accepting the coffin and listening to the tenants' grievances.

Like his Consevative predecessor, Sir Desmond Plummer, Cutler soon had total confirmation that he was known by the public, only he learned of his notoriety in a more unpleasant way. Scrawled on the wall of a tube station he saw the message: DEATH TO HORACE CUTLER!

Sir Horace came up the hard way, labouring all hours for the family firm. He once told me that for much of his working life he never had more than one week's holiday a year. As the voice of London, Cutler's soon became the best known in the capital, and the GLC's projection of a Mister London rose to new heights. His words and actions were reported by press, radio and TV almost daily as he involved himself in such diverse matters as passing over most of the GLC's 236,000 homes to the boroughs, cutting bureaucracy at County Hall, presiding over arrangements for the inaugural London marathon - and trying to bring the Olympic Games to London.

Again, the capital had a firm, positive voice. Horace often said: 'At least wherever I go, people know who I am.' He was right.

Four years later the political pendulum swung once more and into County Hall swept Labour. The party's first action was to ditch Andrew McIntosh, the moderate leader who had led them to victory, and in his stead the new Left wing Labour group chose Ken Livingstone. The rest is recent history.

Sir Horace Cutler once chided 'Red Ken' on being 'the unknown leader.' He goaded: 'The council has a new leader but no-one knows who he is.'

That situation did not last for long. The sheer outrageousness of Ken Livingstone's statements ensured that he would soon be known throughout the land. Again, London had a firm voice to speak out for it - and the government didn't like it.

Ken Livingstone - the only GLC leader not to have been knighted - complained with justification that the national press misquoted him and ignored his policies, picking and choosing from the trivia instead. So he decided to double the size of the press office and start his own newspaper, *The Londoner,* the world's biggest giveaway with a distribution of nearly 2,750,000 copies.

At every stage the Livingstone administration was involved in controversy and confrontation with the government.

Within months of assuming power, the new GLC slashed London fares. As Labour predicted, passenger numbers on buses and trains reversed the downward trend of years. It chose to forfeit grant from the national exchequer rather than back down on its fares commitment to electors. The government was not pleased. The resultant financial burden was to be borne by a huge increase in rates.

Under Ken Livingstone's leadership, for the first time a major council in Britain had a women's committee, a powerful group which put the woman's stamp on the council's every word and every action. Political correctness was born. Money was given to all manner of minority causes; massive attention was paid to racial issues; gays were encouraged to 'come out' and donations were given to various associations supporting a gay lifestyle. Again, the government didn't like it.

London's new voice was taunted by the Tory opposition. It couldn't build houses but it had a foreign policy, they jeered. Certainly South Africa and Nicaragua appeared in council documents, and the leader forged links with the PLO and the IRA.

Back in 1982, Ken Livingstone said to me: 'We've got to talk to the IRA at some time, we might as well start now.'

It took another ten years for the government to reach the same conclusion.

Whether Londoners supported or abhorred the words of the Voice of London, they couldn't ignore them. His party had an election mandate to speak out for London and for Londoners.

Ken Livingstone did that, day in, day out. In publicity terms, could anyone have achieved more? Could a mayor of London have made more impact?

The government may want London to have a strong voice - but not too strong. It may want the new mayor to be powerful - but not too powerful. Memories are long.

Until its abolition in 1986, the GLC had a chairman, who was the ceremonial head and wore the trappings of office, and a leader who held the political power. This caused confusion and embarrassment enough among even Londoners and the news media, let alone visitors from abroad. Happily, the assembly will not have a chairman, so that difficulty is in the past, and the new title of 'mayor,' being more familiar and traditional, will give the new incumbent a prestige which the old GLC 'leaders' had to earn by words and deeds.

But there are problems with this new title of Mayor of London - London already has a mayor. In fact it has 33. Two of them, in the cities of London and Westminster are lord mayors and one, the Lord Mayor of London, has a very high profile indeed. To the uninitiated, Tony Blair's new Mayor of London is clearly outranked in title by the ancient and prestigious title of Lord Mayor of London.

Time may prove London wrong in trying to ape the mayoral title, so successfully used by the head man of New York where there are five boroughs, none led by its own mayor. When you talk of 'the mayor' in New York, there is no doubting whom you mean.

When Sir Desmond Plummer was leader of the GLC, he was so exercised by the confusion surrounding the city and its lord mayor and the GLC and its leader, that he considered changing the leader's title to 'President.' Such a title sounded more prestigious, yet still paled in comparison with Lord Mayor of London, so he dropped the idea.

When Sir Horace Cutler visited Munich, the Germans often addressed him as 'lord mayor' - and every conceivable title except the correct one. Perhaps, as the German word 'leader' translates as 'fuhrer,' it was just as well.

The Prime Minister has already stated that other towns and cities may have their own directly elected mayor. One London borough, Lewisham, seized on this and has thrown what could prove to be an almighty spanner in the works by announcing that it wants one. If followed through and copied by other boroughs, this could have far-reaching consequences for the Mayor of London should they decide on different priorities.

Clearly Lewisham sees its new incumbent promoting his own borough and bidding to attract investment, events and visitors, not confining himself to talking about dustbin collection and repairing holes in the road. If other boroughs adopted similar policies, they could find themselves even more at odds with the mayor and assembly than they were with the GLC.

Indeed, if many London boroughs adopted this course, the new mayor could be faced with the disintegration of his capital and end up as a king without a kingdom.

However this particular situation may evolve, one certain to cause embarrassment concerns the City of London and its Lord Mayor. Overseas visitors to the GLC could never understand who was who. Many, particularly from Europe and the United States, were confused when wined and dined in the comparatively spartan surroundings of County Hall instead of the ancient splendour of the mighty Mansion House or the Guildhall. They had watched snippets of the Lord Mayor's Show on television and seen a figure in scarlet and ermine waving to the crowds from an open carriage at the end of a spectacular pageant. Yet this was not the person they met at County Hall when they arrived as representatives of their nation or state. Nor will it be under the new legislation.

The facts, of course, are that the Lord Mayor of London and the Court of Common Council over which he presides, have authority only within the square mile of the City of London, where few people live. Talk to visitors about the relevance of the 'city' and you encounter yet more confusion. Many with a knowledge of London will assume you are referring to the Stock Exchange and the financial city which has nothing whatever to do with the Lord Mayor and the city council.

Then what of London's other city within the Greater London boundary - Westminster? Again, the Lord Mayor of Westminster carries all the trappings of ceremonial splendour. And Westminster has within its boundaries such world famous landmarks as the Houses of Parliament, Buckingham Palace, Trafalgar Square, the West End theatres and art galleries, Soho, Covent Garden and Oxford Street. Again, the power of that authority is limited to its own boundaries just as the power of the mayors of Hounslow, Tower Hamlets, Bromley and all the London boroughs is restricted to their own patch. Try explaining that to a foreigner. Or to many citizens of Greater London for that matter.

From time to time threats are made to abolish the city corporation and its lord mayor. The new Mayor of London may see this as the answer to removing what at least will be an irritant and at worst a cause of much confusion. Tony Blair has already said that he does not intend abolishing the city, so the confusion will remain unless there is a change of heart, a change of title - or, ultimately, a change in the proposed strategic control of London.

Whatever the city's critics may say, is eliminating it a sensible solution anyway?

When Harold Wilson was Prime Minister, abolition was official Labour party policy and the Labour GLC urged the government to implement it. Tony Banks, a GLC member later to become Sports Minister in the Blair government, proposed a motion which the GLC passed, urging the government to kill off what Banks called 'the most undemocratic local government structure in the country whose abolition is long overdue.'

Whether in a calculated response to that threat or not, the city proposed that Sir Reg Goodwin, the GLC's Labour leader of that time and Banks' political boss, should be made an honourary freeman of the city - an honour Sir Reg was inclined to accept.

The now defunct *Evening News* learned of this and Len Vigars, its municipal correspondent, smelt a story and decided to seek some opinions.

First he rang Tony Banks, a man whose language is colourful and whose vocabulary is somewhat limited in such situations. His response was characteristically unprintable.

Then Vigars rang No.10 and asked if they would care to comment in view of the government's policy for the city's elimination.

A spokesman gave the usual response that the city corporation was 'undemocratic, unrepresentative, elitist and sexist... an anachronism of days long past, a bastion of money and privilege....' Then he added: 'For the record: We're going to abolish it. Off the record: Forget it!'

Despite the political rhetoric, the city corporation continues to flourish because successive governments of both parties have found it useful. Overseas statesmen and other dignitaries are welcomed with great pomp and ceremony, entertained in ancient splendour and wined and dined in magnificent surroundings - and the city corporation picks up the bill.

The corporation has 900 years of tradition and is rich in history, going back to Dick Whittington and the building of the Tower of London. There has been a strange relationship through the centuries with the city giving money to kings and queens. It has vast assets which make it the world's richest city.

Its spending is not limited to hosting the rich and famous either. Four of the principal Thames bridges in central London are owned by the city corporation's Bridge House Estates company which pays for their upkeep. The city is a great benefactor of worthy causes and has a number of surprising outposts: it owns several parks, including Epping Forest, Burnham Beeches, near Slough, Berkshire, and is now responsible for Hampstead Heath.

When the GLC was abolished and its functions were devolved, the future of Hampstead Heath was on the agenda. It was offered to the National Trust which declined, being unwilling to become involved in politics. Eighty per cent of the heath lies in the Labour borough of Camden which wanted control, but Camden was never particularly flush with cash. Weighty ideological objections to the 'undemocratic, elitist' city corporation taking it over soon evaporated when objectors realised how much money could be made available for the heath's future.

In recent times, the city corporation has moved a long way towards meeting its critics. The building of the huge Barbican residential development in the sixties meant that, at night, the city was no longer inhabited only by cats and caretakers. There was now a sizeable electorate in some wards. It abolished the business vote, which gave voting rights to anyone who owned property in the city. Women were permitted to become aldermen, a prerequisite to becoming Lord Mayor, and one woman has already held that prestigious office.

The city seems to have no problem in successfully combining the old with the new. Cherished tradition flourishes side by side with progress. Every year hundreds of men and women are accepted as city 'freemen,' a title which, unlike 'honorary freeman,' can be bought for cash. It allows the title-holder such privileges as being permitted to make donations to various good causes, to drive sheep over London Bridge and go to the police station by taxi if arrested for being drunk.

Another tradition sees the city corporation hosting a welcoming ceremony in which all the London mayors parade up the aisle of the Guildhall to be greeted by the Lord Mayor before being appropriately wined and dined. It is an invitation which, despite outward animosity by Labour mayors, has been accepted to the manner born by most, including Tony Banks, the last GLC chairman, who had so vociferously argued for the city's abolition.

The problem of the city corporation and its lord mayor will not go away. If, during the latest reorganisation of London local government, nothing is done, visitors will continue to be bemused and confused.

In 1889, the city corporation was invited to take over the running of London - not the entire Greater London but a smaller area of central and inner London. It declined, realising that it would have to dilute its prestigious position of independence and dirty its hands in party politics.

Some observers feel that, when the mayoral experiment has run its course and yet another reorganisation is attempted, this may yet be the way ahead.

2. TOOLS FOR THE JOB

Will the new system work? Does it avoid the problems of there being a government at the top wanting to retain overall control, especially of the purse strings, and of the boroughs underneath who consider that they should be master in their own house?

People experienced in walking the tightrope between these two factions in the days of the GLC, are not impressed.

Sir Alan Greengross, former Tory Opposition leader on the GLC and now chairman of the London Region Passengers Committee said: 'The Bill was cobbled together at the last second. Amendments were being drafted at night to be tabled next morning. That's not the way to do it and we will suffer for it. The GLA won't last because it is setting off all the tensions with other bodies that have always destroyed London government in the past. Every time it has failed before it is because of tensions with, first the city, then the boroughs and the government. None of those has been resolved.

'Without tax-raising powers or being given enough money, the mayor will be in the wonderful position of saying "I want to do all these things but the government won't give me the money." To be able to say that is every politician's dream.'

Maurice Stonefrost, the GLC's last director general and formerly its comptroller of finance: 'There will be problems. The government has gone out of its way to continue to keep to itself practically everything it needs to make sure that whoever is running London has got to run round the corridors of government. Until the later years, the GLC could raise its own money on the capital market and it could raise its own precept on the rates and be elected or shot down on that. Under the new system there is no power to levy a community charge.'

Sir James Swaffield, GLC director general for eight years and formerly president of the Society of Local Government Chief Officers: 'The mayor and assembly must struggle hard to get as close as possible to the financial relationship with government that the Welsh Assembly and Scottish Parliament enjoy. If it is just treated as another local authority there will be that second tier relationship which has been so unsatisfactory in the past.'

Norman Howard, a GLC member for 13 years and planning chairman during the Labour administration of Sir Reg Goodwin, who attended the passage of the Bill through the committee stage in Parliament: 'I would rather have seen it tried out in a provincial city. It was cobbled together in haste and there were far too many amendments. Nobody had thought it through. I think they will have to come back and make substantial changes particularly in the financial area. For Tony Blair to let other towns have a similar system before London has been put to the test does not make sense.'

There were 800 amendments to the Bill. Many were not debated and backbenchers virtually took no part.

Opinions are divided over whether the new mayor will be a person of immense power or virtually a PR figurehead. On the one hand, as the representative of five million voters, the mayor could reasonably be regarded as, perhaps, the second most powerful political figure in the land behind the Prime Minister and one who could virtually demand an audience with the PM at will.

Representing five million voters may be technically accurate though Ken Livingstone used to say that to get elected in London, a candidate needed the support of only about 16 per cent of electors because only 30 per cent bothered to vote.

Those who regard the new role largely as a PR function point to cash as being the key. For better, for worse, the government is already strapping the mayor up quite tightly. The rate contribution is to be restricted to about 3p; income from road pricing and from office car park charges is ring fenced, only to be used for transport initiatives; the mayor 'will not be free to use for other purposes' government grants for police, fire service and transport. The GLA's first budget will be set by ministers.

On the face of it, the mayor is not being left with much room for manoeuvre.

Last time London voted and the entire count was at one venue - a referendum on membership of what was then the Common Market -

it was a paper count, probably the biggest ever in the UK. Sixty per cent of the population voted (3.3 million). The whole of Earls Court was taken over and hundreds of officers from the GLC and the London boroughs counted through till dawn. Inside the building, voting forms were conveyed to and from invigilators in supermarket trolleys and the GLC was taken to task for 'trying to influence the vote' after a press photographer at a preview noticed that the waiting line of 'Yes' trolleys was longer than the 'No' line!

There was international interest in the vote, including from Japan. The numbers and weight of large outside broadcast vehicles wanting to record the scene for television caused panic. Earls Court feared its floor would collapse under the strain and in desperation all the lorries were ordered to reverse out down a ramp and into the yard.

There will be no such problem in future. Counting will be done electronically.

The new Greater London Authority will have responsibilities in eight main areas: transport, economic development and regeneration, police, fire and emergency planning; the environment, planning, culture and health.

Duties of the mayor will be to devise strategies and action plans to tackle London-wide issues in these eight core areas and including air quality, noise, waste and biodiversity.

He will represent and promote London at home and abroad and speak up for Londoners.

He will take over a number of existing government policies for the first four core areas costing about £3.6 billion. In addition, the government estimates the cost of running the GLA's new services and provision for future elections will be about £26 million a year. Most of this will be met by central government grant. London council tax payers will contribute about 3p a week on a Band D tax bill.

The mayor and the 25-member London assembly will serve a four-year term; all will be full-time members.

The mayor will pick his deputy from the assembly, be allowed to appoint two political advisers, choose ten of the 400-strong GLA staff and decide what jobs they do. He will not be allowed to appoint the Head of Paid Service, Monitoring Officer or Chief Finance

Officer who, along with the rest of staff, will be appointed by the assembly. The mayor's appointments will lapse when he leaves office.

Tasks for the mayor include setting the budgets for Transport for London (a new body), the new London Development Agency, the Metropolitan Police and the London Fire and Emergency Planning Authority. He will also control new transport and economic development bodies and appoint their members; make appointments to the new police and fire authorities and publish a regular report on the state of the environment in London.

He will also have a general power to do anything which will further the principal purposes of the GLA - to promote economic and social development and the improvement of London's environment.

As far as possible decisions will be taken in full public view - consulting interested parties when drawing up plans and informing the assembly of all major decisions and the reasons for them.

In the key area of transport, the mayor will be empowered to introduce road tolls and to levy a charge on workplace parking - the latter suggested at £3,000 per space. In each case all revenue must be spent on improving transport. Exemptions and other concessions to the charges will be specified by the government because they will apply nationally. Boroughs will be free to implement new charges only with the mayor's consent.

There will be a new body, Transport for London, responsible for delivering an 'integrated and sustainable transport strategy.' With eight to 15 members, it will be chaired by the mayor, and will set fares, have 'a say' in how commuter railways are run and be able to fund new services, make investments and introduce new systems.

It will manage the buses, Docklands Light Railway, the Underground once public-private partnership contracts are in place, a network of important roads, and will regulate taxis and mini cabs, run London River Services and promote the river for passenger and freight movement.

It will also help co-ordinate dial-a-ride and taxicard schemes for transport users with mobility problems, and take over responsibility for London's traffic lights. London Transport and a number of other organisations would be wound up and their resources transferred to the new body.

The government intends to modernise and maintain the Underground's infrastructure through a public-private partnership. When negotiations for this have been completed, the Underground will be transferred to Transport for London.

Boroughs will remain the highway authority for 95 per cent of roads.

As opposed to the mayor's executive role, the 25-member London Assembly has a scrutiny responsibility - to keep a 'check and balance on the mayor' and scrutinise his performance. It will have powers to amend his budget and summon him, senior staff, functional bodies or anyone in a contractual relationship or receiving a grant from the authority.

It will also have the power to investigate issues of London-wide significance and make proposals to the mayor.

Meetings in public will be held ten times annually to question the mayor and there will be a twice yearly 'people's question time' with the mayor and assembly.

The Home Secretary will be empowered to set a minimum level for the police authority's budget if he considers that this is needed to provide an efficient and effective police force. He will also retain statutory powers to ensure that the fire authority maintains nationally agreed standards of fire cover. A large proportion of spending on Transport for London and the London Development Agency will be met by government grants specifically for these purposes. The mayor will not be free to use these grants for other purposes.

Having studied the mayor's powers and the responsibilities of the assembly, Maurice Stonefrost, for eight years the GLC's comptroller of finance before becoming director general, is not impressed that the mayor will have either sufficient money or sufficient freedom to be more than a shadow of the Mayor of New York.

He considers that there is no hope of solving the financial problems of a London statutory body unless the system of government is changed.

He said: 'London is a huge national and international city and needs to be treated as such, yet that is not possible because it cannot fit into the existing structure of Parliament or government. Parliament is the power centre and it won't devolve it. London will find itself sucked down in the name of looking at the country as a whole.'

The mayor may also find himself running out of time to achieve his objectives, just as the GLC did. Because the GLC was usually won by the party in opposition nationally, the constantly changing political complexion of both the council and the government meant that completing any long term measure was a gamble.

Maurice Stonefrost maintains that lack of a long enough run of finance was one of the two basic problems which handicapped the GLC. The other was over-control, an imbalance between the functions and the ability to carry them out.

The GLC, he said, had sufficient headline responsibilities but most were constrained by government controls and were operable only by government agreement.

Some observers were surprised that the Greater London boundary was unchanged in the latest reorganisation.

Sir Desmond Plummer, when leader of the Conservative GLC in the late sixties and early seventies, had in his office a map of the south-east and he would constantly indicate the entire area within the M25 and say: 'This should all be part of London.'

Areas of Middlesex had resisted inclusion when the GLC boundary was set and part of Surrey won exclusion in the Lords.

It has long been argued that for commuting purposes, London's boundaries extend from the South Coast to Watford and beyond, though opponents of large conglomerations argue that the larger the area the more one dissipates the representative role of the people elected.

Learning from the failings of the capital's last strategic authority suggests that, perhaps, the problem went deeper than the GLC. Maybe the constitution of the London boroughs was wrong.

There were some strange shotgun weddings. Hampstead had little affinity with Holborn and St Pancras; Hounslow and Chiswick have nothing in common; there was no good reason for merging Orpington, Beckenham and St Mary Cray into Bromley, or combining Southall with Ealing. In many cases each district valued its own identity and did not want to merge. Sir James Swaffield contends:

'When the GLC was set up, the new boroughs were designed to be as close as possible to the county boroughs which were all-purpose. They had relationships with the new strategic authority, the GLC, but they were encouraged to think like county boroughs. Both these things had an effect on the way the whole thing started out.

'I thought the new, enlarged London boroughs would be delighted to have greater strength, greater status and power, but nothing of the sort. In the past, some of their major needs had been funded by the LCC. They were grateful for that and not particularly keen on taking over sole responsibility for everything.'

Sir James also had some interesting views on council members. He recalled: 'Local politicians became members of the GLC having previously been members of the London metropolitan boroughs and boroughs in Middlesex. Suddenly they found themselves being expected to think strategically instead of doing things which were much closer to people.

'Talking to members I found that quite often they had stood for election to the GLC as a sort of consolation prize because they had failed the selection process for their local council. A number, if they were honest, would say that what they really wanted as a GLC member was to do their best to protect the interests of the area from which they came.

'This strategic function was laid down in statute but I don't think much thought was ever given to how you produce members who thought along strategic lines. You don't see results quickly in a strategic authority and you don't get public acclaim for long term thinking.

'Most members think in terms of the length of time for which they have been elected and want to establish their authority during that period.'

Parochial interests were certainly always a problem for the GLC. When the Conservatives won control in 1977, they came to power promising to create 'a real South Circular Road' in place of the hotch-potch of roads which then made up that vital route.

Their supporters in the area had other ideas when their environment was under threat, so their election pledge was conveniently forgotten.

When Ken Livingstone's Labour administration came to power, plans by the previous administration for a vast lorry ban were halted because, the incoming administration claimed, it would push the displaced lorries to where their voters lived. And so it went on.

With the Greater London Assembly having only 14 large constituencies instead of the 92 of the GLC, cases of members pursuing parochial interests should be fewer.

The type of person entering local politics has also changed over the years. A phenomenon of the last two decades has been the upsurge of party politics by local councillors who see their jurisdiction extending beyond the local council to which they were elected. An increasing number also see local government as a stepping stone to a career in Parliament. They are just as dedicated as their predecessors, but dedicated to different goals.

When Ken Livingstone gained the leadership of the GLC, he announced immediately that he intended to use County Hall as a platform to attack the Tory government. His deputy John McDonnell, spoke of the council becoming 'a rallying point against the government and a rallying point for the left.' Both men are now MPs.

So the success of the new system could depend as much on the calibre of the assembly members as on the mayor. Although the assembly has no individual powers, it could be an excellent sounding board between the mayor and the public.

Maurice Stonefrost commented: 'If the assembly has a good system of support and information, and enough of those members are prepared to use that information and form judgments, it could be good. If it is starved of information and support or if the members don't choose to take advantage of them and simply use the assembly for log-rolling or noise-making or jumping on this week's issue, it will be missing the point of its creation.'

London, and the boroughs, will be watching.

3. HOW IT ALL BEGAN

London had no comprehensive local government until the creation of the Metropolitan Board of Works in 1855. Before that, the capital's needs had been inadequately served by a hotch-potch of parish vestries, boards, commissions, and justices of the peace.

The Metropolitan Board of Works was born under the shadow of cholera which, in the mid 19th century, was becoming the scourge of London. This was the time of the 'Big Stink,' when the stench of sewage from the Thames was so great that Parliament suspended a sitting.

The board's primary task was to provide a clean water supply and set up a main drainage system to dispose of sewage from an area which is now virtually the twelve inner London boroughs. It accomplished these tasks with remarkable sophistication for the times. Rivers, including the Fleet and the Tyburn, were enclosed and became sewers in a system built by Sir Joseph Bazalgette which remains the backbone of London's sewage system today.

Other duties followed and included street improvements, Thames crossings, parks and fire fighting, the last previously run by the insurance companies. One of the board's initiatives led to them buying out the owners of most of the Thames bridges between Blackfriars and Hammersmith and freeing them from the tolls owners had imposed.

The City of London was excluded from the new reorganisation, being served by the ancient city corporation. In 1884 - and not for the last time - attempts were made to extend the city's powers far beyond its historic square mile. According to the scribes of the day, rowdy public meetings ensued as the advantages and disadvantages were noisily debated, but the city was not interested and the parliamentary Bill was withdrawn.

In spite of the MBW's successes, reformers continued to agitate for more effective, centralised local government, and in 1888, Lord Salisbury's Conservative government set up the London County

Council. It inherited the board's existing boundaries, again omitting the City of London, although reformers once more sought unsuccessfully to end this exclusion. The new authority took over the MBW's responsibilities and others followed, most importantly education in 1904 (after abolition of the School Board), and health services in 1930, though some of these were surrendered in 1948 on creation of the National Health Service.

Politically, the early LCC divided into two camps - the Moderates (Tories) and the majority Progressives, which included Liberals, Fabians and others. Subsequently the Moderates changed their title to Municipal Reformers, and won power in 1907, retaining it until 1934 when defeated by the Labour Party who had emerged on the LCC scene about 12 years earlier.

Labour was led by Herbert Morrison, later Lord Morrison of Lambeth, a dynamic, dictatorial personality who lived most of his life in a semi detached house in Eltham and whose last wish was that his ashes should be scattered on the Thames from County Hall. The most powerful man in London he may have been, but Morrison had a habit of kicking off his shoes while he worked and visitors to his office were often surprised to find him in his socks.

Over the years the LCC became a world leader in local government. Long after its demise the excellence of its education service was still quoted as a shining example to others. Its housing, though basic, was practical and homes were built to last. For child care and water treatment the LCC was well ahead of its time, and for parks, its 6,000 acres of open space made London the envy of the world. In health, too, the LCC was successful, building up a remarkable hospital organisation and ambulance service.

One of its earliest landmark actions was to open the Woolwich free ferry in March 1899. Newspaper reports of the day record that six bands played, and thousands thronged flag-decked streets to hear LCC chairman, Lord Rosebery, stand in his horse-drawn carriage, doff his topper and pronounce the ferry 'open free for ever.'

Ships sounded their sirens and a gun salute was fired from North Woolwich Gardens as the 490-ton paddleboat Gordon sailed to the north shore carrying 500 VIPs. The *Kentish Times* reported: 'Shops closed for the day and reopened at night. And what a night it was!

Gauged by the public houses, it was the busiest Woolwich had ever known.'

The ferries' finest hour was the infamous docks blitz of September 7, 1940, when they evacuated much of the population of Silvertown from their blazing homes to the Kent bank.

Frank Bryant, a commodore skipper who retired after completing 300,000 crossings, would never forget that night. He told me: 'The bombers seemed to be coming from all directions. When daylight came a thousand fires still blazed out of control. Both sides of the river were walls of flame and the river was littered with burning oil and debris. I thought the end of the world had come.'

By the time the paddle steamers were phased out they had carried 180 million passengers and 55 million vehicles and cycles. They sailed in all but the thickest fogs, though in one pea-souper a ferryboat drifted up Woolwich Reach forcing passengers and crew to spend the night on board.

Earlier Woolwich ferries are shrouded in the mists of time. Not until 1884 when the Metropolitan Board of Works funded a crossing did a modern ferry become reality.

The LCC also ran penny steamboat services in the Docklands area. Nearly 600,000 passengers used Greenwich pier in summer and 250,000 paid their penny to use the pier to view the river.

The LCC also dabbled in the restaurant business. Following the success of its wartime civic restaurants - originally called 'communal feeding centres' by an anonymous man from the ministry with a flair for words - it decided to challenge private enterprise. Wedding receptions were successfully catered for as the intention grew to rival the Lyons Corner Houses, so popular in post-war London as venues for a good meal amid an atmosphere of glitz and glitter and at a price the ordinary person could afford.

Forbidden by statute to make a loss, the council opened its first major restaurant off Oxford Street. Called The Ramillies, it was not a success and the whole ambitious dream was abandoned.

Under Morrison's leadership. the LCC produced famous three-year plans for health, education, town planning, parks and housing. By the time war broke out in 1939, the LCC had built nearly 100,000 homes, many in tenement blocks, but none more than five storeys high. Numbered among its residents was Karl Marx who had found sanctuary in London after being expelled from many countries. In 1868 he was summoned for non-payment of rates on his home in Dean Street, Soho.

Even in those days there was confrontation with the government. London gained Waterloo Bridge through the stubbornness of Morrison and the LCC who defied the government and built the bridge themselves after being denied powers to raise the capital. War intervened and a temporary Bailey bridge was used for 18 years before the Waterloo bridge of today was opened in 1945.

When Morrison finally retired a year later, he was superseded by another political strongman, Ike Hayward, who retained control until the LCC was abolished. But it was a close thing.

The 1949 elections resulted in a dead heat between Labour and Conservatives. Tory hopes of power sharing were dashed when Labour used its outgoing aldermen (who were appointees) to help elect as chairman John Bowen, who had failed to win a council seat. Bowen then used his vote to help elect enough Labour aldermen to give the party a majority.

There was a royal reception at County Hall later in the year, when`the Queen knighted Bowen, not for his services as chairman - which the Conservative government perhaps found hard to forgive - but for services to a regional hospital board.

Like Morrison, Ike Hayward permitted no deviation from the official party line. Once a miner, he liked to boast of his time in the pits, though his days underground had long been superseded by a position as a union negotiator.

There was virtually no effective opposition party for much of that time and any rebellion from within was speedily crushed by Hayward and his chief whip, Freda Corbett, MP for Peckham, who strutted the corridors together, known to friend and foe alike as Darby and Joan.

County Hall had been damaged by six bombs during the war and was waiting in a long queue for permits to make good the damage. In the hope that personal contact could grease the wheels of action, the general purposes committee invited the minister responsible for war damage repairs to County Hall for lunch. In his friendly speech of welcome, however, the chairman forgot to mention the permits, and the minister, who was expecting to be asked, did not remind him. But the occasion was not a complete loss; the permits arrived soon after.

What must have been the shortest meeting of the LCC was held in the early fifties.

Near the end of the usual Tuesday afternoon assembly, bitter and personal things were said. Amid uproar the meeting gradually broke up, refusing to be called to order by the chairman, and forgetting that, at the end of meetings, there had to be a formal resolution providing money for all the decisions that had been made. So three days later the members reassembled, passed the formal resolution, and went sheepishly home.

The 1939-45 war had changed attitudes dramatically and there was a determination never to return to the grim lifestyles of the past. There was full employment and soon, greater freedom, wealth and mobility which led to many families moving out of inner London for the greener, more prosperous suburbs.

Politically, this was bad news for the Conservatives. Many of these families were Tory voters. If the Tories were ever again to rule London, its boundaries had to be revised to bring back these families on to its electoral roll. At the same time, the need for a strategic planning authority was perceived by government and in 1957, Henry Brooke, Housing Minister in Harold Macmillan's administration and a former Tory leader on the LCC, set up a royal commission to examine local government arrangements in Greater London.

It reported in 1960, proposing an extension of London's boundaries to 616 square miles - previously it had been 117 - absorbing most of the county of Middlesex and areas formerly in Kent, Surrey, Herts and Essex and almost doubling the electorate to 5,500,000. The new Greater London Council was to take over all the LCC's powers, excluding hospital services, which were now to be administered entirely by the National Health Service, and education, to be managed by a new Inner London Education Authority. Outer London boroughs would be responsible for their own schools.

The commission's principal recommendations were incorporated in the 1963 London Government Act, though a proposal to include water provision was dropped and the boundaries were further changed.

Some areas, including a rump of Middlesex, and Epsom and Walton-on-Thames, Surrey, successfully resisted being absorbed into Greater London.

The new council began its official, executive life on April 1, 1964 after operating in tandem with the LCC and Middlesex County Council for a transitional year.

Structurally and procedurally, the GLC (like the LCC before it) mirrored Parliament, giving itself airs and graces above its station which irritated some boroughs.

They called themselves members, not councillors. There was a members' entrance, members' terrace, members' dining room and bar. Controversial debates were likely to end with calls for a division whereupon bells would recall members to the council chamber so their names could be recorded by tellers as they filed through Ayes and Noes lobbies. There were also written questions and a whipping system.

There were 36 divisions during one meeting in the Livingstone era which meant that the mere act of voting occupied three hours. On a number of occasions, before Ken Livingstone introduced a deadline, meetings went on for 12 or 14 hours.

County Hall had been the home of London's local government since 1922. The building, on one of the finest sites in Europe, was described by Morrison as 'the headquarters of the greatest municipality in the world.' Its design was such that it acted almost as a counterfoil to Parliament on the other side of Westminster Bridge.

It occupied six and a quarter acres, had Thames frontage and, in 1907, cost £617,000.

Nearly 100 architects, the famous and the not so famous, entered a competition to design it and the winner, unanimously chosen by the competition panel, was a little-known 29-year-old, Ralph Knott. Although Knott had been among prizewinners in other competitions, little of his work had ever been built and it was said to be this inexperience, plus delay in designing the interior, which led to the building's long construction period. Work began in 1909.

Because of its nearness to the Thames, the building needed to be sited on a vast concrete raft, 5ft. thick. A year after excavations began work was interrupted when builders uncovered the wreck of a Roman ocean-going boat. A superb piece of petrified oak was also excavated and from this was carved the chairman of the council's ceremonial chair.

It was three years (March 1912), before the site was sufficiently far advanced for a foundation stone to be laid by King George the Fifth and Queen Mary.

The building was still only a shell when the First World War broke out and work was suspended for a time. Part occupied by government departments during the war, it was 1922 before it was taken over by the LCC, having cost nearly £4 million to build. Even then the council continued to meet in Spring Gardens, Westminster, because the members' area in County Hall was not ready.

By this time the building was already too small. Bureaucracies had flourished. County Hall's 1,000 rooms on eight storeys, with miles of corridors were insufficient to house the staff. Desperate for space, the council scoured inner London - a search which continued when the GLC came to power and which resulted in a strange collection of outposts and offices. One in Wellington Street, Covent Garden, had enjoyed a colourful past as a gentlemen's club and included a bordello at the back. There, an ornate landing across the entire rear of the building connected to a rear door and separate staircase so gentlemen could leave discreetly.

In the spacious courtyard at County Hall, two other blocks were added and subsequently, in the seventies, a circular, state-of-the-art third building was completed across York Road and connected by an enclosed footbridge.

In contrast to the warren of offices in County Hall, the new building was open plan, air conditioned and the windows had blinds which came down (or were supposed to come down) automatically when the sun shone.

Up the grey granite steps of the main building, through the heavy bronze doors and across the vestibule was a carpeted ceremonial staircase, strictly reserved for members and important guests. This led to a dignified marble and oak-panelled principal floor with imposing council chamber, members' offices and committee rooms.

Acoustically, the council chamber was excellent but the system of keying in the speaker led to some comic situations. Members used microphones suspended from the ceiling which were switched on by an operator as speakers rose from their seats. Usually the opening words were lost before the appropriate mike was switched on and sometimes, if a new and consequently unknown member was speaking, or one had popped up unobserved, whole passages would go unheard.

Staff were allowed on the principal floor only on members' business, and provided they were properly attired - morning dress for men, skirted suits or appropriate frocks for women. Staff were liable to be challenged by security messengers and dispatched to a more appropriate area if their dress or their purpose was deemed unsatisfactory. At least one timid young man was reduced to tears when bawled out for not wearing a tie.

If a visit to the principal floor was imperative, staff were expected to use the staircase nearest the room they sought so minimum time was spent traversing the hallowed corridors. The wise soon learned that, to avoid hassle and challenge, the secret was to carry a file of papers.

Gradually restrictions were relaxed and when Ken Livingstone's administration won power, staff and visitors wandered the first floor at will. Jeans, T-shirts and trainers were all acceptable dress, almost *de rigueur.*

County Hall was famous for its corridors, seven miles of them. Finding the way around was never easy even for staff, As if seven miles of corridors and 1,000 rooms was not problem enough, many rooms had been divided, making numbering no longer consecutive and dead-end corridors were created. Cross corridors and other obstructions to circular access complicated what the unknowing expected to be a straightforward route. Visitors needed to be escorted and staff not gifted with a sense of direction were known to have become so lost that they would leave the building and start again from the main door.

The corridors and the oak panelled principal floor were used in many films and TV productions, including 'Scandal,' the story of Oscar Wilde and 'A Perfect Spy.' They were also used unofficially for roller skating by the caretaker's children and, during the long council breaks, for 'recess cricket' by the Treasurer's department.

Whatever one's business at County Hall, the outstanding memory was likely to be of the magical, shiny floors, polished to look like glass. This immaculate finish was achieved at about 9 pm, long after most staff had gone. But those working late were liable to emerge from a cross corridor on to a sea of liquid polish.

The choice was either to go back, find another route and hope for an unlocked door at the end of it - not favoured if your train was about to depart - or take a chance that the floor was dry enough to walk on. It was tempting, if naughty, to pick your way along a tacky stretch of corridor, leaving footprints, your shoes clinging more firmly with every step. If the next stretch had been waxed more recently, the floor would be more slippery than ice. The remainder of the journey could be completed only gingerly, clinging to the wall for support. Many a suit ended up at the dry cleaners after the challenge of the polished floor had been accepted and lost.

Knott's County Hall had ten entrances, making security its Achilles heel. With so many offices, an attic, a basement and sub basement (where a vagrant was once found dead beneath the central heating pipes), clearing the building was an impossibility.

Realising these security weaknesses, eyebrows were raised when Ken Livingstone's administration announced that County Hall's committee rooms were to be opened at night and weekends so that local organisations could meet there free of charge.

Apart from the odd complaint about discarded beer cans, no major problem seemed to result.

VIP visits were a nightmare and on occasion councils had gone to extraordinary lengths to ensure their guests' safety.

In the early fifties, during a state visit to London, President Tito of Yugoslavia was a guest of the LCC and was received in the council chamber. At every strategic point on the principal floor stood a plain clothes policeman in a raincoat, presumably hiding a revolver.

The council's ceremonial head found the officer in charge standing on a manhole, rocking it gently and wanting to know what was underneath. He was not happy on being told there was a gap between the two floors for pipes and wires, big enough for people to move around in.

In a desperate measure to keep out any would-be assassin, officers of the council were ordered to occupy all the seats in the public gallery so that the council could honestly tell people waiting outside that the gallery was full.

Security was even tighter in 1954, when Soviet leaders, Leonid Bulganin and Nikita Khruschev arrived on a goodwill visit. The Russians were so worried about their leaders' safety that they secretly sought - and were secretly given - permission to site a machine-gun in the caretaker's flat at the top of County Hall. Its field of fire covered Westminster bridge and, ironically, the Houses of Parliament.

That was typical of Soviet concern for the safety of their leaders during the trip, no doubt fuelled by the 'Buster' Crabb incident in which Commander Crabb, a Royal Navy frogman, disappeared after allegedly being ordered to examine the propeller of the cruiser on which the Russians had arrived.

On the day they visited County Hall, there was no way the Russians' safety could be guaranteed to the satisfaction of the KGB along miles of London's congested streets, so they travelled by boat to Westminster Pier. Just across the Embankment from the pier was the former New Scotland Yard where, in those days, most newspapers had a resident crime reporter. In view of its juxtaposition to County Hall, newspaper editors asked their crime reporters to ring through when the Russians arrived.

But as the Soviet leaders' boat neared its destination, somebody locked the famous green door to the street, imprisoning all the reporters in the press room. The police were 'unable' to find another key until B and K were safely in County Hall.

Typical of the problems of security concerned a visit by the Queen in the seventies. Her activities were confined to the first floor and one corridor had been cleared and sealed as far as was possible. As she left one room for another, however, there was a clatter of running feet on the stairway only a yard from where she stood.

Her anxious bodyguard commanded: 'Stay where you are!'

The running feet stopped obediently. It was no would-be assassin.

Just a man, unaware of the royal visit, racing down the stairs to catch his train home.

There was exceptional security for a visit of Harold Wilson when Prime Minister. The main courtyard was packed with hundreds of uniformed police. Even the council's press officers were asked to mount guard in the foyer and keep an eye out. There were probably 250 PCs standing almost shoulder to shoulder in a vast semi circle 30 yards from the County Hall steps. Inside was a cordon of sergeants, also ranged in a semi circle and behind them, a line of inspectors. On the steps waited various commanders and superintendents - a truly mighty police presence.

I was posted just inside the main doors with an ideal view of the car park. The PM was about to arrive and vigilance was at its peak. Suddenly a little old man carrying a case entered the car park and headed for the County Hall steps. He reached the cordon of PCs who, to my surprise, parted to let him through. True he was not your archetypal terrorist (whatever that may be) but I didn't expect him also to make his way unchallenged through the ring of sergeants, some of whom looked after him curiously. On he came, through the inspectors, up the steps, past the top brass and into the foyer without a single challenge.

Rushing in where angels feared to tread, I stopped him and asked where he was going. Simultaneously a sinking feeling in the pit of my stomach told me I ought not to have become involved.

He cocked an ear at my question and said: 'Just a minute.'

Then he placed his case on the reception desk, opened it and brought out an old fashioned hearing aid, wired to an enormous battery.

Plugging himself in he asked: 'What did you say?'

Having reached the point of no return, I repeated my question.

He replied: 'I've come to watch the chess.'

Security had forgotten that somewhere in the vastness of County Hall an evening chess match was planned. The GLC was playing the civil service. He said he was going to the junior officers' dining room, deep inside the building, where it was being played.

'Do you know your way around County Hall?' I asked.

'Know my way around?' he repeated. 'I helped build it.'

4. FISKE'S QUIET REIGN, 1964-67

To the surprise of the pundits, Labour won the first election to the new GLC in 1964, one fought on a system of boroughs electing two, three or four members to the 100-member council, depending on their population. Considering that Greater London's boundaries had been changed to include parts of the Home Counties deliberately to increase the likelihood of a Conservative win, the election was a shock to Tory headquarters.

Political control of London, through the GLC, looked set to continue where the London County Council left off: the iron grip which Labour had held for 28 years through Herbert Morrison and Ike Hayward threatened to remain unchanged.

For the first year of its life, the GLC sat in tandem with the LCC, virtually shadowing its actions and preparing to take over 12 months hence. Its first meeting on Monday, April 27, was all over in one hour, eight minutes. William Fiske, a modest giant of a man who disliked publicity, was council leader, Sir Percy Rugg led the Conservative opposition, and Harold Shearman, later Sir Harold, was elected chairman.

That first meeting is recorded on a 10ft. by 7ft. canvas by A.R. Thomson RA, a deaf artist, who was commissioned by the council and paid 2,500 guineas. The painting took him a year. When Thomson had made his initial sketches, each council member was required to attend a one-hour sitting so his face could be faithfully captured.

Another artist, also invited to quote for the work, said that he found the council chamber setting and including 250 members and guests 'not a task I care to tackle.'

Much of this first year was spent by the council getting to grips with its new responsibilities, appointing staff and preparing departmental and committee structures.

Its first serious business concerned government proposals to ban smoking in cinemas. The new GLC, which licensed places of public entertainment, said it hoped no decision would be taken until it had been given an opportunity for a debate. The council could do little apart from hope and plead in such situations because it would not become an executive body until April 1 of the following year.

At the third meeting more 'hopes' were expressed. These concerned rumours that the British Railways Board intended to shut down the Richmond to Broad Street line. The LCC and eleven boroughs were said to have voiced 'profound concern.' GLC member Ellis Hillman urged that no decision be taken until the council had a chance to voice its views.

Nearly half a century later, the line is flourishing as never before, thanks to being revived by GLC money.

Members became immersed in continuing the LCC's new and expanding towns policy and preparing to move more than one million Londoners out of the overcrowded capital. Three New Towns for 150,000 to 250,000 people were planned and arrangements were in place for transfers to Swindon, Andover, Basingstoke, Peterborough, King's Lynn, Thetford, Norwich, Basildon, Aylesbury and elsewhere to accommodate the London families considered surplus to the planned population of six million.

The GLC had assumed responsibility for the Royal Festival Hall, a proposed South Bank entertainments complex, a site for a National Theatre, a Museum of London at Aldersgate Street in the city - and two zoos at Crystal Palace and Battersea, created by the LCC in the early fifties.

During Bill Fiske's term of office, the 1,100-seat Queen Elizabeth II Hall and the Purcell Room were opened on the South Bank. Next door, work was continuing on the Hayward Gallery. Together with its riverside gardens, the entire complex cost £2.7 million.

The new strategic authority did not take over the LCC's widely respected education service, which had passed to a newly created Inner London Education Authority (in the new 20 outer boroughs it was handled by the local councils). A later Tory leader, Sir Horace Cutler, would accuse ILEA of damning education with political dogma and 'destroying the finest education service in the world.'

Whatever the opinions, it is a fact that if a child was absent from an LCC school, the schools inspector was often on the doorstep before midday, demanding to know where the child was. In the last years of ILEA, in the borough of Islington at least, older children were offered pairs of Levi's as an incentive to attend.

Education was changing significantly in many ways. Children were arriving at school in their tens of thousands with more than 130 languages other than English as their mother tongue. Many teachers complained that, with every section of society now having rights but not obligations, trying to enforce discipline could create more problems than it solved.

Bill Fiske was a shrewd campaigner and veteran of 20 years on the LCC, though at this time he and the GLC were exercised by such things as the lack of conformity of street lighting over their extended domain. Sodium lighting gave everything a yellow hue, mercury vapour made people look alien green and fluorescent lamps reflected a ghostly white light. It was cause for much concern, said Gladys Dimson, a GLC member The new strategic council would be the lighting authority for 500 miles of metropolitan roads. Another 130 miles were the responsibility of the government and a further 1,200 miles handled by boroughs acting independently.

News that the Ministry of Defence was about to release the 1,000-acre Woolwich Arsenal site - later to become the town of Thamesmead - caused excitement. Here was an opportunity, perhaps the last within Greater London, for extensive housing. A survey of the capital's housing needs was already underway. Housing was still the capital's No. 1 priority and there was much emotion and idealism behind the programme to clear the slums and build homes for the homeless.

The war had been over nearly 20 years yet the need for tens of thousands of homes remained. In parts of the capital, families were still living in 'ten-year temporary hutments.' These prefabricated, single-storey homes, affectionately known as 'rabbit hutches' because of certain design similarities, were much praised by many who lived in them and were still in use decades after their planned life had expired.

Bomb sites all over London still awaited development, and many air-raid shelters were left standing as the cold war and fears of possible conflict with Russia dragged on. Covent Garden's fruit and vegetable market was moving, dramatically changing the traffic scenario at its new home in Nine Elms, Battersea, and offering an opportunity for imaginative redevelopment at the central London site it was vacating.

The first positive action by members during this continuing transitory stage was an attempt by Geoffrey Aplin to rename Festival Pier, at the Royal Festival Hall, as Lord Warden Pier. Churchill had just died and the name change, said Aplin, would commemorate the place where 'the body of the greatest Lord Warden of the Cinque Ports' was disembarked from London's river.

His suggestion was referred to the LCC who, apparently, didn't think much of it and no action was taken.

One subject raised at meeting after meeting concerned taxi drivers ripping off visitors arriving at Heathrow. These were the days when the only direct means of transport from the airport to central London was by taxi. Exorbitant fares were often charged leading to a series of complaints to GLC members.

Before the council-in-waiting was a year old came the first of many disputes with the government. Procrastination in supplying various planning permissions was delaying vital development, the council complained.

When the transitional period ended, the GLC held its inaugural meeting in its executive role on Tuesday April 6, 1965. Almost the first item William Fiske's council had to consider was the redevelopment of Piccadilly Circus following Sir William Holford's controversial plan to separate pedestrians from traffic by building 'walkways in the sky.' His proposals were accepted for detailed study.

The GLC was saddled with the enormous task of preparing a Greater London Development Plan, a strategic map of the capital into which each borough council would slot its own town plan. This would be the basis of London for the next 25 years, though there would be nothing to show for it until the framework had been decided and a public inquiry held. That was years away.

But the council was anxious to make its presence felt with a milestone project. With major planning out of the question and no responsibility for buses or trains, the one area where the council could make an impact was with roads, and particularly ideas for a 'motorway box' around central London. So this proposal was pursued with great enthusiasm.

In addition to the motorway box, another motorway scything through the middle of Greater London was also proposed with links to a government motorway (in part the forerunner of the M25) round the outside. Together they were known as the 'Ringways,' purpose built roads to take through traffic away from the capital's residential and historic areas.

This would prove to be one of the most controversial issues in London's local government history and one which would drag on for years. Fiske optimistically announced that construction would start in the 1970s and that there would be public inquiries 'if necessary.'

With hindsight, his statement must rank with the most naive of all time. Protesters fought many stretches of the proposed motorways tooth and nail, yard by yard. Most were never built; others were scaled down and modified to meet changing times.

For the next year, much of the council's activity concerned work necessary to achieve its vision of a bright, new, modern London - slum clearance and land acquisition for road widening.

It also found time to consider the possible necessity for road pricing. Although this was quietly discussed in committee it was leaked to the *Daily Mail,* causing some consternation.

London's vulnerability to flooding from the Thames became a hot topic propelled to the fore by a series of abnormally high tides. In those days before the Thames Barrier was projected, river walls were raised periodically to protect low-lying areas.

Among new tasks being handled by the council was censorship of films by a Film Viewing Board, later to be known colloquially as the 'dirty pictures committee.' Many films, tame by today's standards were refused certificates in the following years, including 'The Christine Keeler Story,' which the committee of the day considered 'depraved and corrupt.'

Another project destined to run for years was development of Lee Valley Regional park, inherited from the LCC which bought 78 acres of surplus land for £400,000 and 13.5 acres from the British

Railways Board. Interest in recreation also saw the council build an artificial ski slope on 500 square yards of Crystal Palace.

Pay negotiations with staff were handled on the first occasion with amusing naivety. With the serried ranks of council and Staff Association lined up on either side of the table, continuation of the cut and thrust experienced in dealings with the LCC was anticipated. However, Staff Association negotiators recall that the committee chairman, clearly no poker player, began by saying:

'I am empowered to offer three per cent, three-and-a-half if pushed.'

The meeting was soon over.

Negotiations with the London Fire Brigade suggested greater experience. Committee chairman John Henry, formerly Mayor of Lewisham and himself once a fireman, would put a large bottle of Scotch on the table and say: 'When that's gone I expect there to be agreement.'

5. THE PUBLICITY REVOLUTION

As one administration followed another at County Hall, press publicity and public information formed a larger and more important part of its business. With ever more sophisticated information technology and the election of an all-powerful mayor for London, the next administration promises to have the highest publicity profile of all.

Not until the London County Council was fighting for its life after 76 years of running inner London did it consider that, perhaps, it had contributed to its own downfall by not trumpeting its achievements. With abolition staring it in the face, the council reflected on its past and realised that performing tasks successfully was no longer enough. It was necessary to broadcast its achievements so they were appreciated by the public at large and applauded by commentators and opinion formers.

So it was that in its death throes, the year when the LCC and the GLC operated in tandem to smooth the transition between the two bodies, the LCC acted. Examining the small press department staffed by local government officers, it decided to recruit Geoff Lewis, a sub-editor from the *Daily Mail*, to reorganise its press and public information services on a professional footing. Thus was sown the seeds of what became a publicity revolution.

As year followed year, dissemination of information became one of the council's principal tasks. The result was that a once secretive local government opened the doors of committee meetings first to the press and public, and later - years ahead of similar action by Parliament - opened council meetings to TV. From having little communication with the public, London's strategic authority ended its days in 1986 producing almost 700 press releases annually and giving visual impact to the news by arranging photo calls for press and TV every few days. How things had changed!

Len Vigars was municipal correspondent for the now defunct

Evening News and was the first London local government specialist in Fleet Street.

Recalling the last years of the LCC, he said: 'There was virtually no interest in local government and planning, probably because no-one outside local government could understand it. Under the LCC, most decisions had effectively been taken behind closed doors in committee and you only learned what they wanted to tell you. On council day, I would be given a copy of the agenda to make of it what I could. There was no one to interpret it or give any help. I would have to go along and beg for back-up documents.'

To the establishment at County Hall, the press office was just another job into which local government staff were posted whether or not they had any skill, knowledge or interest in the work. One such person was a member of a narrow religious sect which forbade him reading newspapers, watching television or listening to the radio and who would often spend his lunch break Bible-punching in The Cut, near County Hall, where a flourishing street market attracted crowds. Asked how he reconciled his beliefs with his job, he would explain: 'It was God's will that I should take the job, so I can read newspapers during office hours.'

Of those early days, Geoff Lewis, later director of public information, said: 'What information the old LCC press office produced was rewrites from the council agenda - pretty flat, pretty dull, quite informative. I felt we ought to liven them up.

'As every committee report was signed by the committee chairman, there seemed no reason why the odd sentence shouldn't be taken out of a report and put into the chairman's mouth as a quote, to personalise the story and make it more usable for the press.'

Some say that this single act marked the nemesis of the GLC, ultimately leading it into a highly party political arena where it was never intended to operate. Personalising press releases gave committee chairmen power, a new stature, a high profile which projected them personally into the news. Richard Brew, who later became leader of the GLC Tories in opposition, once reflected that a senior chairman had 'as much power as a junior minister.'

And so it proved. Each administration demanded more and more of officers whose salaries were paid by the ratepayers and who were expected to work for the council, not become the tools of politicians.

Said Lewis: 'We had created a monster and it was impossible to stop it growing.'

As employees of the council, not of the political party ruling it, the publicity machine worked only for the administration and was allowed to become involved only when an item had been before a committee. At that point it became council policy. At the outset, political parties were not to be mentioned by name, nor were individuals to be attacked by name; constituency matters were to be paid for by the politician concerned; statements which were blatantly political were to be passed to the political party's press office for them to issue.

However, the new breed of career politician realised that statements from Tory Central Office or from Labour party headquarters were seen by the press as tainted and were not given the same credence as words from a more independent source like County Hall.

The once strict rules which governed how public money could be spent on publicity were gradually eroded. Some members with political aspirations beyond County Hall began insisting on issuing press releases on items which did not warrant such high profile publicity, simply because the item might be used by the local paper where they hoped to become a parliamentary candidate.

Blurred at the best of times, the dividing line between what was party business as opposed to council business was scorned by later administrations who were less and less inclined to accept any distinction - or to pick up the bill for constituency statements.

The next stage in the publicity revolution, when William Fiske was Labour leader of the first GLC, was to increase the press office staff to six, half promotions from within County Hall, half professional journalists from outside. In part this was prompted by a PR consultants' report which highlighted the public's ignorance of the GLC.

Consultants also recommended that the council should have a professional design unit. Yet more staff were recruited, causing Desmond Plummer, then leader of the Tory opposition, to warn that 'all these new officers should not regard their jobs as safe' after the next election. Nevertheless they were all retained and their numbers increased when Desmond Plummer won the election of 1967. Politicians were quick to realise that, while other departments continued their precious work of planning and providing for London and its population, the publicity department was dressing the shop window and writing the sales pitch.

During Plummer's leadership, Geoff Lewis set up local government's first all-professional press office, recruiting more journalists from the national press - poachers turned gamekeepers from Fleet Street - who could identify newsworthy stories and promote positive publicity. Or take action to limit the damage. The council offered salaries comparable with those paid on national newspapers, with the added carrot of better conditions and longer holidays. The posts were soon filled.

Press officers were allocated committees and encouraged to attend them to become personally known to the chairmen and committee clerks and to technical experts who wrote reports or supplied the data. They would then be able to write with a deeper knowledge of their subject.

Press officers were given committee papers as they were written, including confidential ones, had frequent meetings with chairmen, with authors of reports, and attended meetings and briefings as they thought necessary. The result was a pro-active publicity machine to manage the news: the first of the spin doctors was born.

Press officers knew virtually everything that was happening at County Hall and had the authority to brief themselves fully before the news broke on any item they expected to arouse media interest. The system allowed stories to be written so far in advance of being approved by committee, that they could be checked by officers for accuracy, words prepared for the politicians, and be issued within minutes of a committee decision being taken. Now there was time and the skill to angle stories for maximum exposure.

In the words of Geoff Lewis: 'We became more sophisticated, more conscious of press requirements. Now we were producing news stories rather than items from the agenda.'

As the publicists' role became more understood and accepted, senior officers consulted them on delicate matters where damaging fall-out could result. Some of the GLC's top officers were not only professionals *par excellence*, they were world authorities whose views were sought by writers and broadcasters from home and overseas. After the publicity revolution they, like politicians, were chaperoned at meetings with reporters. This was to ensure not only that conversation did not stray beyond the parameters of the agreed topics and that the council's interests were safeguarded, but also to make certain the reporter did not get lost afterwards along the seven miles of corridors at County Hall.

I recall sitting in at one such interview which ranked very high in the 'watch for fall-out' category.

Israeli troops had occupied Jordanian land on the West bank following one of the Arab-Israeli wars, and Israel had asked the GLC to send a planner to help reorganise the seized territory. In an unthinking moment, the council agreed. The Foreign Office, engaged in its perpetual dilemma of balancing our country's stance between the warring nations, learned of the GLC's action and blew a gasket. Two men were dispatched from Whitehall to confront the council's director general and demand the planner be brought back. Immediately.

The GLC sat tight, crossed its fingers and wondered if news of the gaffe would reach the media, in which case it could expect all hell to break loose. The council thought it had got away with it, until a young radio reporter named Ann Chapman telephoned.

Was it true, she asked, that a GLC planner was helping replan the occupied territories?

She asked to interview a senior officer and was invited to meet Bernard Collins, the Council's planning chief. At the meeting which followed, Collins, a man the press had once labelled 'probably the world's top planner,' gave a masterly demonstration of obfuscation. Without telling a whisker of a lie, he tied Ann in knots.

No, she was told, we had not sent a planner to Jerusalem, but we had sent one to Tel Aviv. (True). There was nothing unusual in that. We had another in New York (True). Exchange visits to swop ideas and learn from other big cities were commonplace and were part of local government. (True). Next month, a GLC member was going to Madrid and a traffic planner from Bangkok was coming to London

(True). Our man in Tel Aviv was there to talk about planning systems. Planning systems were his speciality. (True).

Ann left bewildered, not knowing enough of the story to ask the right questions. We talked as I led her through the corridor maze when the interview ended. I longed to know who had tipped her off, while the reporter in me was bursting to say: 'You should have asked......' Ann would never know how near she was to the story. Some years later, while on holiday in Greece, she was murdered.

With the GLC now a reservoir of good stories, London's *Evening Standard*, decided that it, too, should have a regular presence at County Hall. It appointed Mike King, a member of its Parliamentary team, to double up as County Hall correspondent, and he and Len Vigars set about making the GLC more user friendly to the media.

Desmond Plummer was quick to appreciate the advantages this could bring, not least to the GLC, and soon the two reporters were given lobby status - aping yet another Parliamentary system. As time passed, the national press and television appointed GLC commentators, and Radio London and LBC set up studios in County Hall. In contrast to the days when local government was rarely mentioned in the national press, GLC stories now appeared daily. Sometimes there were half a dozen in the evening papers.

In the Plummer years, this initiative grew into an all-embracing public information branch with the addition of a specialist news photographer (adding to eight employed by the architect's department). Together with graphic designers, they produced a flood of information for the public and news media, plus sophisticated publications and posters. A telephone helpline for Londoners was also set up.

Because few of London's 108 local papers ever attended council meetings, the GLC flirted with using a news agency to report business and circulate it free of charge. Predictably, the experiment did not last long. The agency journalists reported items dispassionately, which did not please some members who felt their views had not been correctly reflected. The idea was dropped after two or three meetings.

During the Labour administration of Sir Reg Goodwin (1973-77) the helpline service was extended further by opening public information centres in some boroughs (another Geoff Lewis initiative). But all this paled beside the enormous growth of publicity when Ken Livingstone's administration ruled in 1981-86. He doubled the size of the press office, published a regular newspaper which was delivered to all 2,750,000 homes in the capital and created outreach teams to drum home the political message throughout London. Publicity and open government under the GLC had come a very long way in a fairly short time.

As the thirst for publicity became greater, press photo calls were ever more newsy and innovative, publicity stunts more bizarre. No longer were ordinary cheques presented as in days of yore. Now they were written on giant pieces of pasteboard, once on a brick. Tapes were cut with 4ft. long decorative scissors. The GLC even borrowed an elephant (which Ken Livingstone rode) to publicise a temple of peace being built in Battersea Park by Tibetan monks.

Another stunt saw Livingstone parasailing along the Thames when a capricious wind dropped him unceremoniously into the water where his life jacket kept him afloat.

At a potentially more serious event, silver-haired Sandy Sandford, when chairman of the central area planning committee, chose to publicise a new cycle facility at Hyde Park Corner by riding round it on an old push bike, wearing morning suit and a bowler hat. Thrusting out an arm, he boldly pedalled into the swirling traffic and was soon lost amid speeding cars at what was then London's busiest road junction.

Fears that enthusiasm for publicity might result in a by-election were eased when Sandy, a wartime Pathfinder, ultimately negotiated a path through the traffic and returned safely to pronounce the trip: 'A bit hairy.'

Gremlins await the unwary. Every GLC department learned to organise a dummy run whenever possible in advance of every public event, to make sure the car park to which visitors were being directed would be open on the big day and with directions clearly marked; that there would be sufficient chairs in the hall; that the loos were in working order and that none of the transparencies for the film show was upside down or out of sequence.

Even when everything that could be rehearsed had been rehearsed there was always the chance of a problem from the unforeseen. Such a situation caused Sir Desmond Plummer more than a little anger on one occasion.

Over the years, the GLC had spent millions raising the river walls along the Thames, an interim flood prevention measure until the Thames barrier was completed. It was a massive and very successful operation which, for years, saved homes from flooding along the tidal Thames as far as Richmond.

When work was completed, a riverside ceremony was arranged for Sir Desmond at which he proposed to praise the GLC's foresightedness in working for London's safety. Television and the rest of the news media were present in some numbers, and tugs and riverboats cruised to the site with instructions to sound their hooters and horns at a signal to be given when Sir Desmond's speech ended. It was a simple signal, the waving of a handkerchief.

But the organisers reckoned without one of the assembly having a streaming cold and, in the middle of Sir Desmond's speech, pulling out a handkerchief with a flourish to blow his nose. After that it was sheer pantomime. The lead tug mistook this act as the signal, souned its hooter and all the other boats followed in a deafening cacophony that drowned out the leader's speech, forcing him to abandon it.

Maritime events seemed to be fated for the GLC. Sir Francis Chichester had just completed the first solo sail round the world, when word reached the GLC that there was a possibility of bringing his boat, Gipsy Moth, to London for permanent public display. Sir Francis and Gipsy Moth were big news at that time and getting the boat for London would be a major coup. John Howes was ordered to drop everything and concentrate on negotiating to get the boat and arrange a berth for it.

After a week of telephoning, persuading and cajoling, everything was arranged for Gypsy Moth to be taken to Greenwich where she would be berthed alongside the Cutty Sark. Another major media ceremony was arranged, the pictorial attraction of the two famous boats in such an historic setting would be a photographer's dream. Having Sir Francis in attendance put the icing on the cake, his words ensuring a publicity coup.

But the old man of the sea was not enjoying a good day. When a *Daily Mail* reporter approached him for an interview about his epic voyage, Sir Francis turned curtly and said: 'Piss off.'

You can't win 'em all.

A potential page one story which threatened publicity that neither the GLC nor Scotland Yard's anti-terrorist squad wanted, concerned London's sewers. It happened at a time of heightened IRA activity when members of the royal family were thought to be on a hit list.

Sewers can be dangerous places. Heavy rain can cause a sudden surge of flood water, while the ever-present methane gas can build up without warning. Both can be life-threatening. Even experienced sewer workers are forbidden to venture 'below' without a safety man, and when he blows his whistle, it's a case of everybody out. Fast!

We knew that an unknown, unauthorised person had been into the sewers because one of our workmen found a coat down there. Serious enough in itself, there was additional cause for alarm: it was found underneath Buckingham Palace. The incident was kept under wraps and, so far as I know, was never explained.

For me, that meeting was particularly significant. During the course of the conversation, our sewers chief said that there was trouble enough in the sewers without intruders going down: rats were becoming a major problem. He went on to say that the GLC was having difficulty keeping down rat numbers because they had learned to avoid some baits which contained poison and had developed immunity to others. He added: 'I can see the day coming when we develop a super-rat that we can't kill.' His words gave me the idea for a novel, *The Scurrying,* which was successfully published a couple of years later.

Not all the cover-ups and interviews concerned matters of national importance.

Another story the GLC decided would be best untold concerned a Christmas tree.

Each year the council received a giant fir from the people of Finland, a gesture of friendship and an appreciation of London's firemen who helped the Finns during the Winter War of 1940 when Stalin's troops invaded. Year after year the tree was displayed on the members' terrace at County Hall, overlooking the Thames. Each year, festooned with coloured lights, it vied for prominence with that other famous Christmas tree from Scandinavia, the gift from the people of Norway which graces Trafalgar Square.

On this occasion the GLC tree needed to be put up in a hurry because a Finnish choir was coming next day to sing carols round it. As usual, a contractor was instructed to set it up. No complication was anticipated, but because of the tight time schedule, work was done at night and unsupervised.

Next morning, when County Hall opened for work, instead of the Christmas tree's foliage sloping gracefully to the ground in a natural crinoline, all the lower branches had been hacked off and a large section of trunk was visible under an inelegant green miniskirt.

The contractor must have doubted his hearing when, with the concert only hours away, he was ordered: Put all the branches back!

Holes were hurriedly drilled into the trunk, the severed branches pushed into them - and nobody noticed the difference.

Authors occasionally asked to meet GLC experts to confirm facts and obtain material for their books. Provided the appropriate officer or politician was willing and could spare the time, there was rarely a problem.

One such fiction writer, however, turned out to be pursuing a potentially dangerous theme. He wanted to talk about London's roads and asked to meet Richard Brew, the affable chairman of environmental planning in the Plummer regime.

The GLC was painfully aware that there were vulnerable junctions on its main road network where traffic chaos resulted if an accident occurred. They were known as 'pinch-points.' There were about eight pinch-points in those days where, if accidents occurred simultaneously, central London could become gridlocked.

That was precisely the scenario the author was proposing to create. His plot concerned the fictional kidnap of the Queen. Road chase was to become impossible because London had been brought to a standstill by simultaneous crashes at the pinch-points.

Much to our alarm, he had done his homework well. Not only did he know the location of half the troublespots, he had also worked out the ramifications of the traffic build-up in surrounding areas. He asked Richard Brew if there were any other vulnerable junctions he should include in order to cause a total snarl-up. The normally obliging Brew was not able to help. He could imagine that sort of information falling into other hands.

The new breed of press officers identified closely with their committee chairmen, setting up media interviews, accompanying them to TV and radio studios and generally looking out for publicity opportunities. They also had the power to stop transmission (it did happen) if they thought the member in their charge was being unfairly treated. Inexperienced politicians did not take kindly to being invited to speak on a particular subject only to discover once the interview had begun that the reporter was really wanting to probe some presumed scandal in the member's private life.

There were some areas of business about which the council was particularly sensitive of media interpretation. The few reporters who, in the GLC's opinion, treated it unfairly, soon became known. With views coloured by memories of unfortunate experiences, an historic impasse was once reached when TV was making a complex documentary on homelessness, *Longfellow Road.*

Days of preparatory work had been done by both sides and all was set for the final day's filming. A dozen council officers were lined up to make their contributions when the council's housing chief insisted on having a preliminary sight of the film. The producer said No and neither side would back down. It was probably the shortest visit to County Hall a TV crew had ever made.

Many committee clerks, PAs and others also showed great loyalty to their chairmen, irrespective of political persuasion. There was an occasion when this loyalty was, perhaps, taken a little too far.

When his chairman was out of town, one officer, later to become an MP, learned of some action proposed by a member of the committee without the chairman's knowledge and, presumably, to his detriment. The officer responded by grabbing the perpetrator by the lapels, lifting him off his feet, banging his head on the oak-pannelled walls and leaving him in no doubt about what would happen if he ever attempted to 'cross' his chairman again.

Being identified with a chairman could become a double-edged sword. At the next election, when the ruling party was voted out of office, as usually happened, the officer was seen as a political animal and was mistrusted by the incoming regime. Many politicians cannot accept that anyone can be strictly apolitical. They suspect that the slightest political inclination will manifest itself in a person's work - potentially dangerous in any situation and particularly so in publicity.

It is a matter of history that when Sir Horace Cutler won the 1977 election and was returned to County Hall in a landslide victory, his publicity campaign was handled with great professionalism by Mary MacKenzie, a former GLC press officer of many years' standing. She went on to work for Tory Central Office, among others, yet Mary, as she shared in Cutler's triumph, told me that she had only ever been a member of one political party - the Labour party.

Sir James Swaffield, the longest-serving director general of the GLC, agreed on the problem.

He said: 'When a new administration comes in, they don't trust any of us. We may not agree with them but that doesn't mean we try to sabotage what they do.

' The notion is that the longer you serve an administration the more you absorb its colours. The facts are that they make the decisions and we carry out their wishes.'

The professional political publicist first made an appearance at County Hall when Sir Reg Goodwin won the 1973 election and brought with him Peter Walker, a Labour parliamentary candidate for Croydon, whose title was head of the leader's office. Although Sir Desmond Plummer, the previous leader, had assistance from a political professional paid for by Tory Central Office, Peter Walker became the first overtly political figure to have his salary paid from the rates.

He saw all press statements on behalf of Sir Reg to satisfy himself that the political slant was satisfactory. After the initial, mutual distrust had evaporated, the system worked well. The new leader's office, staffed by two young men in their twenties, soon found its feet and, as the leader's representatives, were not inhibited about 'sending for' the director general if a problem arose. Until then, it had been the DG who sent for you.

Prior to this outside appointment, existing GLC employees had staffed the leader's office, a system to which the Conservatives reverted when Sir Horace Cutler's team superseded Labour in the election of 1977.

When Sir Horace was defeated by Labour and Ken Livingstone came to power, he freely admitted favouring the American system in which the in-coming administration brings in its own chief officers.

The phrase 'if you're not with us, you're against us,' was rife - if wrong - during the Livingstone era.

Experienced officers who had heard all these misgivings expressed before, dismissed them for the nonsense they were, but some old hands were encouraged to retire and known left-wingers were brought into the administration at senior level. Ken Livingstone also wasted little time in increasing the size and scope of the publicity department.

Having voiced his intention of using County Hall to attack the government, the old distinctions between what was council business and what was personal or political propaganda became almost indistinguishable.

His personal office was headed by Bill Bush, vice chairman of a constituency Labour party in Wembley, who later became a BBC psephologist until joining Tony Blair's team at No. 10. As a political adviser, Livingstone brought in Veronica Crichton, a talented press and public relations officer who later schooled MPs of the Blair government in TV presentation. When she left mid term, she was superseded by Nita Clarke, the publicist behind so many of Ken Livingstone's stunts, and who later become the wife of Tony Benn's son, Stephen.

The arrival of the Livingstone administration also soon marked the departure of the GLC's last link with its original publicity machine.

Geoff Lewis, the man who masterminded the publicity re-volution and a former chairman of the Institute of Public Relations, retired early.

He said: 'It was a combination of things that caused me to retire. I wasn't happy about the way we appeared to be pressurised into getting involved in politics. I didn't think that was the way we ought to go. The straw that broke the camel's back was when Paul Boateng, chairman of the police committee, said in public that a report I had written was racist. I asked him afterwards to explain the problem but he just brushed it aside. I was a bit upset.'

Geoff Lewis's departure opened the door to Tony Wilson, fresh from success with ultra left Lambeth borough council, to become head of public information. Influenced more than ever by members, the council's information machine was now the most party political in its history. Whereas in the past, mention of a political affiliation was sufficient to disqualify a job applicant, such allegiance suddenly became an advantageous entry on one's cv.

It could be argued that this was necessary in the council's final years when it was fighting for its life in an openly political battle with the Conservative government; others may point to the inevitability of this from Day One of the Labour administration in view of Ken Livingstone's stated objective of attacking the government.

There was always something happening at County Hall, as the news media learned in its daily contact. Not all the stories it produced were political and not all saw the light of day.

Occasionally politicians chose to work behind locked doors, no doubt so they could ponder undisturbed on the weighty problems of running London. Or were there other reasons?

On one hilarious occasion a politician shut himself in his office high above the Thames embankment, intent on some non-council business with one of the female staff. Unknown to them, as they prepared for a passionate interlude, a television cherry-picker had parked below to take some aerial shots along the river. As camera and crew were hoisted noiselessly into the sky, they came level with the office window, catching the couple *in flagrante delicto*.

Imagine the member's dismay as strange faces and then a television camera appeared at the window, 30 feet up. For one uproarious minute they met eyeball to eyeball before the couple covered their embarrassment. It wasn't quite the footage Blue Peter was expecting.

6. PLUMMER'S TWO TERMS, 1967-73

Victory for Labour seemed a foregone conclusion when elections for
the 100-seat GLC were held in 1967. The Labour administration of
Bill Fiske had settled in quietly running the enlarged capital and
there was no burning desire for change. The scent of presumed
defeat was so strong in the nostrils of some Conservative
associations that they fielded weak candidates on the assumption
that they wouldn't get in.

Ladbrokes ventured into these unchartered waters, running a book
on local government for the first time and making Labour racing
certainties. Cyril Stein underlined his company's presence with a
champagne-soaked press launch and followed the political pundits in
virtually discounting the Conservative challenge. The odds against a
Tory majority of 20 were 500 to 1.

Len Vigars who attended the party for his paper, *The Evening
News*, recalled: 'I phoned over my copy and the story was in the
paper when I got back to the office. A man from the racing room
walked over and said: "What's all this bollocks about odds of 500 to
1?"

'I checked my notes. The figure was correct.

'He said: "You couldn't get 500 to 1 on a three-legged horse.
You've got to have a bet."

'I studied the constituencies and realised that the Tories would
probably hold their traditional seats and pick up most of those in the
outer suburbs. If that happened, it was possible that they could get a
sizable majority.

None of us on the news desk were betting men but we had a whip
round, put in ten shillings (50p) each - no insignificant sum in those
days - and bet a tenner. The election resulted in a Tory landslide and
we won £5,000.'

Elected to office were the good, the bad and the ugly. Those
picked by their associations as sacrificial lambs suddenly found

themselves catapulted to power in County Hall. Conservative Central Office was not pleased. Their London Regional agent, Cyril Norton, visited the guilty constituencies and read the riot act. Never again, he warned, should candidates be adopted on the assumption that they were not going to win.

Among the newcomers was one, Jeffrey Howard Archer, described as director of Medical Research into Children's Welfare. The best-selling author and former England sprinter who was the Conservatives' No. 1 choice for Mayor of London until a ghost from his past scuppered his bid, served only one term on the GLC and was a back-bencher. He is best remembered as an energetic showman who was responsible for persuading the GLC to lay Britain's first all-weather athletics track at Crystal Palace.

Chief photographer Roy Ferriman remembered being asked to attend a party in one of the rooms at County Hall.

He said: 'Several times I had just composed a shot when a little guy hurried over and pushed in. I got fed up with this and finally I took him to one side and told him to cut it out because he was spoiling the pictures. He looked surprised and said: "But I'm Jeffrey Archer. It's my party."

'Whenever we met after that he would pull my leg about it.'

Desmond Plummer, the Tory leader, formerly an England Olympic swimmer and water polo player, had an eventful reign as London's supremo. Formerly Mayor of Marylebone and an LCC member, his leadership was regarded enviously by Horace Cutler, the strongman from Middlesex County Council. Observers said that Cutler was always 'looking over Plummer's shoulder.' Ultimately he was superseded by Cutler, though not until Plummer's became the only GLC administration ever to be re-elected for a second term, winning again in 1970.

Desmond Plummer's council took over the runnning of London Transport's buses and tubes, saw through the GLC's first and only London-wide strategic plan (the Greater London Development Plan) after an 18-month public inquiry, produced the London Rail Study (the first and last comprehensive look at London's railways) and set in motion some important long term projects. These included making a start on building the Thames barrier, and presiding over the initial stages of revamping Covent Garden and Piccadilly Circus. House-building continued to be the priority of the day. In his inaugural address, Plummer promised to speed up the supply of new homes, sell council homes to sitting tenants, create housing outside London, and make greater efforts to restore and improve older property. He also guaranteed help to needy tenants by use of a new rent-rebate scheme.

Most of all, however, his administration probably will be remembered for the Ringways, the momentous plan of urban motorways proposed during the Fiske years.

The 'Motorway Box' had been renamed Ringway One, and there were changes to the outer rings. Now the plan was for three motorways to girdle London's centre, middle and outside, plus a fourth, the outer orbital motorway, planned by the government. The outer two subsequently became merged to form the M25. Each ring was to be connected to the others by a series of feeder roads like the spokes of a giant wheel.

Desmond Plummer, like his predecessor, was desperately keen to do something about London's traffic. The ringways were widely seen as the answer and they continued to enjoy all-party support. Only days after his election, he emphasised that the inner ringway 'must be completed in ten years.'

The ringway system was a child of Professor Sir Colin Buchanan, whose publication *Traffic in Towns* was widely respected and quoted throughout the land. For the first time, an authoritative figure addressed the problem of separating people from traffic and suggested how it should be done. Robert Vigars, a lean, lanky lawyer from Kensington, chairman of the GLC planning committee, was the person delegated to push the plan through.

The logic of the ringways was simple: lorries and through traffic would be taken out of residential streets and shopping areas and diverted to purpose-built motorways. Half of the 13 million road journeys generated by London every day would use the new motorways, resulting in a safer, cleaner and healthier lifestyle for everyone.

But there was a price to be paid - and not only a staggering cash cost of £860m. over 12 years. Ten thousand homes would be swept away, shops and parkland buried under concrete and thousands more families living near the ringways blighted by unacceptable noise and disturbance.   Robert Vigars pointed out that London's roads were inherited from the last century and that a ring road for London was advocated as far back as 1937.

With commendable honesty, detailed maps were produced for public inspection at an early consultation stage and before road lines were cut and dried. Probably for the first time ever, the help of the press was sought to publish them so that everyone could know exactly how far the proposed road was from their home.

But the more open Robert Vigars and the GLC became, the more objections swelled as residents realised the enormity of the proposals. Ultimately several stretches of motorway met with tidal waves of protest as those who were to lose their home or their peace and quiet were joined by political agitators and others who opposed road-building in principle.

Vigars decided to put the record straight by going on the offensive, spelling out the ringways' purpose, pointing to the advantages and what supporters saw as the dire alternative.

Roads were not 'monsters ploughing willy-nilly through residential areas,' he told doubters. Planning the exact line of a road was done with very great care and after lengthy consultation with local interests, which was why it took so long. Every effort was made to avoid disrupting important local centres and to reducing, as far as possible, the demolition of homes.

In particularly sensitive areas roads would be routed in tunnels and elsewhere in cuttings which would be covered over and gardens planted above. Londoners would be the beneficiaries. Studies showed that the system would cut accidents and journey times each by 20 per cent. The problem of rush-hour traffic would be resolved by improved public transport which was the other side of the GLC's transport coin.

Vigars stressed that London could not hope to provide for the tremendous increase in inter-suburban travel forecast for the next decade by tinkering with existing roads. What was imperative was to provide a new concept of urban motorways. Without new roads, congestion would become so appalling that it might become necessary to deprive Londoners of the use of their cars, an action he was not prepared to consider.

The ringways lobby stressed that the 30-mile inner ringway encircled an area the size of Leeds. Four cities the size of Glasgow could be fitted inside Ringway Two. These arguments ultimately led to the production by the GLC of a scale map which showed that the next 13 largest cities in Britain could all be fitted inside the massive area of Greater London - and each of those cities had its own ring road.

For three years the GLC had begged the Labour government of Harold Wilson to be allowed to deal more generously with those dispossessed. To no avail, Desmond Plummer urged that the GLC be permitted to pay towards sound insulation, buy up fringe properties for environmental reasons and knock down others which became virtually uninhabitable.

No matter how logically and reasonably the council's case was put, protests had now worked up such a head of steam that the argument had become unwinnable.

Desmond Plummer, who had previously announced that Ringway One must be completed by the late eighties, was forced to concede that there was now no chance of completion before the late nineties.

Robert Vigars turned the tables on the motor industry and, at a meeting of the Motor Agents Association, accused them of not playing their part to make motor vehicles more environmentally acceptable. If manufacturers could solve the problems of noise and fumes at source by developing and fitting more efficient exhaust and silencer systems, it would make road-building more acceptable to residents and cheaper for ratepayers.

He threatened: 'If the motor trade wants more roads quickly, it must make this contribution. Perhaps the GLC should refuse to build new motorways or promote new traffic schemes until the motor trade agrees to sell only noiseless, fumeless vehicles.'

London's traffic congestion became a major national topic when Prime Minister Ted Heath was trapped in Downing Street, unable to get to the House of Commons. In a rage he ordered: 'Get me Desmond Plummer!' The GLC leader was in Tokio. Heath, nevertheless, pursued him on the telephone and reportedly tore Plummer off a strip when he finally got through. Sir Desmond caught the next plane home.

[The story was to have an encore 15 years later when another Prime Minister, Margaret Thatcher, complained that MPs were delayed in reaching the Commons because of a new pelican crossing the GLC had sited at Waterloo station and which caused enormous jams in its early teething stages].

In the second administration of Plummer (now Sir Desmond), the chore of pushing through the ringways became the responsibility of Richard Brew, chairman of the newly created environmental planning committee.

If the title was mocked by supporters of 'green' policies, it at least acknowledged a change in council thinking. Under Brew, the council changed tack, pressurising the government for concessions to those affected and softening its approach to residents.

Europe's longest stretch of motorway to be built underground purely for environmental reasons was planned to run beneath Blackheath - one and a half miles costing £39m.

The council announced that the £64 million West Cross Route through Kensington and Chelsea would not be built until the GLC was assured of additional powers to deal with the environmental hardship caused to occupiers of properties alongside the road. The Government at last conceded - and Sir Desmond rejoiced that now 'humane and adequate' compensation could be paid. But it was too late.

By now the GLC had been forced to accept that the ringways could not be completed before the end of the century. In an effort to get one into operation, they amalgamated Ringways One and Two, linking the North Circular Road with the lines of the East and West Cross Routes, so saving from demolition 7,000 homes in Hampstead and Highbury. Residents of these areas, along with those in other districts now to be spared in Chiswick, Barnes, Tooting, Streatham, Croydon and Bromley had beaten the mighty GLC.

Towards the end of Sir Desmond's six years, attitudes to road-building were changing. A huge anti-roads lobby was winning massive public support. Labour saw the writing on the wall and withdrew its support. With the election approaching, Richard Brew hurried white-faced into a confidential meeting of the leader's committee, having spent the previous day 'on the knocker' in Kensington and experiencing the bitter animosity of residents towards the West Cross Route.

'We' ve got to do something about the West Cross Route, Desmond, or we are going to lose the whole of the vote,' he said desperately.

He was right. The Conservatives defiantly nailed their colours to the ringways mast and sailed on to oblivion at the polls.

Pedestrianisation of streets and shopping centres was all the rage, and media commentators were berating the GLC for lagging behind. London was being compared unfavourably with major cities in Europe and some in the UK.

Perhaps in desperation, Bond Street was offered as a trial candidate. Alas, the council overlooked that Asprey and the other standard-bearers in this swankiest of shopping streets expected their visitors to arrive by Rolls-Royce or taxi, not on foot. Painstaking negotiation finally resulted in the smallest crumb of comfort, New Bond Street being made one-way, a situation not improved upon to this day.

Hurriedly, the easier option of Carnaby Street, then the centre of pop culture, was substituted. Even here the GLC was so uncertain of new-fangled pedestrianisation that it was afraid of upsetting tourists if their coaches and taxis were not allowed in. Nevertheless, with some misgiving, the scheme proceeded. Londoners were told that it would be continued indefinitely - if there were not too many objections.

These minor tokens to pedestrians were not acceptable, particularly to the *Evening Standard* whose columnist, Simon Jenkins, campaigned vigorously for action to improve Oxford Street where 16,000 shoppers an hour - double that number in the run-up to Christmas - jammed the narrow pavements. There was no way of shirking action when readers' letters began supporting the call and other journalists talked of London's obsession with cars.

I went along to listen when the council's top traffic planners were called together to suggest a solution. Traffic Commissioner Dudley

Dennington surveyed his troops through tinted spectacles and said: 'We've got to take the traffic out of Oxford Street. How are we going to do it?'

A long silence was at last broken when one brave soul said lugubriously : 'It can't be done.'

Dennington replied: 'If a Boeing came down in Oxford Street we would have to divert the traffic. Where would we put it?' Everyone knew there was only one answer - along already congested Wigmore Street.

Without any positive proposal, the meeting broke up and the planners returned to their departments. Eventually a scheme emerged. Not full pedestrianisation of Oxford Street, but a popular alternative. Cars were banned, pavements widened and mature trees planted and seats added to give it a park setting. Car traffic was banished to Wigmore Street.

Plummer's arrival at County Hall as leader had coincided with a mystery which was strangely mirrored 30 years later when Tony Blair moved into Downing Street - the cat disappeared. Just as a cat was a well known incumbent of No.10, so Hector was one of the characters of County Hall. A large tabby, Hector had few friends. He could usually be found occupying a spot in front of the Italian marble fireplaces in the foyer whether or not a fire was burning. There he would sit, defying visitors to stroke him.

When Hector disappeared so soon after a change of occupant, the finger of suspicion fell on the new chief, just as suspicion fell on Tony and Cherie Blair when the Downing Street cat vanished. As with the Blairs, Plummer denied responsibility. The mystery was never solved.

Housing was constantly in the news during each of Sir Desmond's terms of office. Various initiatives were tried to break the back of the London-wide waiting lists which had risen 10 per cent in five years even though tens of thousands of homes were being built annually and 750,000 had been completed in 25 years since the war.

Selling council homes to sitting tenants was new and an immediate success. Within two weeks of the policy being announced more than 3,500 applied to buy. Alarmed at the threat of so much stock being sold off, the government suddenly limited to 600 a year the number that could be sold. By then, more than 15,000 potential purchasers were waiting, the lucky ones being chosen at monthly draws until the government relented.

During the Plummer years 10,000 council homes were sold to sitting tenants, nearly as many were in the pipeline and applications to buy were running at 100 a week when the GLC election brought that enterprise to a halt.

GLC mortgages were a good deal. They were offered to people who had been turned down by building societies, and loans were for a fixed term and at a better rate than could be obtained commercially. During the initial flurry of purchase, the £30 million set aside for mortgages was soon gone. Again the government interfered, refusing to allow the fund to be increased. Amid much acrimony, the scheme was suspended, leading Sir Desmond to protest that he had had a 'bellyful of government interference.'

When loans were resumed, they were extended to buyers of flats and maisonettes. In the last months of the administration the council decided to build 1,000 houses for sale whilst also building to rent.

Housing continued to be the main battleground with the government and another dispute erupted when Parliament blocked GLC plans to standardise rents throughout London to facilitate movement between the boroughs. This entailed an increase for most of the council's 236,000 tenants and the government said 'No.'

One of the major inroads into housing was under the council's New and Expanding Towns policy (inherited from the LCC) and the government-supported Industrial Selection scheme. In both, workers moved with their jobs. Under these schemes, tens of thousands of homes were built by the GLC at 32 locations.

Four years into the Plummer regime, a quarter of all families were being housed outside London, including at 20 seaside towns from Dovercourt to Weston-super-Mare. Here the council was building retirement homes where elderly couples were able to realise a dream and at the same time help the homeless by releasing their larger family home in London.

Dick Fedorcio journeyed to a corner of old London on the Isle of Wight for a photo shoot and was unprepared for what he found. The new arrivals had been reaping the bounty of the Hampshire countryside and picking sloes. The pastime was not restricted to a couple of families, they all seemed to have been doing it.

Said Dick: 'The first woman we called on insisted we tried her sloe gin. Next door the woman said: "You haven't lived till you've tried a glass of mine." At the next call a man was brewing bitter and had a dustbin full of it.

'Home brewing and winemaking were the fashion and everyone seemed to be trying it. It was like going on a trip to a distillery.'

Several designs by GLC architects won prizes including one at Thetford, Norfolk, which Labour Housing Minister Anthony Greenwood described as 'the best I have seen.' But there were storm clouds on the horizon. Robert Vigars observed that policies were almost too successful. Manual jobs were being lost too fast - at more than 30,000 a year. But still the policy continued.

The East End's tallest tower block - 26 storeys in Rowlett Street, Poplar - made news when the architect, Erno Goldfinger, chose to live in the penthouse for eight weeks (paying full rent) as a social experiment to study at first hand the living conditions he had created. An amused Sir Desmond said that perhaps this should be compulsory for all architects.

As a result of Goldfinger's experiences, the council redesigned its ventilator grilles, omitting copper because Goldfinger found it vibrated in the wind. Among the most persistent complaints he met concerned central heating that did not work, flat roofs which leaked and builder's surplus cement blocking the drainage systems.

After his report, Sir Desmond announced that there was no doubt that 'Londoners like living in the sky.' But this development was different from others. All the tenants had previously lived together on the same estate, so they knew each other. Not for them the isolation experienced by later tenants of tower blocks.

In a move to ease the burden on council tenants, government approval was sought for a lower minimum rent for the needy so that no one was called upon to pay more than 10pc of their income.

The GLC's poorer tenants were also encouraged to apply for the new rent rebates and, in a flamboyant gesture to guarantee the promised secrecy of information, when the applications had been processed, Sir Desmond set fire to them on the roof of County Hall.

The role of the caretaker on GLC estates was changing during this period. Now they operated in a pool instead of singly, equipped with walkie-talkies. Another sign of the times was the arrival of a new-age fleet of rent collection vans with bullet-proof windows and sophisticated alarm systems.

Sir Desmond was a tough negotiator who took his job very seriously and rarely drank. When he entertained in his office and his guests were tippling on gin and tonic, he would settle for tonic water.

But there was no abnegation in his appreciation of a good car. He had a gold-coloured Mini Cooper in which he drove a government minister at the ceremonial opening of the Blackwall Tunnel Southern Approach, and when he bought what he modestly called 'a runabout,' it turned out to be a state of the art Bentley.

Sir Desmond's interest in driving, however, was not appreciated by Bert Waterman, the leader's chauffeur.

'Driving him was the bane of my life,' he would say. 'I know London, that's my job. But Sir Desmond - and Lady Plummer, too - would insist on taking what they regarded as short cuts. They were forever making me turn round and take the route they knew.'

The Plummer years were momentous times for public transport. The 1968 Transport (London) Act transferred London Transport to the GLC, making the council responsible for transport policy, financing the buses and tubes and everything except day to day running which remained with a newly titled London Transport Executive. Barbara Castle, Labour's Transport Minister during most of the two-year negotiations, heralded the change as 'the biggest advance in London's transport for well over 30 years.' Privately the word was that she was mighty relieved to divest herself of what she regarded as an albatross.

For their part, the GLC had played their cards carefully, insisting that before takeover the government must wipe out London Transport's £250 million debt and the £12 million annual interest charge. They also pushed the government into agreeing a limited fares increase outside central London to provide some working capital.

More people were travelling on the Underground and, helped by tourism, fares revenue exceeded expectations by a considerable margin.

Aided by government grants, the Piccadilly Line was extended to Heathrow and stage one of the Jubilee Line was approved. With the LT ship on an even keel after another £20 million grant from the council, the GLC turned its attention to smaller experiments, including a dial-a-bus innovation at Hampstead Garden Suburb where a 16-seat minibus could be called to collect customers from their doorsteps along a flat-fare, flexible route to Golders Green.

London's first bus lanes made their appearance in Park Lane and on Vauxhall Bridge in February 1968. Their controversial introduction was slow and only 12 more were in operation (and 15 in the pipeline) four years later.

Clearways were the flavour of the time in the struggle to speed traffic flows and in one 14-month spell 100 were put in place and another 100 promised. London's first residents' parking meters also made their appearance along 25 miles of streets in Kensington and Chelsea. The charge: £7.10s (£7.50p) per quarter.

In another search for answers to London's traffic problems, the GLC began flirting with monorail. Planning chairman Robert Vigars was sent to the United States and Canada to study systems operating there, but returned with a negative report.

Interest switched to electric cars - just as it has again today. Sir Desmond foresaw these as being 'the answer to many of today's problems.' He expressed the hope that designers could make them sufficiently robust to withstand impact, yet nippy enough to get away at the lights and keep up with the other traffic.

Today, 30 years on, electric cars are still that elusive 'six or seven years away,' but this time, according to David Bayliss, formerly the council's chief transport planner, that estimate is realistic whereas in the past it never was.

There was more trouble with the government over planning. Unwillingness to submit its own architect's drawings to the GLC for approval led the council's respected historic buildings board to protest that the government put itself outside the law.

Historic Buildings was chaired by the Countess of Dartmouth, later to become Countess Spencer, step-mother to the Princess of

Wales. Friend and foe alike recognised Lady Dartmouth as an immensely capable lady. It was to her that Sir Horace Cutler turned to organise the financing of his 1977 GLC election campaign, though she declined because she was nursing her husband who died soon after. She was also chairman of the council's Covent Garden committee - some said to put her out of harm's way because she was a loose cannon; others because she was a threat to the leadership.

Raine Dartmouth accused the government of producing 'ghastly developments which wrecked our beautiful city.' She referred to changes at Knightsbridge barracks as a 'monument to government vandalism' and protested against there being 'one law for the rulers and another for the ruled.' Only a GLC outcry prevented similar vandalism at St Martin's-in-the-Fields and the National Gallery, she said.

Raine was not a lady to mince words. There was never cause for misunderstanding. Geoff Lewis, when assistant director of the council's public information branch, remembered one phone call to the countess on important council business which ended with her ladyship saying: 'In future, Mr Lewis, would you talk to my butler.'

In its dealings with public information, Sir Desmond's administration was the last to adhere to the rules differentiating between matters which were council business and those which were party political.

Brian Buckle, Sir Desmond's personal assistant recalled: 'He always meticulously observed the political divide. He issued labels to some of his political correspondents to put on their letters to him so they would not be opened by staff.' He also brought from Tory Central Office Cyril Townsend, later to become an MP, as his political aide.

Sir Desmond was the first leader to have a PA, his predecessor had only a secretary, though changes to the personnel structure were not the only ones Sir Desmond made.

On his election, he refused to be tucked away in an office at the end of the principal floor in County Hall from where his predecessor had operated. He chose to create a new suite of offices in the middle, close to the prestigious crescent terrace. The best rooms in the building were on the first floor and, as more and more of these were allocated to committee chairmen to give the administration more status, the director general became the sole officer to survive on that floor.

In a revolutionary move to discourage car commuting the GLC threatened to get tough on office parking. In a two-prong attack, they warned that big office blocks of the future may not be permitted to have their own car parks. Instead, space could be provided at strategic points partly at developers' expense, and that space would be shared by staff and visitors. Parliamentary powers needed to enforce this draconian measure were never sought. It was considered too big a political step to expect companies to pay towards providing car parks and then have to pay again to use them.

The second element was a proposed clamp on existing office parking, first by persuading a scaling down of requirements and, as a last resort, taxing it. This was another proposal needing parliamentary powers and which was never pursued to the point of action, though it has been revived by the Blair government and is now being promoted as a source of transport revenue for London's mayor.

In the course of studying ideas on office parking, GLC officers working with government planners devised a scheme called 'counter pay.' Meters were placed at the entrance and exit to car parks, counting and charging vehicles when they entered in the morning peak and when they left in the evening - a system which could be related to traffic generation at those crucial times.

Some think that this 30-year-old idea is superior to the one presently favoured by the government where a company is charged a fixed sum, perhaps £3,000 a year, for each parking space, irrespective of how frequently it is used or whether it is used at dawn or during the rush hour.

The Plummer administration looked again at road pricing and Sir Desmond appeared on television to warn that this was an option which London had to consider seriously.

Enthusiasm for this form of road rationing was never strong. There was concern about the unfairness of a charge which so favoured the company car, the moral dilemma of people living in the border areas and the need for a buffer zone to stop over-parking on the fringes. Eventually the idea was pigeon-holed as 'a possibility for the next decade.'

County Hall was never short of ideas or the willingness to try something new. The thinking of many of today's 'innovations' was done yesterday by the GLC.

For example, spurred on by the enthusiasm of geologist Ellis Hillman, a Labour member and author of the book *Underground London,* the council investigated building an underground freight railway and transferring surface goods to it. Studies were made of a possible £100 million project for 17 depots each servicing about one square mile. The hope was to consolidate daily delivery services of bread, milk and mail. Reluctantly the council concluded that savings in road traffic would be only 5 per cent. Better results could be achieved by restricting vehicle types and hours of access.

Another innovative scheme was Operation Moondrop - yet another suggestion being made to the new mayor - of night deliveries to shops, so freeing roads during the day.

There was greater success in actions to halt the scourge of lorries parking in the street at night. In those days, while the drivers slept, London's roads and pavements were littered with parked vehicles every night, 14,000 of them. The first steps were also taken towards banning heavy lorries from Central London when surveys showed that, on one day, between 500 and 700 juggernauts were thundering along Piccadilly and round Parliament Square. Thus began a ban on lorries of 40ft or longer from six square miles of central London.

London's first tentative steps in recycling were taken under the Plummer regime, with the setting up of 38 depots but to handle only bulky items like fridges, TVs and beds.

Lotteries, too, began to make news. Borough councils watched with interest as, in an attempt to acquire more cash for the arts, sport and other worthy causes, Sir Desmond's GLC sought parliamentary approval for a London-wide lottery. Gambling of that type was frowned on in 1970s Britain and the GLC's idea was finally squashed by the House of Lords in a 76-60 vote.

This was an era of innovation and of planning.... planning with a vengeance. There was town and country planning, land use planning, environmental planning.... We had become a nation of planners. As chairman of theGLC's strategic planning committee, Robert Vigars usually had a committee agenda of inordinate length.

Members recall one very hot afternoon when Vigars was ploughing through a long list of items with his customary diligence and Raine Dartmouth sat there rustling the bag of sweets she tended to take to meetings. Suddenly she left the room, returning after a couple of minutes.

'We all assumed she had been to the loo,' one of those present told me.

The sweltering meeting continued when suddenly the doors were propped open and into the hushed room came a waitress pushing a trolley which rattled across the floor and stopped in the aisle opposite Lady Dartmouth. The cover was taken off and there was a pot of tea with three cups and saucers for Lady Dartmouth and those sitting either side of her.

The chairman looked irritably towards the disturbance and remarked that it was very thoughtless of Lady Dartmouth to provide tea only for herself and her friends. Others might like a cup, too. So he adjourned the meeting - much to everyone else's delight - for what was certainly the first and last tea break the efficient Bob Vigars ever called.

7. THE GOODWIN YEARS, 1973-77

Free travel on public transport, first for pensioners and ultimately for all, was first mooted as the solution to London's traffic congestion when Labour, headed by Sir Reg Goodwin, was voted into County Hall in 1973. In what was probably the most radical strategic policy ever for London, the two principal elements were: low fares leading to free travel, and municipalisation of private rented accommodation allied to a standstill in council rents.

Shortly before the election, Labour had changed its stance on urban motorways. Supporters of a ringway system for London since LCC days, the party had become increasingly disenchanted with the theory that motorways were the answer to the capital's traffic problems and convinced that better use of public transport was the best and most acceptable answer.

Twenty years ahead of the government, the GLC's traffic planners were already satisfied that building additional roads often was not the answer to urban congestion. Their surveys proved conclusively that additional traffic capacity merely encouraged additional journeys and that traffic increased to fill the extra space. Whereas visits to a major shopping centre may have been made only once a week because it was difficult and time-consuming, when the journey was transformed by a new road it became an outing to be enjoyed every other day. As a result of Labour's change of heart, an anti-motorways backlash helped Goodwin sweep to victory on a Homes Before Roads ticket.

Sir Reg Goodwin came from a middle-class family. He was a man who had seen poverty and deprivation at first-hand and decided to devote his life to doing something about it. A deeply religious man not given to small talk, he was general secretary of the National Association of Boys' Clubs.

Sir Reg was a forceful and respected leader, quick to grasp issues and make up his mind. A polished speaker, he was said to spend hours in the seclusion of his office working on his speeches. True or not, his contributions to debate were always excellently argued and often were the high point of the debate.

Unlike Sir Desmond Plummer, Sir Reg did not have the ability to choose which car to use. Except when official duties required him to use the leader's Daimler, he ran around London in a battered old Ford Prefect, driven by his wife, known to all as 'Lady Pen.'

His two committees responsible for the main elements of Labour's revolutionary policies were both chaired by women, Evelyn Denington (Transport) and Gladys Dimson (Housing), both veterans of the LCC and both chosen without resort to quota systems or pressure from a then unborn women's lobby. And both were 'chairmen,' not chairwomen or chairs.

Evelyn Denington, a former schoolteacher and a veteran of 30 years in local government, was adamant. She would say: 'Chairman is a title of honour; it has nothing to do with gender. I am proud to be called chairman.'

She would tolerate 'madam chairman' but her reaction to anyone who called her 'chair' ensured they would not repeat the error.

She was certainly not a darling of the Left. To Labour's small left-wing rump, led by Ken Livingstone, she was No. 1 on the hit-list. Yet she had shared the radicalism of youth. At the famous Labour Party conference of 1945, she seconded the motion which ensured that the national manifesto included full support for nationalisation of the mines, steel and the railways, a commitment which led Herbert Morrison to comment: 'That's cost us the next election.' But he was wrong. Labour won in a landslide.

When the portfolios for the new GLC administration were handed out to press officers, I was given Transport, and so worked closely with Evelyn in her two years as chairman. She was not a person one warmed to instinctively, though I soon learned that beneath a sometimes very frosty exterior beat a heart of gold.

She worked tirelessly in pursuit of the council's manifesto pledge to introduce free bus travel for pensioners. No delay was permitted, no excuse tolerated. Every obstacle was faced and negotiated with great single-mindedness of purpose. With Andrew McIntosh and Norman Howard for Labour and Richard Brew (Conservative) negotiating behind the scenes, free travel was in operation only four months after the election and well ahead of schedule. It was a triumph for which Evelyn Denington richly deserves to be remembered.

London Transport strongly resisted free travel, not least because it caused problems with conductors' bonuses. For whatever reason, many conductors were frequently unwilling or unable to collect fares and a bonus system was instituted to encourage them to greater effort.

Evelyn Denington liked to refer to free travel as 'giving the elderly a lifeline to the outside world.' At that time London was home to 1,223,500 pensioners, though she did not expect all to apply for a free pass.

She monitored the scheme closely and became angry when told of couples garaging their car and travelling free on the buses. The scheme was not designed for those people, she would say. It was never intended that well-off Londoners should leave the car at home and travel for nothing. The problems of vastly increased car ownership which may have led to a desire to keep cars out of cities no matter what, and the dangers of pollution from car exhausts, were problems for the next decade.

Other stories to reach her concerned groups of pensioners boarding buses with sandwiches and flasks of tea and joy-riding all over London, a practice which became common. She would mumble that this was not the purpose of the scheme.

'We introduced it to combat the twin evils of old age - loneliness and infirmity. It was to enable elderly people to visit their children and keep hospital appointments,' she said.

Then she heard from pensioners' groups that the reason for much of the joy-riding was companionship and a need to keep warm because they could not afford to heat their homes. That put a different complexion on matters and introduced a factor the originators of the scheme never foresaw.

The original free travel scheme was restricted to London Transport's red buses and available only outside peak hours to women of 60 and men of 65 irrespective of whether or not they were working. It became known as the 'Cinderella pass' because holders were required to be home by 4 p.m., when the pass turned into a very expensive pumpkin. The extension of concessions to the Underground, to buses not operated by London Transport and to surface rail came later. Nevertheless, there was still an initial take-up of 800,000.

There was no way of checking the precise cost of the scheme and a token £8 million was put into the budget. It was a hopeless underestimate. When, in the nineties, more sophisticated systems were used to check precisely who was using the buses and tubes, the true cost of the present scheme was found to be more than £100 million.

As the extended concession became a lifeline for so many, the GLC continued in its blissful ignorance of the sums involved. By 1977, London Transport's guesstimate had soared to £27 million and the GLC swallowed hard before including such a sum in the budget. The implications for ratepayers were already becoming horrendous.

Guiding the GLC through other transport matters palled beside the monumental gift of tree travel, but Evelyn was an independent spirit.

Wearing seat belts in cars was not compulsory in those days and, despite considerable evidence of the benefits, there were some who opposed their introduction. The GLC was proposing a free vote among members and, as chairman of the transport committee, Mrs Denington was invited to give a preliminary radio interview. Naturally, she was expected to give weighty support for their introduction. Knowing her fairly well, I thought it prudent to ask what she was going to say. It was just as well.

'As I understand it,' she said, 'if I'm involved in a crash and I'm not wearing a seat belt, I'm liable to be thrown through the windscreen and killed. If I am wearing a seat belt, I'm liable to be trapped in the car and burnt to death. I'd rather be thrown through the windscreen.'

On another occasion, a two-man television team had arrived from Tokio to report on the London rush-hour. We decided to take them on a bus ride from Liverpool Street station, Evelyn acting as guide and explaining the bottlenecks. There was a problem and we got off to a late start by which time the worst of the rush was over.

There was no point in cameramen coming all the way from Japan and not seeing anything so, as we stood in the bus queue, I said to

Evelyn: 'You stay here and I'll get on the bus before it turns round and bag the front four seats upstairs.'

'You'll do no such thing!' she snapped. 'I'd be furious if anyone did that to me. We'll wait our turn.'

Then she walked to the head of the queue, explained our situation and asked if the other passengers would kindly not occupy the front seats. That was typical Evelyn.

On the housing front, London's strategic new broom was sweeping all before it. The GLC announced the beginning of negotiations to buy and repair 7,500 privately owned houses and flats 'to prevent the market declining and to rout bad landlords.'

The cost: £1 billion. That was just the first phase of the vast municipalisation programme.

At the same time, house-building was being pursued with such fervour there was no doubt that the target of 5,000 new homes in the first year would be achieved. The council was also attempting to double to 2,000 the seaside and country homes the GLC had bought or built for retired Londoners. And it was pressing on relentlessly with its new and expanding towns programme, aimed at easing the housing crisis by moving 20,000 people a year out of London.

The capital's population was now about 7.1 million, midway between the target of six million and the population 14 years earlier.

In co-operation with government policy of the time, it was also busily selling council houses in London, offering very competitive mortgages, and experimenting with such innovations as renting couples the shell of a house and inviting them to plan the interior with the help of GLC architects.

Director of housing was Harry Simpson, a man who had worked his way up from rent collector to being an inspirational authority on housing. He was a former director of housing in Northern Ireland and in the borough of Lambeth. At a fund-raising event in his memory, John Major, then Prime Minister and a former treasury minister, said that Harry Simpson had taught him all he ever knew about public finance. The PM also welcomed to the event Gladys Dimson who, he said, 'not many of you will know is godmother to one of my children.'

Although the GLC was London's strategic authority, it continued to be involved at both ends of the housing market - building big estates on the one hand, choosing the wallpaper and fixing tenants' garden gates on the other.

Gladys ruled the roost in housing development and was not always easy to please. Council officers who travelled with her to out of town estates would try to keep out of her way by sitting in different railway carriages. But there was no escape. When the journey ended they were called to account and expected to have at their fingertips all the information she required.

London's involvement with out of town housing was not always welcomed. On one occasion when Richard Balfe had taken over as housing development chairman, a GLC party was visiting north Wales in support of a proposed development.

The atmosphere was so ugly that the GLC party was tempted not to venture into the public meeting and finally did so only with much trepidation. Balfe, now a Euro MP, a brilliant speaker who usually wore a green cape and often carried a stick, was somewhat disadvantaged when the fiery opposition put their case in Welsh. He knew the basic complaint was that London was 'dumping its unwanted citizens' onto the municipality. In fact, many were Welsh families returning to their roots.

Undeterred, Balfe calmed their fears and spelt out the facts brilliantly. One of his party said: 'In the end he had them eating out of his hand. He was great.'

For a time, everything in the garden was rosy. London's strategic authority was certainly a winner for the hundreds of thousands of existing and prospective council tenants.

Almost the first act of the Goodwin administration was to keep its promise to roll back the 'scourge' of the ringways, abandoning three-quarters of the network at a stroke and so saving 10,000 homes from destruction and freeing thousands more from planning blight.

Simultaneously, the public transport alternative received an injection of £15 million (equal to a 1p rate), a commitment which soon began to bear fruit. Helped by stable fares, free travel for pensioners and a hike in the cost of petrol, peak-hour commuting to central London fell for the first time after 13 years of relentless rises.

The long years of decline in bus passengers was also reversed, with passenger journeys up 26 million in the first year, even though at one time 400 buses were off the road because of staff shortages. Bus and tube miles went on to increase year on year for the entire term of the administration.

Every committee was buzzing with activity. Strategic planning, another of the duties awaiting the new mayor and London Assembly, saw GLC planning chairman Norman Howard announce a five-year plan to control speculative office development which many thought had been spiralling out of control. He announced that growth would be limited to 17 million square feet, all but three million outside the central London honey-pot and most diverted to the more impoverished east side.

The dawn of pedestrianisation was promising a safer, more relaxed age for shoppers. The Hon. Tom Ponsonby (later Lord Ponsonby), chairman of the council's central area planning board, was dispatched to Europe to study overseas methods and he returned with many good ideas which formed the basis of future policies. Soon, 24 of the capital's main shopping streets were in the pipeline for car exclusion.

On the tube, extension of the Piccadilly line to Heathrow, paid for by the GLC and the government, was nearing completion and work was progressing on the new Jubilee tube line.

Yet even in these early, euphoric days, storm clouds were gathering. Inflation was rising strongly and shooting interest rates through the roof. Less than six months after the election, Illtyd Harrington, the GLC's finance chairman, announced that interest payments were now costing the council £7,000 a day more than just one week earlier.

In his first budget Harrington, never lost for a winning phrase, criticised the previous Tory administration for 'putting off until tomorrow what should have been done yesterday.' But there was no denying that much of the multi-million pound hole in the council's coffers was due to Labour's hugely expensive policies.

Whatever the cause, the council's solution was to increase the rate 46 per cent to 9.5p in the £. (The Tories claimed with justification that the actual rise was nearer 85 per cent because sewerage and the ambulance service had been taken away by the government and given to new bodies). But if ratepayers were the losers, at least all the sacred cows had remained unscathed. Though not for long.

The shape of catastrophes to come became evident only four months later when the council announced that London Transport's operating costs had soared from £15 million in 1973 to £34 million for 1974 - even before calculation of a much vaunted pay deal for LT's staff. The dream of free travel for all was beginning to recede.

Labour's problem was that their best intentions for improving London Transport services came to little because the pay offered was too poor to attract staff. Indeed LT's chairman once said he was 'embarrassed' at the wages they were compelled to offer. Labour was caught in a classic vicious circle.

To break out, LT's staff were offered a very attractive package of pay and conditions - but no productivity deal was asked in return. Sir Horace Cutler, leader of the Conservative opposition, goaded Labour on its negotiating naivety. The staff must have thought Christmas had come early, he said. The true scale of the give-away soon became apparent. It had cost £80 million. The GLC was stunned.

Because of this, Sir Reg Goodwin was forced to change his mind on a proposed second fares standstill and instructed London Transport to put up fares by a massive 36 per cent from the following April. The change of direction was blamed on a combination of the new pay awards and inflation which 'turned out to be far more than anything we could have reasonably expected.' Clearly there would be no free travel during Sir Reg's administration. Even the lesser strategy of stabilising fares had been blown out of the water.

The first clash between London's strategic authority and the government was not long delayed. While the Labour government of Harold Wilson urged restraint and hinted at cuts in rate support grant, the GLC pressed on with its expensive and grandiose manifesto commitments.

Early in its honeymoon period, the council proudly announced it had bought 500 vacant homes - five times the number purchased by the previous administration.

It trumpeted the biggest loan in GLC history - £215 million - three and a half times larger than the previous biggest raised seven years before. At the time, Sir Reg welcomed it as 'a great deal for the people of London.'

Whenever the GLC dealt on the money market the sum involved was so huge it would have affected market prices. So business was completed in a cloak and dagger style that would have done justice to James Bond. The GLC party would leave in an unmarked car and drive to the rear entrance of the Bank of England where they would be met by the Governor. Business would be completed over a glass of sherry after which the GLC party would depart as anonymously as they came.

Like its predecessors, Sir Reg's administration spent long hours considering how to tame London's traffic. It produced an impressive five-point plan, not unlike that being suggested today. It aimed at building on the previous council's park-and-ride scheme at outer London railway stations; introducing a network of express bus services; bringing in tougher curbs on cars entering central London, and making greater use of rail and water for freight transport. It also proposed to ban lorries from the area inside the North and South Circular roads.

Park and ride, perhaps the easiest of the options, was off to a prompt start. Later, the railways were browbeaten into abolishing parking fees at a handful of stations in an attempt to encourage greater use, though this failed to change drivers' habits and was abandoned.

Ideas for a network of express bus routes, and the transfer of freight to rail and water proved tougher nuts to crack.

The proposed clampdown on motorists took several forms: one was aimed at charging them for bringing their cars into central London, another at parking once they arrived and a third to reverse the previous requirement that new office blocks must have car parks

Road pricing in central London - still called supplementary licensing by the GLC - was now being widely canvassed as a cure for the area's traffic ills. Having been briefly considered by Sir William Fiske's first GLC and examined in some detail by the Plummer regime before being consigned to the back burner, it was now finding additional supporters. Yet fundamental doubts remained. Inequality among car drivers and difficulties of policing stymied progress. When the Goodwin administration finally threw out the idea, Jim Daly, who had succeeded Evelyn Denington as transport chairman, said:

'I consider that any method of road rationing which gives the wealthy and the company car driver an advantage at the expense of the ordinary working man is socially unacceptable.'

Instead, the GLC opted for seeking powers to tax office car parks. It urged the government to make changes in the company car system. Eventually, in what it called a 'clampdown on the company car perk,' the GLC sought to levy a tax of £6 a week on 30,000 company parking spaces, exempting car parks with ten spaces or fewer. Although parliamentary powers for this were never granted, a similar scheme is presently being proposed by the Blair government at an annual charge of £3,000 for each parking place, a not dissimilar sum to that suggested by the GLC 25 years ago.

Unlike Evelyn Denington, who championed the buses, Jim Daly, a polytechnic lecturer who later became a prominent SDP member, was a rail man. He wasted no time in proclaiming the advantages of universal ticketing, the forerunner of today's travelcard, and in ordering that Piccadilly Line trains should stop at Turnham Green during peak hours.

Unkind commentators sneered and pointed out that this was Daly's local station. However, there was no denying that Turnham Green was in the middle of a large commuter area served by four Underground stations through which LT's line connecting Piccadilly and Heathrow passed without stopping.

Jim Daly also championed the near derelict nine-mile North Woolwich to Tottenham Hale line, and the North London Line which periodically was threatened with closure. The latter ran parallel to the North Circular Road for 16 miles and linked Richmond to Broad Street via 19 stations. If workers along the North Circular could be persuaded to take the train, it could make a noticeable improvement to traffic on that busy artery.

He persuaded the GLC to pump £500,000 into the line to buy off service cuts proposed by British Rail, and then insisted that London Transport include the line on their underground map to 'lift it from comparative obscurity and give it prestige.' LT did not take kindly to associating their up-market service with the tatty rollingstock and tumbledown stations of the North London Line, but Daly insisted. Salt was rubbed into the wound when he held a photo-call in the ticket hall at Holborn tube station when the first of the new maps went on display.

These joint initiatives gave the line the desired fillip and soon passenger traffic was increasing.

Bus lanes and the consequent cut in hold-ups had eliminated the 400,000 miles previously lost to congestion. Nearly 130 bus lanes were in operation and had generated an extra 2.3 million passenger miles. Before the administration had run its course the number of lanes would pass 200.

The bus lane programme had become more venturesome, with several lanes against the traffic flow and another double-width. Peak-hour only operation went some way to placating motorists who reacted angrily when forced to queue while, alongside, road space reserved for buses was empty.

This problem was also an occasional bone of contention with the taxi organisations, always keen to stand up and be counted as part of the public transport system when it suited them. And it certainly suited them if this allowed cabbies to use bus lanes. Generally they were accommodated without fuss, though occasionally bus lanes served so many routes, or were in areas so popular with taxis, that allowing taxis to use them defeated their purpose.

Such a disagreement had just occurred when Jim Daly was disturbed in the early hours of the morning by an incessant ringing of his doorbell. By the time he got downstairs the caller had gone. It happened again the next night, and the night after.

Relating the incidents to me, Jim said: 'It's got to be a taxi driver. Who else is on the streets at that time of the morning?'

Backing his hunch, he telephoned the taxi associations. Oh no, it wasn't them, they protested. None of their members would do such a thing.

Jim was in no mood to be fobbed off. He warned: 'If it happens again, I'll ban all taxis from Oxford Street.'

That night he slept soundly. And thereafter.

In other service areas, too, London's strategic authority was busy.

The GLC had always been among the leaders in the disposal of household refuse. Now electricity from rubbish burnt at the state-of-the-art Edmonton incinerator was raising nearly £750,000 a year from sales to the national grid, in addition to that being generated for its own needs.

On the roads, although the cycling renaissance had not then arrived, cyclists were represented by a vociferous, if small, lobby - and the Goodwin administration listened. Cyclists' needs featured in all environmental improvements. They were also allowed to ride on footpaths in a dozen GLC parks and, as almost the last act of the administration, London's first cycle network was established over three square miles of Balham.

There were many glimpses into the possible London of the future as various innovations were tried to halt the continuing rise in car use. A shop to home delivery experiment was begun over 13 square miles of Greenwich and Lewisham, involving many of the big retailers. Plans were laid for London's first Speedbus route, along a ten-mile corridor from Parliament Hill Fields to Peckham Rye.

London Transport hoped to run a limited-stop service along this route as well as clipping 25 per cent off other bus times in the area. Studies were continuing for a futuristic super-tram link between Croydon and New Addington, and a dial-a-bus service was running experimentally in Hampstead Garden Suburb.

With control over 47 parks and vast sports facilities, including Europe's biggest collection of football pitches on Hackney Marshes, Tony Banks, chairman of the arts and recreation committee, called a meeting of all London's football league clubs to consider mutual help. Banks is an enthusiastic football fan who does not hide his love affair with Chelsea. Less well known is his fleeting infidelity at this time with Watford FC, when he was angling for a Parliamentary nomination there.

The County Hall meeting, the first such contact between London's principal local authority and the capital's many professional football clubs, helped lay the groundwork for tangible co-operation in a subsequent administration.

Everything about the GLC had always been big. Traditionally it had been Europe's biggest landlord with more than 230,000 tenants. Every year redecoration consumed 500,000 rolls of wallpaper, 250,000 gallons of paint and occupied an army of 1,500 decorators.

Now that vast housing empire was growing month by month as private landlords were bought out and the GLC built new homes with great speed. Half way through their term of office, Tony Judge, chairman of the housing management committee, boasted that 100 families were being housed every working day. But times were changing fast: the government was struggling to balance its own books and was calling for local councils to draw in their horns.

There was a shortfall of £319 million when the council presented its second budget. Despite an agonised decision to break faith with tenants by putting up council rents - thus slaying the second sacred cow following the increase in fares - and making across the board cuts in services, this still resulted in the rate being hoisted 80 per cent to 16p in the £.

Illtyd Harrington said that but for the £36 million from increased fares and transport grant from the government, ratepayers could have faced a charge of £150 million instead of the £81 million fares subsidy they were being asked to pay. Only the faithful were paying heed as added: 'This increase is not due to profligacy but because we are not receiving our fair share of Government grant.'

On the left wing, Ken Livingstone argued that if Labour had pursued its manifesto programme without any rent or fares increases, the rate would have been 22p - up 137 per cent. For that the party would not have been condemned more than for 80 per cent and with the higher rate they would have kept their election promises and not broken faith with all the users of public transport and the council's tenants.

Worse was to follow. Sir Reg was already warning of increasing costs, including in hitherto untouched housing. After two years in power, the Labour administration stopped selling council houses. Predictably, the best were being snapped up by sitting tenants and the less desirable left with the council.

Almost simultaneously it was realised that London was losing too many skilled workers - and too much industry - to the Home Counties and provinces. Prosperity in the south-east generally distorted the figures, and planning chief Norman Howard pleaded with the government to separate London from the rest. When they did so, it showed that whilst the industrial base of the south-east showed a rise of more than 21 per cent, London's registered a fall of 34 per cent compared with a decline of just 5 per cent in the rest of England and Wales.

The government had introduced a scheme for industrial development which required certificates (IDCs) for developments above a certain size. The figure set was too restrictive and was driving industrialists away. Again the GLC and government locked horns as the council lobbied for change. By the time the government listened, it was too late.

Moving families and jobs from London to the new and expanding towns was hurriedly reversed. The council withdrew from house-buying outside London, then tried to renegotiate deals which were pending, and finally resorted to selling site acquired for homes.

Interest charges were running at 13-14 per cent and rising when Illtyd Harrington spoke of inflation and rising costs 'bringing a new dimension of complexity to the budget process.'

As the pillars of the council's strategic policies collapsed around it, Labour began reaping more returns from its earlier initiatives. Although the council's successes were getting it deeper and deeper into debt, this was a boom time for London Transport.

Following the new pay deal, staff shortages were history. As services improved and the number of miles covered by buses and trains continued to grow, there were more give-aways. Pensioners could now travel on the underground outside peak hours for a 20p flat fare. Free travel to toddlers under three was extended to the under-fives. These reductions, allied to those for children under 15, meant that 40 per cent of all London Transport passengers were now travelling either for nothing or at a cheaper rate than previously.

Another project that began to bear some small but popular fruit at this time was the pedestrianisation of Leicester Square. But it didn't come about quite as intended and was rushed through to counter bad publicity expected on another front.

Pedestrianisation of leafy Leicester Square is now taken so much for granted one forgets that, not many years ago, the garden in the centre was an island surrounded by a smelly tide of traffic where pedestrians crossed at their peril. Few tarried in the garden where winos occupied most of the seats; few knew there was a finely sculptured statue of Shakespeare in the middle. The surrounding black ornamental railings seemed to frown on access and the garden was simply used as refuge for people crossing from restaurants on one side of the square to cinemas on the other.

When the previous GLC administration had been set on driving motorways through London, one lesser known plan concerned the transformation of Charing Cross Road into a six-lane highway, demolishing the bookshops so much a feature of that area. When the major ringway proposals were abolished, the safeguarded line along Charing Cross Road remained. Apparently, it was thought that some minor tinkering with the alignment might be desirable.

The *Sunday Times* discovered that the planning blight had not been lifted on the road and telephoned the press office late one Friday. I took the call.

Yes, there had been a plan to widen Charing Cross Road to six lanes but the GLC had scrapped it, I said.

Why wasn't the safeguarded line abandoned with the rest of the ringways system? If the road was to be abandoned, why hadn't the worried booksellers been told? The council was going ahead with road widening by stealth, wasn't it?

So the allegations continued. It was obvious that the GLC was in for a roasting in that weekend's paper. We needed to deflect criticism and take the heat off with a positive story. Did we have a contender?

A three squares study, for the possible pedestrianisation of Leicester Square, Trafalgar Square and Parliament Square had been commissioned by the GLC a year or so before and seemed to have disappeared without trace. I asked Jim Daly what had happened to it when I went to his room to warn of the storm about to burst and to suggest a pre-emptive strike.

'We'll do that,' he said. 'Announce an experimental weekend ban on traffic in Leicester Square. I'll put out a row of oil drums as a first step to permanent pedestrianisation. Do a press release on that.'

We did. And it worked. A row of oil drums was placed across one side of the Square to bar traffic along Coventry Street... and the pedestrianisation of Leicester Square had begun. Piece by piece the scheme grew and on April 20 1976, a concert by the London Fire Brigade band marked the extension of the scheme to weekdays and couples danced where traffic had rumbled for decades. Later the square was repaved and landscaped until it finally emerged as the popular attraction it is today.

Because of police objections to the re-routing of traffic, the GLC was never able to make progress with the more difficult pedestrianisation of Trafalgar and Parliament squares. The GLC could manage only two minor improvements: giving buses priority over a small part of the road surrounding Trafalgar Square, and introducing limited pavement widening in Parliament Square. Like Sir Reg Goodwin, the GLC's traffic planners found that good intentions and reality could be worlds apart.

There were failures as well as successes among the council's more innovative experiments. Its well-intentioned policy to direct new development away from central London failed because firms simply refused to build there. Problems were exacerbated by an oil crisis which led to many developers going to the wall.

Hampstead's dial-a-bus experiment came to an abrupt end, unable to cover its overheads even if every bus were full - no longer a consideration in today's climate. Experience showed that the Lewisham shop-to-home delivery service probably generated more, not fewer journeys, as customers stayed home to receive the supermarket delivery and then drove off to a fashion store or the DIY shop.

Speedbuses fell foul both of local residents and traders and no satisfactory solution was found to the displaced traffic. The Croydon tram link was abandoned as 'not feasible,' only to be up and running 25 years later.

Although these GLC dreams failed when put to the test, all produced masses of data on which subsequent schemes were successfully launched

For Sir Reg Goodwin and Labour, the financial chickens were fast coming home to roost. Illtyd Harrington bemoaned 'staggeringly high' interest rates - inflation at one time touched 28 per cent.

Yet while the council was drowning in an ocean of debt, some of its own bills remained unpaid. Businesses owed a staggering £15.8 million in rates which they were disputing. The law allowed them to retain 50 per cent of any increase pending appeal. Tenants owed £2.7 million in back rent.

As always, pensioners were the least of the bad debtors. When a Lewisham tenant died the council found 29 rent books going back 41 years and showing that in all that time she had only once been in the red - by one shilling. Her rent books are kept in the council archives as a cameo of the ideal tenant.

As the drain on the GLC's cash resources continued and new borrowing cost an arm and a leg, there was now insufficient money to resurface roads. They had to be patched instead. London Transport had to make do with only 50 of the 660 buses it wanted to buy. Borough councils were told there was no hope of progress on the 50 town centre schemes they had lodged with the GLC and which cost £130 million in highways investment alone.

The last sacred cow, Labour's housing programme, was finally put to the sword, £50 million being sliced from its budget. Privately, Sir Reg warned that house-building was resulting in ever increasing debt as interest charges soared. If the programme was continued at its intended level, the Labour party could be faced with levelling an astronomical, vote-losing rate of 50p in the £ when the party went to the polls two years hence. It had been less than 5p when it came into power.

Faced with this scenario, there was a rates standstill in the last two Goodwin budgets and the rates contribution to public transport remained frozen at £80 million.

With its policies now in tatters, the GLC ordered London Transport to prepare for another fares rise of 25 per cent and a further 20 per cent six months later. On the buses, this later increase was even advanced a month in a desperate attempt to claw back an extra £1.5 million. The phasing out of government transport grant further compounded LT's financial problems, yet still the government was not satisfied.

As Whitehall pressed for more economies, Jim Daly protested forlornly that there was 'no more fat on the carcass,' while Sir Reg warned that any further economies could mean laying off staff and cutting the services they had worked and sweated so hard to restore.

And so it went on. Yet another fares rise was in the pipeline when the next election brought a merciful halt to Labour's misery.

The final political indignity of breaking its pledge to tenants and raising council rents annually - another rise was also in the course of preparation at election time - further increased the administration's embarrassment. The Tories said Labour had a death wish. Labour claimed it was a victim of a unique inflationary spiral. In a *Sunday Times* interview, a desperate Sir Reg Goodwin lamented that it had been like 'planning for a different era.'

8. THE CUTLER ERA, 1977-81

Labour's defeat in May 1977 was a foregone conclusion. The Labour government of James Callaghan was deeply unpopular and the effects of sky-high inflation had helped wipe out Labour chances of retaining the GLC. With the election more than a month away, I received a 'thank-you, won't be seeing you next term,' letter from a chairman I had served. He was not wrong. The Tories romped home, polling more than a million votes, 52.5 per cent of the total.

They came in with a new leader, Sir Desmond Plummer having given way to Horace Cutler - or as Sir Desmond remarked acidly to the press: 'I'm making way for an older man.'

Cutler did not rise to the bait though privately he said of Sir Desmond: 'Brilliant administrator, lousy politician.'

Evening News reporter Len Vigars recalled: 'I was with Horace in his room when news came through that the Conservatives had won the election. Horace got down on his knees.'

His victory marked the turning point of a Conservative revival nationally which, two years later, saw Margaret Thatcher win the country. She and Sir Horace had an enduring affinity; both were extroverts, dominant personalities with a strong sense of PR and believed in strong government. Mrs Thatcher referred to the capture of London as 'the jewel in the crown,' and was the first to congratulate Horace. Above the fireplace in his office, he had a large picture of her which he would talk to when things were going well.

The day after his victory, an elated Sir Horace waited impatiently to greet her on the steps at County Hall, but Mrs Thatcher's driver mistakenly took her to the members' entrance at the side of the building on Westminster Bridge.

Jack Barker, clerk to the council, said: 'I saw a lady trying to push open the heavy door, went to help and saw it was Mrs Thatcher. I knew she was expected. Even in those days, the lady was not for turning. She declined to go out and drive round to where Sir Horace was waiting. I led her through the building, hurriedly got word to Sir Horace that she had arrived and they met on the ceremonial staircase inside County Hall.'

If photographers outside the building were disappointed, the picture to emerge subsequently, taken on the County Hall terrace, became a classic.

Bearded and always wearing a bow tie, Sir Horace was a show-man and a highly controversial leader. A man with an exceptionally short fuse, he had his share of enemies though those who worked closely with him found him generous, humorous, and a man of vision. All said he would have made an excellent mayor of London.

Mick Brown, head of Sir Horace's secretariat throughout his leadership and for two years in opposition, said: 'He appreciated loyalty above all else. If he thought he could rely on you he would do anything for you. He saw the funny side of everything and he was a politician to his fingertips.'

Mary MacKenzie, who masterminded his election campaign, said: 'Horace was very efficient, very capable, always knew exactly what you were talking about and was a delight to work with. He never procrastinated and he had a feel for PR. But he was very feisty. You had to be prepared to take him on.'

Sir Horace had great energy despite being well into his sixties. His day always began early, his first phone call to County Hall would be punctually at 7.15 when he would expect Mick Brown to be there.

Mick added: 'He said to me: "While you are here you're going to work like a slave, and when you're not you can forget about it." In all the years I worked for him, he only once called me at home.'

Conservative colleagues who noted the picture of Margaret Thatcher on the wall, also remember one other unusual aspect of the famous inner sanctum which was his office: the door to the corridor had a handle only on the inside. Its use, to enable him to work undisturbed while all callers approached through the secretariat, had a more symbolic, even sinister significance. During rows with his cabinet, Horace would say: 'If you don't like it, there's the door.' He would indicate and everyone knew that if you opened the door and walked out there was no way back. The door also enabled Sir

Horace to get out in a hurry in the event of danger. It came in useful once. A lawless intruder with a hefty punch thumped Bill Brereton, the security chief, and his assistant during a tussle in the anteroom but he failed to reach the inner sanctum.

Sir Horace's vision was of a GLC with a truly strategic role and his administration soon got to grips with policies to achieve that. They included transferring the council's 236,000 homes to the London boroughs, reviving the inner city, improving bus services and cutting the council's staff. Cutler confessed to having a 'pathological obsession' about bureaucracy. When asked how many people worked at County Hall, his stock reply was: 'About half of them.'

He was angered not only by what he saw as an unnecessarily large workforce, he was equally scornful of unnecessary council committees. He claimed to have inherited from Sir Reg Goodwin's administration 130 decision-making bodies which he whittled down to 29.

He frequently talked of 'good housekeeping' and pledged a value for money administration. When his four-year term ended, staff had been slimmed down by 5,200, saving £50 million a year, and the rate was 25 per cent higher than when the Tories won power, compared with the 210 per cent increase imposed by his Labour predecessors. Although financial conditions varied much between the two terms, Cutler's administration succeeded in keeping rates below inflation which had averaged a difficult 15 per cent a year compared with 20 per cent during Labour's reign.

In striving to find the council's true role, Cutler set up an inquiry under Sir Frank Marshall, formerly leader of Leeds City Council. Long before Marshall reported, however, Cutler had begun ridding the council of what he regarded as the biggest of all financial millstones - housing. The more houses the council built, the deeper it got into debt. He argued that, although the council should retain a strategic role, it had no place in day to day management. Borough councils were more closely in touch with the needs and problems of tenants, he said, and should have the responsibility for managing and allocating homes.

Hardly had the ballot forms been counted than the first steps in the proposed transfer of council estates was announced by housing chairman George Tremlett, author of books on pop music and a rumbustious politician, never short of ideas or the ability to promote them.

The first transfer of estates was soon accomplished - 5,900 homes to Tory-controlled Bromley. Two years on and agreement had been reached for 75 per cent of the housing stock to be jointly managed or transferred to 21 boroughs, and to 24 district councils outside London. With them went several thousand staff. It required a Parliamenary order to foist the final 70,000 homes on unwilling Labour councils in inner London, an action which the next Labour GLC tried unsuccessfully to stop.

George Tremlett also announced an immediate restart to the sale of council homes to sitting tenants, a scheme halted by Labour. The Tories called it the Sale of the Century. After two years, the council was trumpeting 3,000 sales and was on course for its four-year target of 10,000. Sales resulted in a surplus of £61 million, even though many had been sold at a discount.

Sir Horace pledged: 'In future the GLC will not poke its finger into too many housing pies. We will not fall into the trap of trying to do everything ourselves.'

In addition to ploughing tens of millions into traditional methods to build and improve homes in the inner city, the Tories set up a novel 'homesteading' scheme for first time buyers who could not afford normal house purchase. It was aimed at bringing back into occupation thousands of empty properties, many boarded up and largely derelict.

Couples were challenged to: Find a dilapidated property in inner London that you would like to own and would be prepared to restore for your own occupation, trace the owner, then contact the GLC. The property would be surveyed, valued and, if suitable, bought by the council. On the same day, it would be sold on to the homesteader on a mortgage deferred for three years. If buyers wished to apply to the local borough council for an improvement grant, the GLC would arrange a loan for the remainder of the work.

Such was the demand that some couples camped outside County Hall all night to register their interest. Government restrictions initially limited cash to £10 million, but so great was the enthusiasm that 15,000 names were put into the hat for each of the first two monthly draws.

Conditions, which were changed from time to time, required couples to be first time buyers who had lived or worked in London for 12 of the previous 18 months, that properties must have been empty two years, valuation did not exceed £15,000 and they should need at least £2,000 spent on them.

To publicise the scheme the council invited Mrs Thatcher to meet the first couple to become homesteaders and present them with a five-litre can of paint and a set of brushes. It was a bitterly cold day, so cold that Mrs Thatcher warmed her hands on the tea urn before making the presentation. Unfortunately the paint tin was not quite up to the occasion. It was badly dented and, despite being deftly turned so the PM wouldn't notice, she did.

'Not a very good advert for Dulux,' she observed, turning the can again so the unblemished side faced the cameras.

More than 1,000 houses were bought in this way and the council began homesteading flats. Eventually the idea was widened to include industrial units, the first of which - 64 small businesses providing 200 jobs - had just been completed when the election arrived and the Conservatives were thrown out.

After the success of homesteading, George Tremlett turned his attention to squatters, 'some legitimately homeless, others just skivers,' he said.

Illegal occupiers were squatting in 1,400 GLC properties, many in multiple residency. All were given 28 days to regularise their occupation with a view to becoming tenants, or face eviction. Ultimately there were 1,900 tenancy applications involving 5,000 people. Legal action was taken against the rest.

Among several more innovative ideas, Sons and Daughters was aimed at helping the 10,000 Londoners living with mum and dad to have a home of their own nearby. Another scheme, Ready Access, offered hundreds of flats unsuitable for families, to single adults willing to share. Hard-to-lets came on the market and couples queued all night to take on properties that those on the housing list did not want. In tower blocks a pilot plan was launched to stimulate tenants' pride in their immediate surroundings and to combat vandalism, by carpeting landings, providing entry phones and redesigning some corridors to give semi private access.

There was nationwide interest in what the GLC called its Four-day Improvement Package, a brainchild of the Goodwin administration. Tenants who chose to take part, were given a £20 disturbance allowance and, whilst they remained in occupation, bathrooms and kitchens were ripped out during an intensive four-day modernisation. Even the Labour government offered its congratulations, and councils from all over Britain came to see how it worked. About 15,000 inter-war homes were modernised in this way, at one-fifth the cost had they been vacated.

Afterwards, 83 per cent of tenants pronounced themselves satisfied and more than two-thirds considered it worth the subsequent rent increase.

At the same time the council was asset stripping - in Sir Horace's words, 'getting rid of the 14,000 properties they had no statutory reason to hold.' It was not part of a strategic authority's role to hold property, he argued. The GLC owned West End theatres, offices, shops, derelict buildings and vast acreages of land bought for housing and road widening. The council also discovered hundreds of odd parcels of land owned but forgotten. One long, thin strip, acquired in 1889 for widening the Tower Bridge Northern Approach Road and just wide enough to accommodate an advertisement hoarding, was worth thousands, despite its limited size and shape.

The land bank was also broken up and more than £100 million a year recouped from the sale of property and sites as far afield as Dorset and Gloucester.

Second prong of the Tories' election manifesto was to improve the reliability of London Transport, particularly buses. Planning chairman Shelagh Roberts, later to become an MEP, was pictured on Westminster Bridge with her arm raised and saying: 'I will make the buses run on time.' It was an unwise hostage to fortune and a task beyond even the redoubtable Shelagh.

Delegated the nitty-gritty of this awesome task was Harold Mote, formerly Mayor of Harrow. Mote said that he was born in a taxi 'and hadn't stopped moving since.' He had four children and was legal guardian to another ten, including four of a brother officer killed in action and four Malays. Harold Mote was a lieutenant colonel by the age of 23 and after the war built up a chain of electronics companies and drove a Rolls-Royce.

Nobody's fool, he once told me that when business took him behind the Iron Curtain, he would spend the first ten minutes in his hotel room immobilising the electronic bugs.

One morning at County Hall, I inadvertently walked into a 'dirty tricks' incident in which Labour hoped to trap Mote. He was suspected, wrongly as it transpired, of being instrumental in banning Labour from using a public hall in his Harrow constituency. Unknown to him, the telephone conversation was to be taped.

Was Labour about to succeed where the KGB had failed?

After the initial pleasantries there was a long pause and then Mote asked: 'What's that echo I can hear... that banjo-ing noise?' At that point I made a discreet exit.

Harold Mote once made news following a punch-up between members at County Hall in which he was alleged to have blacked the eye of another Conservative, Roland Freeman. Mote smiled at the allegation and said to me: 'If I had hit him, he'd have stayed down.' (He had been captain of an army boxing team in his youth). The *Evening Standard*, however, felt sufficiently satisfied with its facts to run a story headlined 'The mote in Freeman's eye.'

But Harold had a downside in publicity terms. For a politician, he was soft-spoken and inclined to be hesitant. Some broadcasters would wince when Mote was offered up as the right man to put the council's case. Worse from the television viewpoint, he wore glasses which reacted to light. On one occasion when I accompanied him to a TV studio, as the studio lights turned brighter and brighter, Harold's glasses became steadily darker until his eyes almost disappeared behind two black rings. A frenetic producer came up to me and pleaded: 'Can't you get him to take his specs off. He looks like a Mafia godfather.'

His room at County Hall resembled a military operations room. In the centre was a huge coffee table map of London's bus routes. Several times I watched him scramble over it to reach central London and trace the pertinent routes with his pipe stem. The outcome of his hard work was a 'short term bus plan' affecting 84 routes, 40 of them significantly.

He was also determined to probe the reasons for bus delays. For years London Transport had rightly bemoaned that road congestion made buses late. But were there other reasons? As with statements such as 'there are a million gays in London,' the reason for bus lateness had acquired the authority of the printed word without any corroborative basis. Harold Mote was not so easily swayed.

He analysed the cause of 325 major delays and turned up some unexpected facts. Sixty-six were caused by accidents, 44 by road works and 33 by vehicle breakdowns, half of them buses. Traffic signal failures accounted for another 45, seven were delays caused by protest marches and demonstrations, 50 by heavy traffic in shopping areas, two-thirds related to football grounds. Bad weather was responsible for 14. Reasons for the remaining 66 were unknown.

Despite these efforts, in a half term report to Londoners, Sir Horace admitted that attempts to get the buses to run to time was a 'conspicuous failure.'

The corner was finally turned in the last eight weeks of the administration when passenger miles were up 4.5 million. At their worst passenger miles had been down 36 million in a year - 22 million through staff shortages, five million through 'traffic congestion' and eight million through breakdowns. One of the principal problems was that, unlike the much-loved Routemasters they were replacing, the new buses were not sufficiently robust for London's traffic. At its peak, 500 buses were off the road, about ten per cent of scheduled services.

Busmen hated to see the reliable old Routemasters pensioned off, but the model had its day of glory in July 1977, when a specially painted silver bus was driven through the gates of Buckingham Palace carrying an official GLC party attending to present a loyal address to the Queen, congratulating her on her silver jubilee.

London Transport was very much a man's domain in those days. When Mary Matthews took over the London Transport publicity brief for the GLC, she was invited to LT headquarters in St James's to meet the top brass and dine in what was affectionately known as the 'officers' mess.' It seated, perhaps, 60 and was usually full. When Mary visited, there wasn't another woman in sight, so she asked how many women were members. After much discussion, her hosts concluded that only two women were eligible, both were doctors and both outposted!

Relations between the GLC and London Transport, often strained, came to a crunch one day at an infamous lunch planned at LT's headquarters when the top brass of the two organisations were meeting at a get-together hosted by Ralph Bennett, LT's chief. Other guests were already assembled when Sir Horace arrived in the foyer downstairs. LT had just introduced a security pass system and the doorman asked to see Cutler's.

Sir Horace said that he didn't have one but that he was Horace Cutler. To which the doorman replied: 'I don't care who you are you're not getting in without a pass.' The man left to telephone. When he returned Sir Horace had gone.

Alan Greengross, the GLC's transport committee chairman, took up the story: 'We were having drinks on the roof terrace when the message came up that Sir Horace had been turned away. The blood drained from Ralph Bennett's face and he dashed off and got a taxi to County Hall.'

There he found Sir Horace in the members' dining room having lunch. Ralph Bennett came in apologetically and Sir Horace bawled him out in front of everybody. Relations between the two, never harmonious, deteriorated further and Bennett parted company with LT soon afterwards.

Among new faces elected to County Hall in the Tory landslide was Dr Mark Patterson, a Harley Street haematologist with an international VIP clientele, and who unsuccessfully contested a Parliamentary seat in Ealing. Mark was a humorist, a cavalier characer, frequently seen stomping along the corridors of County Hall with a large Havana between his teeth.

He was numbered among the council members and press officers who occasionally met for a sundowner at the Crown and Cushion pub in York Road. Sometimes he would arrive in a flashy red Masserati - in striking contrast to another member, Sir George Young, later a junior minister in John Major's Department of

Transort, who would usually turn up in leathers and on a motor-bike.

Dr Patterson may also be remembered as possibly the only member to tell a gratuitous, blue joke in the dignified surroundings of the council chamber. As he sat down, almost alone in laughing at the punch line, cries of 'Disgusting! Disgusting!' from Labour's Illtyd Harrington rang in his ears.

On another occasion, honey-haired Marion Roe, later Tory MP for Broxbourne, had just finished her contribution to the debate and adjourned to the bar. Mark Patterson had just preceded her and was drinking with some reporters.

'What did you think of my speech, Mark?' she asked.

Patterson pondered a moment before replying: 'Actually I was sitting there... admiring your tits.'

During the Cutler administration fares went up most years in line with inflation which was always in double figures. Flat fares were introduced over 500 miles of London's outer suburbs in what the Tories called a 'new dawn' in bus travel, and important extensions were planned on the Underground, with the government paying the lion's share. But money was tight and Whitehall was slow to stand its corner.

Sir Horace complained bitterly that government dilatoriness had lost the chance to build the proposed LT station at Heathrow's new Terminal Four on the first choice site below the terminal buildings, and that if Whitehall didn't get a move on, the second favoured site below the multi-storey car park would also be lost.

Relations with the government were even worse for the second stage of the Jubilee Line from Charing Cross to Fenchurch Street, and Sir Horace threatened that the GLC would go it alone.

In a press statement he claimed: 'We started the Piccadilly Line extension into Heathrow without the Government, the GLC and LT dividing it 50-50. Later, shamefaced, the Government joined us and are now crowing about it. I suspect history will repeat itself.'

In a mid term report to Londoners, Sir Horace announced that for the first time the GLC had become free of all debt except in housing - a milestone in local authority financing, he called it. Funds had been boosted by selling surplus land and property and from now on the council would operate a policy of 'No borrowing, pay as you go.'

On the roads, despite an increase in vehicles, traffic continued to move marginally faster, as was shown by the Council's intensive three-year survey over 1,340 miles of the network. An £855 million 15-year programme 'to give London the roads it needs and fill the yawning gaps in the strategic network' was approved.

Planning chairman Shelagh Roberts promised: 'This is not a return to the ringways. They were unacceptable in social and financial terms. Nevertheless, demand for better roads is being urged on the council from every quarter.'

These were the days when sharing vehicles was seen as making a positive contribution to cutting congestion. London's first car pooling scheme began at Heathrow where drivers with similar journeys to work were encouraged to use one vehicle. Sharing taxis was also investigated.

Various forms of taxi-sharing were common overseas and London's cabbies agreed to give it a try when the law was subsequently changed to permit it. Cabs would operate along predetermined corridors, displaying destination boards. Whether occupied or not, they could be flagged down and the fare shared. Some deviation from the route would be allowed to enable passengers to be dropped close to their destinations.

But sharing never succeeded. The Brits, it seems, value their privacy. Taxi-sharing proved a very damp squib when a simpler system was ultimately permitted at main line rail termini, and car sharing seems popular only in the United States although even there it is now in decline. Since car-sharing was first mooted, a new and very important factor has emerged in deciding with whom to share a car: Does the other person smoke?

Behind the scenes the council was getting to grips with lorry traffic and London became perhaps the first city in the world to produce a freight strategy.

Former chief transport planner David Bayliss said: 'This was another example of the GLC doing the thinking and the technical analysis. Even today, apart from the New York port authority, you could go almost anywhere in the world, ask about their freight policy and they would stare at you blankly.'

In Croydon, the Cutler administration set up Britain's first shared lorry terminal for small haulage firms. Eventually 20 more would be dotted around the capital. Hauliers rented space and shared service and fuel facilities and offices. Proposals for London's first major strategic lorry park at Beckton moved nearer, and the first lorry ban made possible by construction of the M25 was given the go-ahead over 50 square miles in North London. An estimated 3,500 lorries would be affected daily.

Road pricing (supplementary licensing) hit the headlines again following a provincial seminar at which a GLC officer was speaking. Details leaked out, newspapers speculated that London was proposing road pricing and Sir Horace hit the roof.

'I'll have that officer's head on a pole,' he stormed.

When the facts were explained he released a press statement saying that charging private motorists a fee for entering central London had never appealed to the GLC and there was no evidence it would be workable.

Although road pricing was a non-starter the council looked at the conventional and the unconventional in its search to improve the capital's traffic flow. With an eye on Tokio where the paraphernalia of roadworks must be cleared away for the start of the rush hour, the GLC considered speeding up the process by imposing double or treble shifts on the contractor, and bringing some order to the needs of public utilities which seemed forever to be digging up stretches of road to get at their pipes and cables underneath.

It was yet another pathfinder idea which looked workable on paper but was very different in practice. Perhaps from this initiative emerged today's system where contractors are charged a rent for occupying a stretch of road - the sooner they finish, the less they pay. Attempts to programme public utility works failed because their need to dig up a road was often dictated by an emergency.

In a joint experiment with the Department of Industry, 62 electric vans were bought by the two bodies. Half way through the six-year study, the gap between these and conventional vehicles had reduced. Reliability had consistently improved and manufacturers modified the vehicles as shortcomings became apparent.

The capital's road safety record was good though there was worrying conflict between traffic and pedestrians in the Strand. To improve safety and cut down delays in the Strand, a vast subway was built outside Charing Cross station where 13,500 pedestrians an hour crossed the road at peak times. At 32ft wide, about three times the usual width, it helped banish the fear so many people have of underpasses. It also served an unofficial secondary purpose as a safe dormitory for the homeless.

The GLC was always in the news. Sir Horace would say: 'Friends say to me, "I saw you on the telly again last night, Horace. You must be on TV more than anyone else in London."' Probably he was right. Either way, it was something Horace liked to hear himself say.

There was one occasion when, in his chauffeur-driven leader's car returning from a TV studio, he said to no one in particular: 'Well, what did you think of that?'

His driver, Bert Waterman, rushed in where angels fear to tread. 'I didn't think much of it,' he said rashly. He began to elaborate - and Cutler bit his head off. It wasn't what he wanted to hear.

Ivor Watkins, from the press office, who was also in the car, later said: 'I thought what Bert said was wrong anyway. Horace had made a number of winning points and I told him so. Horace grunted and buried his face in his papers. Next morning he telephoned the director of public information, said that he thought I was very shrewd and would the director arrange for me to accompany him in future when he made television appearances.'

Bert Waterman was not the most diplomatic of drivers. He tells the story of the night he was driving Harold Mote, then council chairman, to his home in Harrow where he was once mayor. Reaching a crossroads Bert was momentarily perplexed by having unexpectedly to negotiate two mini roundabouts.

He swore and added, inaudibly he thought: 'What --- idiot put those there?'

Whereupon Mote leaned forward from the back and said: 'I did.'

Harold Mote was in the news again when the London Fire Brigade was engaged in its perennial argument about the use of helicopters both for emergency rescue and for fire fighting. They can fly from one side of London to the other in 14 minutes and carry much water, but they are expensive. For years fire chiefs argued that they would rather have the money spent on additional fire appliances. Antagonists also pointed out that rotor blades could spread the flames and that helicopters could not land in busy areas.

Harold Mote, not a man easily convinced of the impossible, decided to make his point by landing one on a council estate - an act for which his knuckles were severely rapped.

After years of lobbying, the GLC finally won Parliamentary permission to promote a weekly lottery which nearly 20 borough councils joined. The venture had a short life and a not particularly merry one.

Both the size of the lottery and its top prize were restricted by law and the £1,000 it offered was little attraction to punters even in the seventies. In less than two years it had folded, though income from it bought televisions for old people's homes, paid for sponsorship of young musicians and enabled substantial gifts to be made to the Old Vic and Scott's ship Discovery.

More and more money was being given to the arts and by the end of the Cutler administration, the grants budget neared £4 million, including lifeline gifts to 80 small cultural organisations.

On the other side of the cultural coin, operating in its role of entertainments licensing authority, the council was battling to stem the tide of porn in Soho. It mounted a 'Clean up Soho' campaign spearheaded by Bernard Brook-Partridge and Brian Cassidy (later to become an MEP). Its particular aim was to remove lurid posters and sexy front of house advertising. Inevitably newspapers wanted pictures of the two men posing in front of the offending material which they did, usually with muscular bouncers peering suspiciously from the club doorway.

Asked what the GLC would do if their gentle persuasion did not achieve the desired result, Brook-Partridge replied: 'We'll gun the buggers down.'

During this puritanical surge the GLC's film viewing board was active. Film companies could appeal to the board for a London certificate if they had been refused one for national viewing. On one occasion the committee were going to a private showing in Soho when the man on the gate at County Hall decided to use his authority. Refusing to raise the barrier to let them depart, he walked to the hired mini bus and teased: 'Off to see the dirty pictures, are we? Off to see a bit of porn...Another freebie. Another morning off.'

In full flow, he poked his head through the driver's window and was horrified to see Sir Horace sitting quietly at the back. He rarely attended but this film, *The Beast,* had achieved much notoriety.

'Oh, I didn't see you there, sir,' he stuttered. The barrier was raised almost before the words had left his lips.

The inevitable rows between London's strategic authority and the government, centred on jobs, particularly on government insistence on vetting office developments above a certain size and refusing to allow the council to guarantee loans to industry. Protesting that the council was 'suffocated by too much government control,' the GLC claimed that bureaucracy had driven away many thousands of jobs and was discouraging firms from setting up.

Half a million jobs had been lost to London since 1961 and for a time replacing them became top priority for the Tory administration. When the government again decided to deny councils the right to guarantee industrial loans, Cutler described it as a crushing blow which had 'done as much for East London as the blitz.'

Devolution of more powers to the boroughs had been part of Tory thinking as it searched for its true strategic role. Shelagh Roberts announced sweeping changes. In future, only planning applications of truly strategic importance should be referred to the GLC. This, she said, would cut by two-thirds the 8,000 planning applications the council dealt with each year. The present system, unchanged for 12 years, caused unnecessary expense and frustration and discouraged development, she said.

Two years later the government responded, relieving the GLC of much planning trivia and increasing tenfold the size of office and industrial developments which could be dealt with by the borough councils.

On the domestic front, the question of ethnic minorities staff appeared for the first time on a council agenda.

Observing what it described as 'the balance of opinion of staff and unions,' the council decided against keeping record of the colour or ethnic origin of job applicants. Evidence was that 'white and ethnic minority employees were promoted on merit,' it reported.

Whether London should bid to host the 1988 Olympics led to a two-year GLC investigation headed by Sir Malby Crofton, formerly leader of Kensington and Chelsea council. Two years before, amid much media speculation, the council did consider bidding to host the 1984 Games but the proposal was dropped on financial grounds. The omen looked more promising second time around.

Cutler hoped that an Olympic village for 7,000 athletes could be built in Docklands and retained as permanent housing after the Games had ended. Sir Malby's 170-page report, however, poured cold water on this idea. Retaining the housing estates was not feasible, he said.

Two choices were considered: Building an Olympic park on the site of the Royal Victoria Dock, Newham, incorporating a 70,000 seater stadium, Olympic village and international centre; or renovating Wembley Stadium to Olympic standard, and building a temporary Olympic village two miles away in Kingsbury. Both schemes required a new indoor arena and use of a greatly improved Crystal Palace sports centre.

Costs were made on assumptions, so estimates were necessarily vague. Possible cost of the Docklands option was £750 million, leaving a shortfall of £221 million, give or take £100 million. The less risky Wembley alternative was costed at £436 million resulting in anything from a shortfall of £44 million to a surplus of £81 million. But a bid was never made. The Red Army invaded Afghanistan and the Olympic movement was thrown into disarray. Finally the Games were held in Moscow and half the world stayed away .

For Sir Horace, a scratch golfer and enthusiast for most sports, an Olympics bid was very close to his heart and would have crowned his term of office. Plans were made for an elaborate unveiling of the study at a press conference, but Sir Malby Crofton blew the gaff, handing a copy of his report to a freelance journalist who gave the *Evening Standard* an exclusive. The rest of the news media promptly lost interest and television shoots planned for the following day were cancelled. Sir Horace was beside himself with rage. The bird had flown and there was nothing to be done.

Cutler's was the last GLC administration to host a chairman's reception. Formerly this had been the social highlight of the GLC year: an occasion for free-loading at public expense, or for thanking those who had helped London in the past 12 months and would do so in the next, depending on your point of view.

When Bernard Brook-Partridge was chairman he broke new ground by adding to the guest list two skinheads who had gone to the rescue of a passenger attacked on a train. At an earlier reception, the council's parks department had taken over all the committee rooms which served as restaurants and produced birds from their zoos to fly freely. In one were penguins which escaped and waddled around the corridors of County Hall, for all the world looking like diminutive dinner-suited guests.

It was at one of these receptions that an emergency doctor was called to Charlie Rossi, a tough, indestructible Scotsman from the Gorbals. A likable man who was a London rat-catcher and later vice-chairman of the council, Charlie was suspected of suffering a heart attack. By the time the doctor arrived, Charlie had recovered and was sitting with a large scotch in one hand and a cream bun in the other.

Sir Horace's love of sports came to the fore again in 1981 when he joined journalist and former athlete Chris Brasher in bringing the marathon to London. Perhaps the Olympics was a pipedream but the marathon was practical, Sir Horace said. He worked tirelessly to win over the police and to get important areas of London closed to traffic, then he sanctioned council staff being used to assist in the organisation and, on the day, opened County Hall's facilities to the runners.

'This is my insurance,' Sir Horace said to me.

Twenty years on the marathon is arguably the most important in the world; the one every athlete wants to run. Now it is providing a surplus of nearly £2 million for good causes and has raised an additional £50 million for charity via sponsorship.

Horace's insurance had paid off. He would have liked that.

9. LIVINGSTONE'S LONDON, 1981-86

Ken Livingstone swept into County Hall in May, 1981 spoiling for a fight. Within hours he had seized power from moderate leader Andrew McIntosh in a Left-wing coup and, in his first speech, announced his intention to use County Hall as a platform from which to attack the Thatcher government. Occasional confrontation with Westminster had been the norm with all GLC administrations, but never before had a council, chosen by the electorate to run London, deliberately set itself up as a virtual Opposition to the government.

Andrew McIntosh, a fast-talking marketing consultant, had spent his summer holiday reading - and understanding - the GLC's complex budgeting system which contained details of all council policy and spending. In the words of Sir James Swaffield, then director-general: 'He would have been the best prepared of any leader. Such was his grasp that it would have been a seamless change of administration.'

McIntosh was cock-a-hoop when the election results came through showing Labour had won power, if only by 50 seats to 42 which was fewer than predicted. Michael Foot, Labour's leader in Parliament, joined the celebrations and, as midnight approached, Andrew and two of his trusted GLC lieutenants drank champagne to a new Labour future. He was not to know that, in a very few hours, those two trustees were to join a putsch and vote him out of office.

Outwardly, the next day began quietly. Behind the scenes, however, there was frenzied activity. Andrew McIntosh issued his first press statement reinforcing the main elements of Labour's manifesto and prepared for the evening meeting at which he expected to be installed as Leader of the Council.

Unknown to him, the Left wing of the party had been meeting down the corridor earlier to plan their tactics and complete a raft of committee chairs. When the unofficial meeting broke up, not only was Livingstone leader in waiting, but John McDonnell, later to become MP for Hayes and Harlington, was deputy leader, and the hierarchy of all the committees had been settled. The official meeting to follow would be meaningless.

Sir Horace Cutler was on record as having told McIntosh that he would not be leader the day after the election because he hadn't enough support. Sir Horace added: 'I even got the vote right - 30 to 20 in favour of Livingstone.'

Left wingers said that they didn't want to carry on the old way of doing things and were determined to have a change. John McDonnell was more explicit. 'It was clear that if we were to become a rallying point against the government and a rallying point for the Left within the party, we needed a Left leader,' he said.

In his hour of glory before being ousted, McIntosh made his only statement as leader apparent. In it he freed London Transport of the cash restraints imposed by the Conservatives; stopped all road schemes; attempted unsuccessfully to reverse the transfer of GLC housing estates to the remaining eight (unwilling) boroughs and promised £1 million, rising to £3 million the following year, to help voluntary and community organisations.

Soon Ken Livingstone's outspoken views made him the media's favourite bogeyman. He raised a furore by turning down an invitation to the wedding of Prince Charles and Diana, then by suggesting that people were all basically bisexual, and caused fury by constantly giving vociferous support to all sorts of minority rights.

His unpopularity reached a peak when he made conciliatory noises about the IRA and entertained Sinn Fein and the mother of an IRA hunger striker at County Hall.

Sir Horace Cutler called a special meeting of the council to censure Livingstone for 'misusing his position to further his extreme views on subjects over which the council has no jurisdiction' and particularly for his outrageous remarks concerning bombing in London by the IRA.

Unluckily for Livingstone, one sympathetic statement about the Republicans coincided with a murderous IRA nail bomb atrocity at Knightsbridge barracks - which led to the *Sun* asking: 'Is this the most odious man in Britain?' The newspaper clearly changed its mind in due time - it paid him to write a weekly column.

In the early days of 'Red Ken's' administration, sections of the press were gunning for him, using foul means as well as fair. He caught one reporter checking the contents of his dustbin, and George Tremlett, housing chairman in the Cutler administration, was wined and dined by a newspaper who wanted the low-down on Ken's sex life. Tremlett wasn't interested.

Because he was so often misquoted, Livingstone began taping his own speeches. As a hate scenario built up in some quarters, one man threw a pot of red paint over him and on another occasion he had to beat a speedy retreat through the back door of a pub in Hampstead to avoid violence.

Such was media interest when he snubbed the royal wedding that requests for interviews threatened to monopolise his entire week. 'The reaction was absolutely hysterical,' he recalled. Ultimately he was forced to refuse some interviews, including one from an Australian woman who offered sex in return.

Livingstone always denied that boycotting the royal wedding was a snub; it was a decision taken by the Labour group, he said. In fact Labour considered passing on the invitation to two old age pensioners, an idea which was never pursued. Instead the council arranged a free open-air rock concert at the Crystal Palace concert bowl on the afternoon of the wedding.

Labour spurned the invitation, Livingstone said, because his GLC was keen to distance itself from what he called the 'junketing of previous administrations.' But there are several flavours of junket.

On the eve of Thamesday, at which Italian boat crews were competing, some of us were talking to an Italian dignitary when Ken came up and, before the introductions had been completed, said: 'I want to go to Bologna.' A visit to the Left-wing capital of Italy surely is as much a junket for a Left-winger as a weekend in Rome for a Tory.

In the early days, Ken Livingstone's personal exposure totally overshadowed the policies Labour was trying to implement. In the privacy of Labour group meetings, he didn't get it all his own way, though the Left always had sufficient votes to force its views through in the end. Illtyd Harrington, one-time deputy leader of the GLC, said he tried to drag matters back on course, telling the Labour group: 'I'm all for expressing our views on international affairs and minority rights but that is not why we were elected. Our job is to run the government of London. The lady in No.10 Downing Street is rubbing her hands because public opinion is hardening against us.'

Ken Livingstone, on the other hand, saw the Labour GLC as trying to win hearts and minds. To him, working to bring peace to Ireland, and challenging sexism and racism were legitimate issues. Of Prime Minister Thatcher, he said: 'I thought that if you really resisted her, you could grind her down and defeat her.'

His were not isolated views. Others in the hard Left ruling group saw trying to bring down the government as their main objective.

Tory front bench spokesman George Tremlett protested that the new administration's aim was to destroy the state, not serve the people. Tory spokesmen had long taunted Labour on having a 'foreign policy' which included proposals for action on South Africa, Nicaragua and Palestine as well as some fairly unpopular views on Ireland.

Central point in the new council's manifesto was 'Fares Fair,' a commitment to slash London Transport fares by 25 per cent - a proposal of Andrew McIntosh, not Ken Livingstone as folklore has it. At the same group meeting where this was agreed, Norman Howard had urged free travel, which barely found a seconder.

To pave the way for 'Fares Fair,' in the weeks before the election Labour's top brass had been meeting secretly with Sir Peter Masefield, then chairman of London Transport, to discuss the ramifications of the cut. Although Sir Peter was delighted at this element of Labour's policy, some members of the LT executive were unhappy at the party's radicalism. One said of John McDonnell that he was 'so far to the Left I couldn't see him with a pair of binoculars.'

With the election won, cutting fares became the top priority. Fruition was several months away, though immediately there were more buses on the road as Labour ended Tory restrictions on overtime and rest-day working. Within days, transport chairman Dave Wetzel, himself a former bus driver, visited Catford garage where over 7,000 extra bus miles a week were now being operated. The incoming administration was news and, as this was Wetzel's first official function, a trusted reporter and I joined him on the trip. As was usual, I ordered an official car, not knowing that the Labour group had banned their use. We parked round the corner from the bus garage - for safety and convenience, not deception - but Dave was uneasy at not having arrived by bus. I thought no more about it, until next morning when a mocking story appeared in *The Guardian*. It transpired that a reporter had eavesdropped on careless talk in the County Hall bar. Dave Wetzel later complained that this minor peccadillo probably robbed him of a parliamentary nomination.

In the lull before the fares storm, the media stopped 'correcting' the word when chairmen were referred to as 'chairs,' and the council busied itself preparing for such actions as declaring London nuclear-free, ditching Civil Defence, expressing solidarity with various strikes and offering County Hall's facilities for a 'people's march for jobs.' For the last, camp beds were provided for 500 marchers from Liverpool who were given three nights B and B and ferried by coach to rallies at Londoners' expense. Plans to give GLC staff 90 minutes paid leave to welcome them were abandoned on legal advice.

Suddenly known anti-GLC agitators from the past were on the GLC payroll and appointments unique in the council's history were being made. In time there were highly paid advisers to head new units on employment, race relations, the police, women's issues, equal opportunities - even a wildlife specialist. No longer did council business revolve around the traditional local government areas of housing, planning, transport etc. Other issues were coming to the fore.

A creche was set up to provide day care for the children of working mothers (and fathers) and to facilitate the attendance of women at committee meetings. For attending the women's committee, up to £500 a year could be claimed for babysitting and dependent carers' expenses.

On a broader front, London's million senior citizens had their free travel facilities extended to include the Underground, and the council laid the foundations for its £56 million programme to create

10,000 jobs, setting up the Greater London Enterprise Board and a direct labour force. Though the sum was enormous, the cost to ratepayers was modest compared with the overwhelming benefit to the capital of a of a revitalised community, said Industry chair Mike Ward.

Mrs Thatcher's government decided that a Left-wing GLC was not getting its hands on London's docklands. It disbanded the Docklands Joint Committee, composed of the previous GLC, dockland boroughs and other interested bodies, and transferred responsibility to a development corporation with wide-ranging powers. Livingstone's administration could do no more than monitor what was happening and protest.

The council elected another toothless watchdog to shadow the Met Police. Chaired by Paul Boateng, subsequently a Home Office Minister in the Blair government, the committee was highly critical of the police and made no secret that it considered the police should be answerable to the council, which was the situation everywhere else in the country. Previous governments had appeared sympathetic to London's claim but had declined to act. The Thatcher government was not even sympathetic. Now, nearly 20 years on, London's mayor and new strategic authority will have that wish granted.

First blood was drawn in London's transport battle when the government blocked GLC plans to give British Rail £20 million to buy off a proposed fares rise and keep surface rail fares in line with those on London Transport. At a meeting with Transport Secretary Norman Fowler, neither side would back down. Ken Livingstone pledged that, come what may, fares on London Transport would be cut by 25 per cent in the autumn.

He warned: 'As fares are cut and frozen on London Transport while British Rail's continue to rise, BR will face rapid decline. The effect is going to mean transport anarchy in London.'

To reduce fares and balance LT's books, the GLC had announced a supplementary rate to bring in the £69 million required, plus another £50 million to meet government penalties imposed for overspending - in effect, a punishment for disobeying the government and subsidising travel.

The rate was duly forced through the GLC and in October 1981,

Londoners enjoyed the first ever across-the-board fares reduction on London Transport's buses and trains. Most 25p bus fares were slashed to tenpence, children's bus fares were halved and the council estimated that the average family's travel costs were cut by £1.50 a week. The council also decided to freeze fares at that level for four years while they considered the ramifications of introducing free travel.

Initial details of the overall 25 pc cut submitted by London Transport fell foul of the Labour group; there were actually some rises - in inner London, no less, the Labour heartlands. These were amended so that no-one lost out. Eventually the overall reduction was 32 p.c., returning fares to their level during the Goodwin years.

Down in leafy Bromley, however, there were mutterings of discontent. The Underground did not reach that borough, nor other Tory boroughs in the outer suburbs of south London. Their fares - on British Rail's surface trains - had all gone up. Why should their ratepayers subside journeys for tourists and residents of inner London who were predominantly Labour? Why should their ratepayers have to pay twice? Bromley decided to go to law.

When the case came before the Divisional Court, Bromley's case rested on three elements: that the GLC lacked the powers to order a fares cut, the amount spent was unreasonable, and that the GLC had not gone through the correct procedures before reaching its decision.

Bromley lost on all points. The case was dismissed with costs and Bromley was on the point of throwing in the towel. Expected support from other Tory boroughs evaporated; most thought that Bromley's claim had no hope of success. But the council's lawyer felt that important points of law had not been addressed and that an appeal was likely to succeed. So it proved.

Heard within days by Master of the Rolls Lord Denning, with Lords Justice Oliver and Watkins, the Appeal Court declared unanimously that the fares cut and the supplementary rate were both unlawful. A key section of the relevant Transport Act stated that the LT Executive had a duty to balance its books 'as far as practicable.' This had been assumed to mean - after taking into account funding by the GLC.

Lord Oliver disagreed. He interpreted the words as being an

obligation on the executive to run its affairs on 'ordinary business lines.' At a stroke that crushed the assumptions held ever since the GLC had taken over the policy-making and funding of London Transport, namely that they had the statutory powers to run LT as they chose, including running it a loss for the benefit of Londoners and making up the difference.

The concurring judgments of Lords Denning and Watkins contained political overtones about 'abuse of power' by Livingstone and of pursuing a political manifesto knowing that it would injure ratepayers more than they first realised (by virtue of government overspend penalties which doubled the amount needed to be raised).

First, Lord Oliver's interpretation of the Act had to be tested. Perhaps he was wrong. The GLC appealed to the House of Lords. Encouraging words reached the council as the hearing continued and on judgment day Ken Livingstone, Dave Wetzel and assorted officers attended the House ready to celebrate. But it was not to be. The GLC lost on all basic points of law. They were stunned.

The five Law Lords ruled that the GLC's cheap fares policy and the supplementary rate which funded it were unlawful. Four judges accepted Oliver's interpretation that the GLC had failed to recognise an obligation that LT should break even as far as practicable. Lord Scarman said it was plain that the fares reduction was adopted as an object of social and transport policy, not because any higher fares level was impracticable. In acting as it did, the GLC had abandoned business principles. That was a breach of its fiduciary duty to the ratepayers and wrong in law.

Lord Diplock disagreed, but held that the policy was unlawful because it imposed an undue financial burden on ratepayers. The GLC's decision was not simply about allocating a total financial burden between passengers and ratepayers, he said. It was also a decision to increase that total burden so as nearly to double it [because of government penalties] and to place the whole of the increase on ratepayers.

He could not say whether the original manifesto sum would have been legally acceptable. That would have lowered fares by 25 pc at a cost to ratepayers of £69 million.

The over-riding factor was that the fares subsidy caused the

GLC to lose £50 million in grants under the government's penalty system. A rates burden of £69m. therefore became one of £119m.

With its main policy in tatters, Ken Livingstone talked afterwards of 'a grim day for British democracy and a massive blow for LT travellers.' The next step, he said, would be to seek a new law to change LT's financing to what everyone thought it was before the Law Lords' judgment.

The Law Lords have not just rejected a GLC policy. Their decision overturned the wishes of the majority of Londoners who decided at the ballot box they wanted the GLC to cut fares,' he said.

Of the rates burden, Livingstone had always argued that 61 pc of rates came from commercial sources which should be prepared to pay a little more to get their workers in by public transport. Most domestic ratepayers who used public transport would be more than recompensed for the increased rates by reduced fares.

Briefly a 'Can't Pay, Won't Pay' disobedience campaign held centre stage, Londoners being encouraged to give the conductor a 'Can't Pay, Won't Pay' slip and tender the old (reduced) fare. But this entailed LT staff being caught in the middle of the row between the GLC and the government. It was pressure from the staff which led to the campaign being dropped.

During its currency, transport chair Dave Wetzel recalled: 'About three days into the campaign I was on a bus in Trafalgar Square. I tendered my "Can't Pay, Won't Pay" ticket and the conductor refused to ring the bell. There we stuck, so I thought the best thing was to take a vote of those on the bus. I got overwhelming support downstairs, but unfortunately, upstairs they voted in favour of the bus continuing. So I stepped off, apologised to people for the delay and said I hoped they would vote Labour at the next election.'

As a result of the law lords' ruling, bus and tube fares were doubled and bus schedules reduced on virtually all routes. Mileage on the Underground was slashed 10 per cent, some branch lines and stations closed, and all stations remained shut an extra half hour in the mornings, opening at 6.30 a.m. Night bus services were largely withdrawn.

In council, when the GLC faced the order to obey the Law Lords' decision and increase fares or be personally surcharged, several

Labour members announced that they would defy the law and accept the consequences. Opposition leader Sir Horace Cutler intended that the Tories should abstain, thereby heaping all the blame for the increase on Labour, but this plan was undermined when the director general gave a controversial ruling on the law, stating that abstaining members would be equally culpable. The sum involved was astronomical; more than members could possibly pay. Many Conservatives were very wealthy - there were reputed to be several millionaires among them. They had a lot to lose whereas some of the Labour members claimed to have virtually nothing.

Ken Livingstone goaded Sir Horace, saying: 'They can have my £200 in the Post Office. What about your million?' In fact Livingstone later revealed that even his '£200 in the Post Office' would be safe. He had arranged to pass it for safe keeping to his sidekick, Bill Bush.

In the event, a couple of Conservatives unwilling to risk their life's savings to make a political point, decided to stay on the right side of the law and vote in favour of the increase which was sufficient to get it through.

Defeat for the GLC it may have been, but the overruling of the popular fares cut, aggravated by the party political words of some of the judges began to turn the anti-Livingstone tide. No longer was he seen as a bogeyman. It was he who had tried to give Londoners cheap travel and had challenged the might of the law.

Not for the last time government ministers misread the mood of London. Their constant castigation of 'Red Ken' accelerated his transformation to folk hero. Former detractors suddenly found his words more reasoned; audiences clamoured to hear him. At one such meeting he was late and Illtyd Harrington, himself no mean entertainer, filled in. Apologising for the temporary substitution of speaker, he said: 'It's rather like coming to hear Bette Midler and having to make do with Vesta Tilley.'

As the weeks and months passed, Livingstone was increasingly seen as a man of easy-going charm and charisma with an appealing, self-deprecating manner. He said he didn't realise he 'talked in a boring nasal drawl until the media pointed it out.' And he spoke about his mum and admitted crying at the cinema watching *ET.*

Typical of the laid-back manner which made him so popular was his reaction to the *Sun* story about him being 'the most odious man in Britain.' Previous GLC leaders would have exploded with rage and reached for the phone to call their lawyers. Livingstone reacted calmly, taking the paper and reading the words. Then said: 'Can I have this?'

'What are you going to do?' he was asked.

Ken replied nonchalantly: 'I want to show it to my mum.'

A year later the adverse effects of the imposed high fares were acknowledged by the government. By then, 16 p.c of bus passengers and 13.5 pc of Underground travellers had been driven away. The six per cent who had forsaken their cars and commuted to central London by public transport were back at the wheel, and road casualties had returned to previous levels after a saving of 3,700 during the cheap fares period.

In a bid to entice back lost passengers, fares were slashed by an average of 25 pc in a scheme called 'Just the Ticket.' But the writing was on the wall. Plans to wrench London Transport from GLC control were being hatched by the government.

Ken Livingstone continued to receive a bad press over some council actions, none more than over elements of its grants policy. Babies Against the Bomb and the English Collective of Prostitutes were two bodies which may have done good work but were saddled with provocative titles which guaranteed ridicule. Individually, their grants were infinitesimal in cash terms, but whenever they came up for a hand-out the press had a field day.

Previous administrations had made substantial grants to arts and cultural groups, but under Livingstone, recipient organisations embraced all types of community interests - what he called his 'rainbow coalition' of single-interest groups. In the last year before the GLC was abolished, when the administration was openly trying to empty the coffers, more than 1,000 organisations were given a total of over £80 million.

Ken Livingstone's detractors claimed he was operating on a false theory: that if he supported sufficient minority causes he would end up with a majority. That is exactly what happened. To have their work acknowledged and be given cash overshadowed all else so far as many   single-issue organisations were concerned. And they were run by activists who would make darned sure   that all the troops turned out to vote at election time.

During a debate in council, Richard Brew, then Tory Opposition leader, suggested that Labour votes were virtually being bought by grants which were also providing a living for about 2,000 Left-wing activists outside County Hall.

Whatever the objections to some grants, there was no gainsaying the popularity of Labour's support for the capital's 400,000 disabled people. The GLC built substantially on the dial-a-ride bus services tried out experimentally by previous administrations. This time, the council was prepared to operate them at a loss.

And they broke new ground with a scheme to enable the disabled to ride in taxis at reduced rates. Begun as an experiment in Southwark in 1983, selected disabled people who were unable to ride in buses and trains could use black taxis for journeys of up to seven or eight miles for a £1 flat fare subsidised by the GLC.

Within two years the scheme had become London-wide with 43,000 users and involving 4,500 licensed cabs. This, together with the dial-a-ride schemes in many boroughs, prompted transport chair Dave Wetzel to herald 'a network of new facilities unparalleled anywhere in the country.' In one summer month there were more than 50,000 such taxi journeys.

Later, when abolition loomed, the cost of a fare was halved and the permitted distance doubled, leading a government minister to remark unkindly that this had been done to 'provoke anxiety and embarrass the boroughs.' [On abolition, the boroughs would be asked to take over the service].

Subsequently, the government gave £5 million to enable dial-a-ride to continue and, on abolition of the GLC, the taxicard system was taken up by all but four London boroughs.

Though the majority of grants were well used, there were occasional hitches which caused payments to be suspended, leading to unpleasant incidents. Recalling one, Mick Brown, the senior finance officer dealing with grants, said: 'At the committee meeting where a decision to suspend payments was minuted, the public gallery was packed. When I stood to give my report the gallery began chanting "Racist! Racist." I said to the chairman, Paul Boateng, that when he called the meeting to order I would continue.'

There were not infrequent allegations of racism against GLC staff. These non-specific claims and generalisations of 'institutionalised racism' were bitterly resented by the Staff Association, the council's white collar union, and by individuals who saw themselves as simply trying to earn a living and uninterested in the colour or race of their colleagues.

The merest hint of racism was sufficient to damn an individual. Such allegations did not need to be proved and were not possible to disprove. If enough mud was thrown some of it was likely to stick. Many staff could never understand why a disagreement between a black and an Asian or a white was automatically considered to be racist when it was, perhaps, nothing more than a clash of opinions or personalities between people whose ethnic or cultural backgrounds were different but totally irrelevant.

There was one horrendous incident in the dying days of the administration when a miscreant set fire to the offices of the ethnic minorities unit on the sixth floor. Three separate fires had been started and three officers could have died. Overcome by smoke, they were rescued by the fire brigade from blazing rooms which were described as 'gutted.'

It was the second fire deliberately started at County Hall in three weeks - the other, in the basement, was put out before damage was caused.

After two months in which the police failed to establish any firm leads, the investigation into the ethnic minorities fire was wound down, leaving Paul Boateng to express alarm at the 'narrow nature of the inquiry.'

Lack of political activism among the staff union disappointed the Livingstone administration. While the council's NALGO members entered the political arena, the Staff Association generally were not the type to go on protest marches.

Sir Horace Cutler referred to the association as a 'sweetheart union' and in the days of Sir Reg Goodwin it voted two-to-one against his offer of a closed shop.

Challenged at council question time about a newspaper statement which alleged Livingstone had claimed that the Staff Association had been 'a total roadblock to everything we try to do,' he replied that it was 'highly selective reporting. In another journal, *Marxism Today,* he was quoted as saying: 'Our problem is that over the last 50 years the Staff Association has had a sort of symbiotic relationship with the right wing Labour leaders. It's been a fist and glove operation and they are as appalled by my election as the Tories are. At the moment they are doing everything possible to obstruct the implementation of our programme.'

There was suspicion from the staff because Ken Livingstone's administration was the only one which had ever tried to get its hands on their pension fund. This was viewed with much concern by some staff who wanted their pensions safeguarded by investment in blue chip companies, not put at possible risk by, perhaps, being invested on an ideological basis to further the council's pledge to boost employment in London. The pension fund was a quiet battlefield for the entire five-year duration of Livingstone's administration. In the event, not a penny was used.

Interestingly, one of the new duties of the Mayor of London will be to oversee the pension fund.

Late during its reign, the Livingstone administration abolished the entrance examination for GLC staff. Recalling the action, Charles Corcoran, formerly a Staff Association officer, said: 'Its predictable results did not endear the administration to existing staff who found themselves having to work with people who weren't up to doing the job.'

More popular was the decision to open the council to another type of applicant by widening the annual talent search round universities to include the polytechnics.

Equal opportunities were pursued rigorously, both among employees and among the 200,000 contractors who annually supplied the GLC and Inner London Education Authority with £700 million of goods and services.

Kit Kat and Blue Riband biscuits were withdrawn from restaurants and Hoover was dropped when the companies refused to give information about their employment policies for women, blacks and disabled people. Although equal opportunities gave added teeth to the policy, there had been a watch on the council's suppliers since the early days of the LCC. Then the council's concern was to support better pay and conditions in the East End sweat shops.

Among the most far-reaching decisions of the Livingstone regime was the setting up of a high-powered women's committee, the first in Britain. Chaired by Valerie Wise, daughter of Labour MP Audrey Wise, and backed by a large support unit at County Hall, it added the woman's view to every report.

Valerie, intensely serious and much younger than the usual women in politics, was subjected to occasional leg-pulls. But even she was ill prepared for comments by a Left-wing mentor about going dancing in his youth. He added: 'At half-past ten, if you hadn't got the women up against the wall, there was something wrong with your technique.' Valerie was aghast.

As befitting a committee which represented more than half London's voters, it took its task very seriously. At times, some say, too seriously. Yet Valerie had an early baptism of fire in the public eye which was a prerequisite for principal members of the GLC. Speaking in support of buskers who, she said, were hounded by the law, she held a press photo-call on the steps of County Hall.

Tony Hosier, who organised the event, recalled: 'Suddenly someone produced a guitar and a reluctant Valerie was persuaded to sit on the steps and put the guitar on her lap. With even greater reluctance she agreed to a photographer's request to strum. The result was a better picture and wider publicity for her cause. But as she left, I heard her murmur: "What on earth have I come into?"'

Valerie was not one to laugh easily. She was cast as Mrs Thatcher in the famous spoof pantomime 'Ken Whittington and his Cat' - an ironic choice in view of later developments. The cast list, with Ken in the lead, makes interesting reading. Paul Boateng was the narrator, Dave Wetzel played Dick Turpin, John McDonnell, the cat, and Tony Banks was cast as Idle Jack. The media chorus included such personalities as Jo Andrews (of ITN), John Carvel (Guardian), Mike King (Evening Standard), Barbara Long (London Tonight) and Anne Jones (Radio London).

Another example of the women's committee's ultra seriousness concerned a GLC proposal to adopt two lions at London zoo. Her members anguished long and hard over the sex of the two animals. Was adopting one male and one female 'sending out the wrong signals?' Would it suggest that heterosexuality was a more desirable lifestyle and therefore would it cause offence to lesbians and gays? Ultimately the council decided to adopt Peter and Leone.

Between examples of ground-breaking initiatives - like a Lewisham experiment of buying a minibus and paying the running costs so that women could be given door to door transport at night - the committee and the women's unit had more than its share of problems. Its chief adviser parted company with the council because of a personality clash with Valerie Wise, a meeting was infiltrated by a reporter from the *Daily Mail,* and was infiltrated constantly by a mole who sympathised with much of the women's work but not their po-faced methods of approaching it.

There was also a row when the organisers of a two-day conference for black women threw out a GLC councillor, Tory Andrew Rolfe, though any GLC member had a right to attend any event held under GLC auspices. His intrusion was said to be an 'insult,' and the women voted 58-nil, with 19 abstentions to insist he left - which he did to avoid the meeting breaking up.

On another occasion the committee arranged an event, having forgotten it was the day of the London marathon. Members protested at the vast male presence in County Hall and worse, the speaker, a prostitute, did not turn up. It was feared that, having arrived and found herself in a predominantly male environment, she may have decided to spend her time.... more profitably.

An insight into the attitudes of some female activists using County Hall was apparent from a question in council about portraits of past male chairmen of the council being removed from a wall on the principal floor by feminists who objected to 'men looking down on them.'

The most frequent complaint against the women's committee was that it was not representative of London women. Doreen King, who handled the committee's press arrangements for a time, said: 'They were dreary, humourless girls and like peas in a pod. All were in their twenties. They wore dungarees, lots of badges and Doc Marten's boots. There wasn't a lick of make-up to be seen.

I remember a security man opening the door for them and saying: "This way, ladies." They rounded on him and said; "We're not ladies.'

'That was typical. It was a thing of style rather than content.'

Even Harvey Hinds, Labour's chief whip and a former canon of the church, was hauled over the coals for calling a woman 'dear,' not an unusual term for a man of the cloth.

Some of the ground-breaking work of the women's committee - and of the equal opportunities and grants committees - so much headlined and ridiculed at the time, is now the conventional wisdom practised up and down the country. Perhaps only an earthquake can bring about seismic change.

In the humourless politics of the day at County Hall when members' loyalty to the Left was sometimes questioned, former Tory chairman Bernard Brook-Partridge decided to spread a little harmless mischief. He wrote a spoof note allegedly to Ken Livingstone from Harvey Hinds saying: 'I have conducted the research you asked for and have put our party in the following groups - hard left, mild left and right.' Names followed. He ran off copies and left them on the photocopier. The head messenger, worried that papers were left in the corridor, asked passing members if they were theirs. Whereupon they glanced at the note, saw the words and said: No, but I'll take one.'

Amid the much-publicised activities of the high profile committees, traditional council work was not neglected. Although the Tories had given away the council's housing stock to the boroughs, their pledge to renovate it was kept by Labour whose £70m. improvements programme was the country's biggest.

Sale of council homes was stopped immediately Ken Livingstone came to power, the council took up house-building again and set a precedent by inviting two tenants, representatives of the 100,000-member London tenants organisation, to sit on the GLC's housing committee with full voting rights.

In the ceaseless struggle to get London's traffic moving freely and to clear away the clutter of parked cars, the GLC became the first authority in the country to use wheel clamps. They called them 'bulldogs.' Statistics showed that there were ten parking infringements every second of every working day on the streets of London.

In May 1983, the first 'bulldogs' appeared on London's streets, the start of a two-year experiment which led to their becoming a permanent tool in the war against illegal parking. The prime motive was to help `clear` the way for buses which were said to carry 36 per cent of London's road travellers in one-fifth of one per cent of its road vehicles.

The last semblance of a dress code ended under Livingstone's regime and some members let it be known they wanted to be called by their Christian names. Chief among them was Dave Wetzel, a friendly, outgoing politician from Hounslow, who became known throughout the hierarchy of London Transport as 'Yours Fraternally Dave,' because of the way he signed his letters.

Ken Livingstone became the first leader to be addressed by his Christian name. As he lolloped along the corridors of County Hall it was not unusual to hear quite junior staff call out 'Good morning, Ken.'

But this relaxed approach did not apply to all things. At County Hall, a lady press officer with a keen interest in the stage, had long ago adopted the language of that profession and tended to call everyone 'darling,' and 'love' and by other rather endearing diminutives. She had successfully served previous Socialist and Tory councils without a problem but some members of the Livingstone administration found her mode of address at odds with political correctness and she was told to change the habits of a lifetime.

We met in the corridor soon after matters had come to a head. 'How are you finding the new administration?' I asked.

'Well, love,' she said. 'Let's face it. Bunch of wankers, aren't they?'

Another important plank in Labour's policy was action against heavy lorries. Balancing the social and environmental pluses against possible economic minuses was enormously complicated, said the council, though half of the 25,000 nightly heavy lorry movements were known to be using London as a through route.

After an 18-month independent inquiry by Derek Wood QC, who heard 2,500 submissions, the GLC decided to ban at night and weekends all lorries over 16.5 metric tons which had no business in

London. Excluded from the ban were 200 miles of key roads which had little or no housing along them, yet when the restriction began in December 1985, the government still protested that the ban was 'irresponsible and mischievous.'

There were more than 5,000 applications for exemptions by firms with out-of-hours business, and the GLC allowed operators a year's grace to fit hush-kits (at £400 a time) or swop their lorries for quieter ones. Two years earlier, when the projected ban had been foreshadowed, the GLC set aside £100,000 and invited industry to join prototype work to make lorries quieter and more environment friendly. This pioneering work had been ignored, said Dave Wetzel.

To publicise the GLC's initiative, the council's publicity department produced a poster with the words: 'For Mr and Mrs Hawkins, the earth moves five times a night.' It was shown to 'Yours Fraternally Dave' who said: 'It's a lot more than that in Hounslow. It's about 50 times a night.' When the laughter had subsided, the council's graphic designers wondered if the latest sexual idiom was as widely known as they thought.

Another popular policy decision was to stop pavement parking, then rife all over London. In its first year there were 6,000 successful prosecutions. Thousands more were in the pipeline when the GLC was laid to rest.

Labour was also examining the old chestnut of getting freight off the roads. This time, however, the administration joined with British Rail in something new - an improved refrigerated rail wagon to handle the five million tonnes of frozen or chilled food transported along London's roads every year. With abolition only months away, a prototype wagon was successfully unveiled at Marylebone station.

The administration also busied itself with DSS benefits, joining with the DSS in an 18-month campaign aimed at ensuring people knew their entitlements. Labour claimed that 30 pc of Londoners were entitled to social security benefits. Ken Livingstone gave the campaign a send-off, travelling on an open-top bus which later toured the whole of London. After six months, £230,000 in lost benefits or 'benefits Londoners were too frightened to claim,' were uncovered.

After outspoken criticism of particular deportations, the GLC set its face against the government's deportations policy generally. Ken Livingstone told the Home Office that the council condemned deportations which had increased steadily in the past ten years and urged that the policy be revised.

He said: 'Deportations are against this council's anti-racist objectives and while they continue there can never be any real racial harmony in London. Communities are under threat, families are fragmented and subjected to police harassment. The GLC will fight for the rights of black or other ethnic minority communities in London to be treated as settled and not be deported.'

He went on to condemn what he described as 'police raids against specific communities,' increasing immigration control, and the exclusion of family members of ethnic minority communities.

Announcing the council's Anti-Racist Year, Livingstone had said: 'We intend to create a better environment for all Londoners to treat each other with equal dignity, respect and justice regardless of thier race, colour or ethnic origins.'

In many spheres, Livingstone's council was forever producing badges - now, probably collectors' items. There were badges to promote Thamesday, Peace Year, Anti Racist Year...Among them was a badge saying 'I spotted a nuclear train.'

On the back of its success in forcing the government to abandon its demand that local authorities must prepare for defence against nuclear attack, the council had declared London nuclear free, ignoring press ridicule and opponents' claims that hospitals used nuclear isotopes.

Nuclear waste passed through London by train on its way from power stations in the south-east to Sellafield, Cumbria, for reprocessing. Use of these trains angered the GLC, and residents were asked to tell the council whenever one was seen. A hotline was opened and badges were awarded to callers.

When the council staged a major anti-nuclear conference at which fears were expressed about terrorists breaking open the nuclear flasks with armour-piercing shells, I decided to test security in the course of writing an article for *The Londoner,* the council's mass circulation newspaper.

It was not difficult to discover that the trains were parked overnight in the goods yard at Willesden Junction. Such was the degree of nervousness among rail staff that if it rained and water ran down the sides of the heavy nuclear flasks and formed a puddle on the track, they would fear the flask had sprung a leak and call the fire brigade - always unnecessarily.

Labour's concern about the potential danger of the cargo was certainly not reflected in any heightened security at the marshalling yard. I went through a gate marked 'authorised personnel only,' past a rail police station and along the line to the freight complex.

Inside, I asked a railman: 'When the nuclear trains are left here overnight, can you show me where they are parked?'

'Certainly,' he said helpfully, leading me out to the track and then pointing to an area 150 yards away where some empty trucks were standing.

I walked to the spot, took photographs as proof of my visit and left the way I had come. No one stopped me or asked who I was.

Labour's industry arm was awash with money. Beginning with a £58 million budget, chairman Mike Ward stated: 'We have the land, the resources and the powers. We seek a partnership with the London boroughs and the unions, and will join with other financial institutions to fund new enterprises, build new factories, construct new workshops. The conquest of unemployment is the greatest challenge our democratic institutions face.'

He added: 'We will set up action teams to help some plants under threat and generate new jobs if closures have been made, promote co-ops and municipal enterprises, provide factory space, finance training, and advice packages to keep new enterprises on their feet.'

Its success in the employment field was an area of frequent controversy. Shortly before abolition Mike Ward claimed that, in the previous two years, it had saved or created 3,000 jobs in more than 150 enterprises. Opponents dismissed the whole policy as a disastrous and expensive failure.

Whatever the facts behind the figures, there was no contesting the excellence of the research by the Greater London Enterprise Board. It created a superb directory of industrial information which continues to be London's industrial bible today and GLEB lives on with support from the borough councils and private enterprise.

If job creation was costing a great deal of money, the prize for securing the bargain of the year went to Tony Banks. As chair of the arts and recreation committee, he was very keen to raise the GLC's profile at its Crystal Palace stadium. At that time the GLC's existence was acknowledged only by a council crest.

Tony Banks arrived with some 'GLC Working for London' banners which he wanted displayed at the track side. The stadium authorities were not enthusiastic. Not a man to be balked, uncompormising Tony, a man used to conducting union negotiations, told them to get on and do it.

The precise location was unplanned but it coincided with the start of the 1500-metre races. At that time our two great metric milers, Seb Coe and Steve Ovett, were rivals whose duels featured on TV whenever they raced. It was a priceless location which, for an outlay of £150 and Tony Banks' determination, earned the GLC television exposure which would have cost tens of thousands.

The administration was busy in many other spheres. It found time to make pronouncements on road pricing - 'opposition is softening;' on speed limits - 'motorway limits should be reduced to 55 mph and on many urban roads to 20 mph'; on season tickets - 'it is the worker's equivalent of a company car and should be granted tax relief,' and on fishing - 'lead weights and dyed maggots (said to cause cancer) are banned from all GLC controlled water.'

Denied any authority over the Metropolitan Police, the Livingstone administration could only shadow police activities through its police committee chaired by Paul Boateng.

Now that the police are at last being made accountable to the people of London through their mayor, it remains to be seen what policy and operational changes may be made.

Ken Livingstone's council set out very firmly what it saw as the weaknesses of the police and the changes it would wish to make had it the power. First, the council would ask Londoners to help decide the most effective structure for the force. Answers to the inner city problems of rising crime and racial tensions had to be developed. He added: 'We want the police committee to carry out in-depth investigations into vandalism and into racial harassment.'

Commenting on a report into the Brixton riots of that time, Paul

Boateng said: 'Policing London has become increasingly marked by a decline in public confidence. Added to this the problem of racism and growing conflict between youth, particularly black youth, and the police, and the events in Brixton and elsewhere in London were sadly predictable.'

Eighteen months later, the committee staged a concert against the Police and Criminal Evidence Bill after its vociferous opposition to it went unheard.

Use of police computers also exercised the committee. A report by an independent consultant expressed concern over the extent they were used to keep a 'check on the lives of ordinary Londoners,' leading Paul Boateng to say:

'We must not allow the police to make computers our masters. They are here to serve, not to keep surveillance. There is a dividing line between the prevention and detection of crime and the harassment of people who become known to the police. This dividing line should be drawn after public debate. We shall be taking action ourselves and together with the Association of Metropolitan Authorities to prevent the creation of a new police Frankenstein in the area of computer technology.

'In view of these doubts, the GLC police committee has decided to consider drawing up codes of practice whereby data collected by the GLC is transferred to the police, to encourage people to argue, through the courts if necessary, for the right of their own access to police records.'

Boateng also called on the Home Office to probe alleged misbehaviour by Metropolitan Police officers policing the miners' strike. The call followed allegations to the GLC police committee that the Met are 'top of the league' in baiting, indiscipline and goading pickets.

Special Branch also came under the microscope. In its manifesto, the GLC had called for the branch's disbandment, saying: 'Surveillance of political and trade union activity must end and all files collected for non-criminal reasons should be destroyed.'

Concerned about what it called the branch's 'development as an agency for political policy,' the police committee invited evidence from the public with experience and knowledge of the Special

Branch for submission to the Parliamentary Select committee on the subject. Londoners who had been interviewed, arrested or had any contact with the Special Branch were invited to come forward and relate their experience in confidence.

The Select committee's ultimate findings were slated as a 'whitewash,' by the GLC for which Paul Boateng described the report as that of 'a watchdog that decided in advance that it wasn't going to bark.' The Select Committee was complacent and had predetermined its decision by refusing to hear the evidence of the GLC individuals, trade union and other sources whose comments might have led to a different view, he said.

Another milestone from the Livingstone administration was a change in the structure of the fortnightly meetings of the council, introducing an eleven o'clock guillotine. They started at 2.30. In the past, meetings had sometimes gone on well into the small hours. By then, Livingstone claimed, some members were drunk and prolonging sittings became almost a game.

Sir James Swaffield, director general for nine years, recalled: 'It was in the early debates that some bitterness and rancour would emerge. As members became more experienced they became more skilled at spinning a meeting out. They would start to flag as the evening wore on and they knew that by about ten o'clock, with a bit of skillful manipulation, they could get slightly controversial issues through more easily.'

For the first time, babies appeared on the floor of the chamber. Director general Maurice Stonefrost recalls an occasion when a baby was being fed near his desk and another afternoon when a 'near riot' ensued when a woman member was holding a baby in the Labour benches and a Conservative asked that 'it' should be removed.

Stonefrost recalled another incident when an unruly debate followed a claim that a junior officer had, without authority, involved the council in considerable expense.

He said: 'The officer was accompanying Mr Livingstone at an open-air event where it had been raining heavily. The event was being spoilt by mud and Ken Livingstone told the officer to 'go and get some carpets."

'Receiving an order from the leader of the council, he didn't ask:

"Have you got authority, sir?" he just did as he was told. The Conservatives raised the matter on which, had it gone to a vote, I would have needed to censure the officer.

'When Ken rose to speak, he said: "Never mind about these carpets, what's happened to the carpets in Rooms 131, 132 and 133." These were the opposition committee rooms.

'Conservative members looked at each other nonplussed: What had happened to the carpets in those rooms? Nobody knew because the likelihood was that nothing had happened at all. The rest of the meeting was devoted to a heated discussion about the carpets in the opposition committee rooms. Everyone forgot the point of the debate and no vote of censure was ever taken. It was just a smart diversionary tactic by Ken. He was good at that.'

10. THE LONDONER

A month after the election, the media's reaction to Livingstone was almost frenziedly hostile. The council's policies were either ignored or trivialised, sometimes with scant regard for fairness or accuracy. It was in this climate that the Labour group decided the answer was for the GLC to produce its own newspaper, delivered through every domestic letterbox in the capital. It would be the biggest free-sheet in the world and would prove the forerunner of a spate of smaller clones up and down the country. I was asked to produce and edit it.

With so many forceful Labour members determined to carve themselves a career in politics and vying with each other for publicity, the post of editor threatened to be a bed of nails. There could be only one Page One lead story; only two stories on the front. Would I really have to tell intransigent politicians: 'Your story isn't strong enough. It's only worth a short item inside.' The job could work only if the editor was freed from interference and guaranteed complete editorial control.

To my surprise, that condition was agreed, and the words 'the editor's decision is final' were written into the job specification. Never, before or since, have I heard of a local government newspaper where an officer-editor has full control. Politicians, the people's elected representatives, insist on reserving the ultimate decisions for themselves. Fortunately, the proposal for a GLC newspaper was being steered through the personality minefield by a wise politician, Dr Tony Hart, whose wife Judith, was a Commonwealth Secretary in an earlier Labour government.

Tony Hart accepted that the competing demands of resolute men and women could be intolerable and make an acceptable newspaper an impossibility - especially as a rigid law required its contents to fall within strict, non-party political guidelines. He foresaw the possibility of senior politicians making unreasonable demands and using their authority to insist on the most prominent display for their words.

The reality proved somewhat different. For the most part, senior politicians accepted the situation; it was their personal assistants and young activists who were less willing to take 'No' for an answer.

In law, the editor is responsible for the contents of a newspaper and, in the final resort, it is he (or she) who goes to jail.

Announcing the decision to produce the newspaper, at a cost of about £87,000 per edition, Tony Hart told the council: 'We believe the job of the world's largest local authority is not only to take action on behalf of the people of London but also to tell them why it is being done.' The newspaper would be a first step in making County Hall less remote by informing Londoners of the council's policies, activities and achievements, and explaining how ratepayers' money was spent.

So began preparations to launch *The Londoner*. The brief was to produce 'a credible newspaper which would be acceptable throughout London.' Members' only requirement was that it was to be an eight-page tabloid with a front page similar to the *Daily Mirror*. The intention, to deliver a copy to every household in London, required a distribution of 2,740,000.

It was to be produced by a staff of two, myself and Mary Matthews, a journalist from the press office, whose claims to fame included being a member of Mensa and having written a 10,000-word summary of 'War and Peace' for *Woman's Illustrated* during a long weekend!

So much which was newsworthy was happening at County Hall there would be no difficulty providing stories for the newspaper. What to leave out - and who would be upset by the decisions - was the hairshirt we would have to wear. Production and distribution were another matter. Here the problems were outside our control and they threatened to be vast.

With one of the council's major policies aimed at boosting employment in London, it was unthinkable that printing and production would be anywhere other than in the capital.

Achieving that seemingly simple objective was another matter. Familiar companies were no longer operating in London.

Some had been driven out of town to where rates and rents and wages were lower; others had gone to the wall. After a month of intensive searching we had to report that we could find no London printer big enough to handle a tabloid with a print run of 2.7 million copies. We advertised again, calling on printers to ask why they had not tendered. The only London printers with the capacity to handle the job were the *Daily Mirror* and *The Evening Standard.* Neither was interested.

The Communist *Morning Star* (formerly the *Daily Worker*) saw a possible contract with the GLC as a lifeline for its rocky finances and tried to persuade us to change our format and make the page bigger to fit their presses, but GLC members wouldn't agree.

We were having similar problems recruiting an advertising agency. Many agencies were very happy to take the council's money for poster advertising, or design. Hard space-selling was another matter. The Left-wing GLC of that time had a non-acceptable public face, and no advertising agent wanted to know.

How to get the newspaper into every London home, in the manner of most give-aways today, proved to be a huge obstacle. None of the distribution companies had a satisfactory London-wide network; nor could they guarantee delivery. We could imagine the outcry if piles of *The Londoner* turned up on building sites or in alleyways. The only solution was to let the Post Office handle it.

This raised the biggest problem of all from the viewpoint of effective presentation. Both the Post Office and the postal union insisted that the newspaper be double folded to letterbox size (four and a half inches wide). Apart from reducing the newspaper's impact by making even its headline unreadable without unfolding it, the few printers in the provinces who could handle the print volume couldn't handle a page requiring a second fold. Machines which could make such a fold were scarce and expensive.

Neither the Post Office nor the unions would budge in their demands. As there was no other means of distribution, we would have to put up with it.

Printers revised their quotations and had to arrange for a second fold to be made - by hand! The successful printer would have to hire a hall and conscript casual labour to fold nearly three million newspapers, painstakingly one at a time, with a ruler. It would take an age.

Nevertheless, at last all the difficulties had been overcome, contracts were signed and the first edition of *The Londoner* was ready to meet its public. It would be produced in Rochford, Essex, by Essex Web Offset. GLC members were not pleased. The council was pouring millions of pounds into job-creation in the capital yet its own newspaper had gone outside to be printed. The Conservative opposition would, and did, tease the administration mercilessly.

Two problems solved, one to go. We turned our attention to advertising.

Such was the GLC's continuing unpopularity, we still could not find an agency willing to act for us. Several companies expressed interest, the financial percentages were excellent, but always they shied away at the last moment. We had to accept that the first edition was going to appear without advertising to help defray its cost.

On May 2, 1981, the first edition of *The Londoner* was being delivered to more than two million homes, distribution arranged by each individual postman according to his weight of mail, but to be completed in three days.

Inevitably there were teething troubles: some postal depots received too many copies, others too few. Elsewhere, delivery lorries were too big to get into the smaller depots.

Postmen received a small bonus, though one or two whose personal political views conflicted strongly with those expressed in *The Londoner,* dumped their consignments and were duly disciplined. The Post Office, too, were breaking new ground and every complaint of mis-delivery was conscientiously followed up.

The day *The Londoner* first hit the streets was memorable indeed. London had seen nothing like it. Unsolicited mail was still fairly new and there had been mumblings in Parliament of how it could be stopped. Suddenly every home in the capital was being given a newspaper the occupier did not ask for, many did not want and they were having to pay for it through the rates.

Telephones were ringing from the moment County Hall opened on that first day and they didn't stop. Scores of callers simply couldn't get through. On Day One, delivery had obviously been heavy in the Tory outer areas and every call was a complaint. *How much did the newspaper cost? ....Who was paying? ....Was this another example of Livingstone profligacy with other people's money? ..How can we stop it?*

Mingled with the grumbles was the inevitable abuse: *Go back to Moscow..... When the Tories get back I hope they sack you first.* Then the threats: *We're sending this rubbish to the district auditor with the demand that Livingstone be surcharged ...... I'm reporting you, personally, to the the Director of Public Prosecutions for invading the privacy of my home.* Everyone seemed to be angry.

Tomorrow was indeed another day. There had been a delivery in the Labour strongholds and callers were all pleased. *This is the sort of thing we want to read.... Marvellous! .....Full of interesting information. ....When is the next issue? ..* Several said they had read every word. Others that it had put a totally different complexion on what they had read in the national press. Yet more asked if the editor would speak at the next meeting of their organisation.

It was a different world.

As other districts received their saturation coverage, public response followed a now predictable pattern. Organisations clearly had been discussing the new phenomenon. Some had studied the law and felt the GLC was breaking it. These complaints were matched almost one for one by others asking for guest speakers.

The council decided the first edition was a success and plans were made for issue No.2 of what was to become first a quarterly, then a monthly publication. Delivery had worked fairly well considering the enormity of the operation. Now was the time to fine-tune the newspaper's content to try to win over the neutrals and make it more acceptable to the antagonists. And to find an advertising agent. We were still being treated like pariahs when we telephoned agencies and personalities who had previously worked for the council. No-one was willing to take us on. All sorts of reasons were offered, some genuine, some simply excuses.

Sections of the national news media continued to pillory Ken Livingstone, often misquoting his words. He was in his usual laid back, unflappable mood when I met him to suggest including a regular feature: 'What I really said,' based on these misquotations.

'I shan't bother to pick up everything, just the more outrageous misquotations,' I suggested.

Ken smiled and replied: 'The more outrageous things I probably did say.'

I felt he had a point, recalling that he had once said to me: 'What's the point of making love if you can't talk politics afterwards?'

Meanwhile news of our successful launch had spread nationwide, not least because of questions in Parliament and statements that some Conservative organisations had asked members to hand in their copies of the paper to be forwarded to the district auditor with a demand for surcharge against GLC members for misuse of public funds.

Other Labour councils wrote to ask how we had apparently 'got round the law' (though this was not the case) and asking Livingstone's advice on how they should set up their own paper. He would reply: 'Find an officer who is sympathetic and let them get on with it.'

Such letters came to my office for replies to be drafted and we were always amused that Livingstone assiduously crossed out our references to giving the task to experienced journalists. Perhaps his views had been coloured by personal experience.

The second issue gave us the desired opportunity to show our impartiality by producing a page of 22 letters. All were genuine. No letter ever used throughout the five-year life of *The Londoner* was fraudulent, though one highly political consultant did once offer to provide us with 'a page of pro GLC letters.' His offer was declined.

Professionally, we were proud of our impartial letters feature, though this impartiality did not meet with universal approval. Transport chair Dave Wetzel once telephoned to complain at 'letting people slag off our policies.' He said: 'We get that in the *Daily Mail.* We don't expect to find it in *The Londoner.'*

Explanations that such was the price to be paid for acceptance as a credible newspaper did not cut much ice.

We were in a difficulty because the Conservative Opposition had taken a policy decision to oppose the newspaper and not contribute to it. Tories I had known from previous administrations said they disagreed with the decision but were bound by it. When Alan

Greengross became opposition leader he told me: 'When we win power we wouldn't necessarily get rid of *The Londoner*. We would change its format to more of an up-market magazine.'

To overcome the difficulties of seeming to be a propaganda sheet, my deputy and I considered attending committee meetings and reporting them, so that Conservative views would appear whether the members liked it or not. On reflection, we considered that Sir James Swaffield, the director general, would rule that we were exceeding our authority. In any event, we were likely to end up being accused of selective reporting and being shown the door.

In the House of Lords, Lord Stewart of Putney found the appropriate aphorism to summarise our problem during exchanges on *The Londoner* when he said: 'One man's propaganda is another's factual statement.'

Most advertisers continued to regard *The Londoner* as too political, but at last we had a respected West End advertising agency representing us, though they were finding the going tough. Even when they succeeded in bringing in business, it seemed that some members were bending over backwards to try to find reasons for rejecting it on political grounds. It was laughable.

It was a supreme irony that our first advert was for holidays in the United States and contained a prominent drawing of the Stars and Stripes. In the high spirits of the occasion we asked our man to see if, next time, he could balance it with an advert for an Intourist trip round Moscow.

Two members wrote to Ken Livingstone protesting that another of our early advertisers, an estate agent, should be banned because he was advocating home ownership which, to them, was politically unacceptable.

Livingstone replied that the council should not censor adverts just because it did not agree with what they offered, so the advert stayed. But the right to free speech of Life, the anti abortion lobby, was given very short shrift indeed. No one with political authority was prepared to speak up for them. Our despairing agent complained that he was wasting his time if members tried to find a reason for refusing every advert he obtained.

Production difficulties faced thus far were trivial compared with those created when the GLC chose to include information on the British Nationality Act - in English, Hindi, Urdu, Gujarati, Bengali and Punjabi. Immigrant communities were anxious to receive bulk supplies of this so it was decided to include it as a loose leaf and so produce a ten-page paper. Now, not only was it necessary to fold every copy by hand, but the printer had to open each copy by hand and insert a fly sheet before folding it - surely another entry for the Guinness Book of Records.

Peter Griffin, Essex Web-offset's managing director, must have thought his printers had drawn the short straw, not won a contract. He blanched at the enormity of this new demand and probably wondered why he had ever become involved. A couple of scotches restored his pallor and he signed up to undertake a task probably unique in the world of printing.

With several editions produced and still no work for London, the print unions were getting restive. Members were pleading for us to find some way of giving the work to London as more mocking letters appeared in the press drawing attention to what the writers saw as the gulf between the council's words and its deeds.

Dutifully, we trawled through the print world of London before each contract, always without success. Finally the print unions sought a showdown with members. The result was an agreement that typesetting (less than 1 per cent of the contract) would in future be handled separately and given to a London firm.

Technically, this was not a good idea, especially as the latest print contract had been won by West of England Newspapers based in Plymouth. However, it showed the council's goodwill and got the politicians off the hook, so *The Londoner's* editorial staff made the best of it.

In those days, type was computer set but page make-up was completed with paste and scalpel: the galley proofs of type being cut and pasted on page-size artboard. That system was common to nearly all major printers, including our new London-based typesetters. There uniformity ended.

The typesetting firm we had now inherited was not geared to newspaper production and worked at a snail's pace. As press day ground on, it was clear that I was going to miss my evening train to

Plymouth and probably miss next morning's deadline when printing was to begin. Anxious to learn how things were going, Brian Doel, managing director of West of England Newspapers, telephoned for a progress report and was not pleased at what he heard. Unknown to me, he and the typesetters had a row, the upshot of which was that I was chucked out into the street with the unfinished paste-ups and all the loose galley proofs pushed under my arm.

I caught the train and completed the make-up of the remaining pages on the floor in the foyer of the Holiday Inn at Plymouth. Later that night, key members of the printer's staff were called to the factory from their homes so that final adjustments could enable printing to begin on time next day.

It was close. But the GLC politicians had made their peace with the print unions. Subsequently, the system continued with another London typesetter and everything ran smoothly.

When each edition was being planned, I would meet Ken Livingstone to ask if there was any particular story he wanted us to run and to discuss how the paper was shaping up. He was always enthusiastic that women's issues should be well represented. We would check through the committees one by one, examining how their activities were to be represented, and he would say: 'I don't mind having a row with him... I don't mind having a row with him... or him.' But women's issues were always close to his political heart.

This gave rise to problems because he was constantly urging inclusion of a woman's page. Most of the council's actions, the only matters the law allowed us to write about, probably concerned men and women equally - fares, housing, jobs, sport. The breakthrough came when the GLC formed its women's committee. Now at last we could legitimately produce a woman's page.

We put the idea to women's committee chair Valerie Wise who was enthusiastic. She was given a deadline with suitable leeway for first-timers and offered our help which was declined. Later, we were told that the task had been delegated to a certain officer who, it seemed, had further delegated it. In short, publication day arrived and not a line of copy had emerged. It was never explained what went wrong but never again was there mention of a woman's page.

Individual women's committee stories were used, though we

tumbled into another trap when the women's committee were having an important conference. We had written the story in advance and on the day we sent along a photographer to give the story visual impact. We thought no more of it until the telephone rang. Our photographer was outside the venue. They wouldn't let him in - because he was a man.

There were eight photographers on the GLC staff. All men. In those days there were few women photographers. The situation was saved when my deputy, Mary Matthews, revealed another string to her bow: she had previously been a writer-photographer for *The Universe*.

Later the women's support unit showed a narrow-mindedness we found difficult to comprehend.

We were deep in the fight against abolition and had produced a cartoon lampooning Margaret Thatcher, who was threatening London's democratic future and all our jobs. We set her on a tightrope, juggling several political balls in the air and dressed her appropriately in fishnet tights. Members of the women's support unit took umbrage at what they regarded as 'a sexist drawing exploiting women' and sent in a small petition of protest. Apparently, no longer was all fair in love and war.

Their likely reaction was imagined a couple of issues later. Writing about some statements in the Commons by Mrs Thatcher which we knew to be wrong, we pondered long and hard over our proposed Page One cross reference - MAGGIE'S BOOBS - See Page Three.

The continuing publication of *The Londoner* was raised several times in Parliament. We were not the favourite publication of Tory MPs, partly because we exposed how they voted on several key issues.

It was Ken Livingstone's idea to publish a chart recording the votes of all London MPs on such crucially important topics as Hanging, Sex Equality, Support for Disabled People, Limiting Rate Support.... There was nowhere to hide. Conservative MPs hated it. For the first time ever, each constituent, every member of every family, would know exactly how his or her Member of Parliament had voted on issues, including abolishing London's democracy.

When the battle against abolition was at its height and the elderly person's free travel pass seemed to be under threat, *The Londoner* included a cut-out coupon which we asked readers to send to their MP. We were later told that Members were deluged by hundreds of thousands of coupons from their elderly constituents demanding an assurance that the passes would be retained.

The Londoner was again in trouble over women when we included a non-political success story about the GLC renovating kitchens in 4,000 council homes.

Housing surely is one of the most important functions for local government and if the council is bringing thousands of old fashioned kitchens up to date and giving tenants a better lifestyle in consequence, why not tell the world about it?

We did just that and illustrated the story with a woman standing in an antiquated kitchen and showing, in a dream bubble, how it could look when modernised. She was black. Whether or not that was a factor I never knew. The words were rather twee, simply padding out the facts.

When some advance copies of the paper arrived at County Hall, my director telephoned to say that some members of the Labour group were incensed. We should have known better than to depict a woman in a kitchen, they complained. They were so angry they were debating whether to incinerate the entire edition - all £70,000 worth. I warned that if they did so, they must be prepared to explain their actions to press and public. There would be no way of hushing it up. Too many people knew the edition had been published and thousands of postmen would be wanting to know why their expected delivery bonus was not forthcoming.

For a moment I reflected on Illtyd Harrington's words to me when *The Londoner* was floated. 'Your job is impossible,' he said.

In the event the Labour group decided not to carry out its threat and nothing more was heard about the woman in the kitchen, though the Left wing was again upset when the GLC opened the Thames barrier, the most memorable of all the GLC's engineering and safety achievements. The opening was to be performed by the Queen, so what was more fitting than to use a portrait of her on Page One?

A frowning Left-winger met me on my next visit to County Hall.

Shaking his head in suppressed anger he lamented: 'I never thought I'd ever see a picture of the Queen in *The Londoner*.'

In a moment of political madness, *The Londoner* had been moved from County Hall to an office on the corner of the Covent Garden piazza. Space in County Hall was at a premium and the newspaper was regarded as a specialist, self-contained unit, which could function equally easily elsewhere. It was a crass decision which cut us off from members and from 90 per cent of our news sources, but our arguments fell on deaf ears.

Discussing it with colleagues whom we expected to be sympathetic to our arguments did not meet with the expected response. They said in disbelief: 'You've been given the chance to work in Covent Garden and you want to stay in the Kremlin? You must be barmy. We're going to be abolished anyway. Go the Covent Garden and enjoy it.'

We took the advice and settled into our new office at No. 1 King Street, an address printed in *The Londoner* and apparently noted by the ill-intentioned as well as those who wished us well.

It was not long before we had our first call from the National Front. It did not please me that they knew my name but I was rather amused they thought it a *nom de plume*. Threats to bomb us followed. We knew that if we reported these to the director general he would recall us to the security of County Hall. We had quickly grown to appreciate our new environs, so we took a vote and decided unanimously to ignore the threats, presuming them to be empty anyway.

We were therefore surprised when workmen arrived with orders to fit a splinter curtain across the huge plate glass shopfront which extended across the entire width of our office and where our desks stood. As it transpired, there were fears that the IRA might choose Covent Garden to make a political point.

A couple more bomb threats followed and we had dismissed them until one morning a large package of excreta was delivered. Joan Robinson, the office manager, had the misfortune to open it. Our caller returned some days later to warn: 'Next time it's gonna be a bomb.'

So when an unexpected package did arrive, it seemed prudent to alert our security and leave it to be opened by experts. The contents were returned later that day. It was Sir Horace Cutler's autobiography, *The Cutler Files.* Horace would have relished that. I can hear him saying: 'That put a rocket under 'em.'

Sadly for Horace, that was the most explosive effect his book had, its publication passing almost unnoticed.

During this era of bomb threats, there was one more alert: an unattended suitcase was left propped up against our window. We vacated the building but before we could alert police, the case had gone. Probably it belonged to one of the buskers who were auditioned in the basement next door for licences to perform in the piazza.

In a crackdown against racism, the GLC announced that any tenant found guilty of racism would be evicted from their home. It was a good story and *The Londoner* led on it. Soon after we published, a widow rang in tears.

Her story was that she had a dog and that when the Indian children in the street went to school, they would kick her front door to make the dog bark. She was scared that one day the dog would get out and bite them. Did that mean she would be evicted? she asked.

We put her case to the Ethnic Minorities unit at County Hall who answered dismissively: 'There is no such thing as racism by blacks or Asians against whites. Whites are not one of the oppressed races.'

I had more respect for a good old Eastender than to convey such crass gobbledegook. When she rang back I told her to write to her GLC member or to Ken Livingstone and to keep their replies.

Why does commonsense fly out the window when we attempt to discuss racial issues?

When the GLC appointed Herman Ouseley (later Sir Herman and chair of the Commission for Racial Equality), as its adviser on ethnic minorities, I went to meet him when he left his job with Lambeth borough council to take up his GLC appointment. I had read up on him and, as we walked together the short distance from Lambeth town hall to County Hall, it seemed a good opportunity to begin an informal interview with the intention of writing a story for *The Londoner*.

'Is it right,' I asked, 'that you have a white wife?'

He turned on me, incensed, and demanded: 'What's that got to do with it?'

Perhaps I'm just an old fashioned journalist, but I would have thought that having an adviser who was going to preach racial tolerance and integration who himself had integrated at the highest level in his private life gave him an added right to be heard.

The Londoner was in its fourth year and the battle against abolition was nearing its fateful end when word reached me that certain politicians considered that the newspaper needed a greater Left-wing slant. After all, my deputy and I had both worked both for the previous Conservative administration of Sir Horace Cutler and for the Socialist administration of Sir Reg Goodwin. Perhaps we had absorbed too much of their political philosophies.

We were asked if *The Londoner* would accept help from a firm of political consultants who arrived fresh from having assisted the Labour party at the previous general election when Neil Kinnock was soundly trounced by Margaret Thatcher. Ultimately the consultants were to replace my deputy and I.

Some Labour politicians, I knew, did not agree with *The Londoner's* policy of using a minimum of political rhetoric and letting the facts speak for themselves. (Perhaps not easy for a politician to accept). In the fight against abolition, we thought it more effective to let Conservative rebels make our case for us. It also helped to make *The Londoner* accepted as a credible newspaper. For one issue, Tory support for anti-abolition was so strong that we abandoned our radical red masthead for one of Tory blue.

My card had been marked, I was told, fairly early in the Livingstone administration when I made an unwise comment about the GLC's commemoration of Hiroshima Day. Invitations were being sent to various CND groups, the Fabian Society and other Left-wing and pacifist organisations. The politicians wanted a bigger turn-out from outside organisations and the publicity department was asked for ideas. I suggested they might like to invite the Burma Star Association.

I accept that there are there are two views on the Hiroshima bomb. Mine is quite firm: Terrible though the bombing was, it ended the bloodiest war in the history of mankind and, based on the first crumb siezed of the Japanese homeland, probably saved many hundreds of thousands more lives than the bomb destroyed.

Coincidentally, in the press office at that time was Henry Donaldson, who had worked on the Railway of Death in Thailand and had seen his friend decapitated by their barbaric guards. I wondered if they would expect him to join the breast-beating and apologise for bringing an end to the war and to his suffering.

There were many other actions to choose from, many other uncontroversial dates to commemorate, if the council wanted to draw attention to the horrors of war. A London council needed look no further than that night in September 1940 when the docks and much of the East End were almost wiped off the map.

Other unsuspecting souls also had their cards marked by some of the more intense political activists who chose to watch and listen to decide who was 'one of us.'

Ivor Watkins, formerly of the *Daily Express* and *Evening Standard,* the head of news, who skilfully steered the GLC press office away from the rocks in many a storm during the Livingstone years, showed his lack of political credentials innocently in the famous pantomime spoof 'Ken Whittington and his Cat,' in which so many members and officers took part.

At the end of the panto, an excited activist told me, most of the cast assembled on stage for a rousing rendition of The Red Flag - and Watkins didn't know the words!

The threatened editorial change at *The Londoner* never came about. My deputy and I were twice replaced only to be reinstated within days when editions were considered too far advanced to be handed over. Finally the consultants fell out with each other and *The Londoner* saw out its days following its original policy of letting the facts speak for themselves.

After abolition, the Wilberforce Committee looked closely at money spent by councils on publicity and the rules on local authority newspapers were tightened up in the light of *The Londoner* experience. Fifteen years on, however, times have changed once more and many boroughs which produce newspapers claim that this is the most effective way to communicate with residents.

When the new mayor is comfortably ensconced, watch this space.

11. SHADOW OF ABOLITION

The first murmurings that the GLC should be abolished were heard in 1973 when yet another local government reorganisation saw the GLC's responsibilities for sewerage given to the newly created water authorities and the ambulance service handed over to a reorganised National Health Service. Critics asked what duties London's strategic authority retained that could not equally or better be accomplished by the borough councils. The call for abolition became a demand in the early days of the Livingstone administration and 16 months after his election, in September 1982, the Tory controlled London Boroughs Association issued a statement saying that getting rid of the GLC was a reform which was long overdue. Chairman Peter Bowness called on government ministers to reinforce the message, but, he thought, without success.

In a press statement, Bowness said: 'Dividing local government between the GLC and boroughs who are often under different political control can only be a recipe for conflict, delay, frustration and confusion and lead to greater intervention by central government. Without the GLC, London government would be cheaper and more effective, duplication of effort and overlapping of functions would be eliminated, staff numbers could be more easily controlled and staff accountability increased. The London boroughs are large enough to run the great majority of local government services, yet they are not remote bureaucracies like the GLC.'

For most of its life, the LBA had been Labour run. Soon after the call for abolition, the Labour-controlled boroughs broke away to form their own Association of London Authorities.

Another general election was looming and Prime Minister Thatcher was making no headway in her pledge to reform the rates or make another headline-grabbing change in local government. So, at the last minute, she turned on the GLC, ordering that its abolition and abolition of the other six Metropolitan counties should be inserted in the Tory manifesto. Critics claim that the measure was proposed with virtually no preparatory work and in spite of caution being urged by some of her ministers. In fact the abolition commitment occupied just seven and a half lines in a 47-page manifesto.

Mrs Thatcher told the story differently. Abolition had been examined thoroughly by her cabinet the previous year and recommended, she said. A final decision was delayed and was added late to the manifesto only because she feared the proposal would be leaked.

Alan Greengross, as leader of the Conservative opposition at the GLC, had been privy to the thoughts of government ministers regarding a possible restructuring of the council. So far as he was aware, abolition was not an option and the word from Westminster was that there would be no change.

In May 1983, he was called to the office of Lord Bellwyn, Local Government minister. Sir Alan related their staccato conversation rather like a Noel Coward dialogue.

'We shook hands and Lord Bellwyn said: "I have some bad news for you. It's abolition. Everything goes."

'We didn't say much. There wasn't much to say really. She had made up her mind. This was the end. I just thanked him and went back to County Hall.

'At GLC headquarters, an overwhelming number of Conservative members genuinely thought you couldn't run London without something like the GLC. We started writing all sorts of papers, some published, some privately to Mrs Thatcher, to try to find her a face-saving solution; trying to produce models that would allow her still to say that she had abolished the GLC, but also to put something in its place.'

He recalls that in subsequent meetings with Mrs Thatcher, she remained dogmatically opposed to replacing the council.

'My personal line was that I could appreciate her frustration with the GLC and I could see that it was no longer the right organisation for London and that I would have no personal objection to it being abolished provided there was a new body to take over. Using the 1963 borough reorganisation as a precedent, we looked at every possible configuration of borough boundaries to give her a Conservative majority for ever. It was pure gerrymandering to try to get her to change her mind, but she was adamant.

'I had a lot of talks with her. They were not heated, they were frigid. To my knowledge, she never shouted at anybody. She had this ghastly habit of turning off when she had heard enough. You would be in mid sentence and suddenly realise she wasn't listening any more. It was really daunting. There wasn't anything you could do. You knew that no matter how long you sat there she was not going to return to that particular conversation. I suffered many times from this when she just turned off. She had heard enough and you had lost her sympathy. The terrible thing was not just that she had turned off, but you could see it.'

He recalled one meeting when she was flanked by Kenneth Baker and Patrick Jenkin, the two ministers who, at various times, were personally responsible for the abolition programme.

Sir Alan said: 'Her whole contention was that getting rid of the GLC would save a fortune which, of course, it never did. I was saying that this was nonsense because all the functions performed by the GLC would still have to be done. Abolition wasn't getting rid of anything, it was merely rearranging the pieces.

'Eventually she said something like: "I'm sorry but I can see no reason to change my mind about the GLC. Whereupon she turned to Patrick Jenkin and Ken Baker who both simpered on about how she was absolutely right and the GLC had to go and that it was a pointless organisation.

At that I exploded. I said I was sorry but I was not prepared to listen to Ken Baker say the GLC was not necessary when, two years before, he had written a book which said how important the GLC was. Or to listen to Patrick Jenkin who went to the Marshall Inquiry, which examined the GLC's functions, where he suggested that the GLC should have more powers not less. I said that I could waste my time elsewhere. Then I calmed down.'

He added: 'There were times in Cabinet when it was very much touch and go whether the policy would be dropped, but always at the crucial moment, just when we were making headway, Ken Livingstone stepped up the abuse. It was uncanny. It made bloody sure that if she was going to change her mind, she wasn't going to do it now. Maybe he was getting the service I was getting.

'On my desk from time to time I received envelopes of ministerial committee meetings. To this day I have no idea who sent them. They just appeared on my desk and from them you could see where there were difficulties and where there weren't difficulties. I was privy to this because someone wanted to help me in the fight. I'm quite sure they were sending them to Ken as well.'

The government case was that abolition would do away with a costly and unnecessary tier of local government and that most of the GLC's functions would be devolved to the borough councils. It soon became evident, however, that the boroughs were unable and generally unwilling to take on these responsibilities and that there were many functions which required expertise which the boroughs did not possess. More and more examples of these were discovered as the GLC's list of responsibilities was examined.

Tasks would have to be taken over by quangos (quasi-autonomous non-government organisations). From the one quango which the government admitted would be required to run the fire service, the list quickly grew to ten, then 20 and was still rising.

Ken Livingstone's response to the announcement of abolition was predictable. He lambasted the government's decision to remove the democratic right of Londoners to have a say in their city's future, and went on: 'Abolition is being proposed for purely political reasons. It is supported by the banks and multi-nationals in the city because they see an opportunity to cease paying a contribution to the cost of maintaining London's vital services and to throw those costs on to others much less able to pay.'

Opposition parties were immediately united in their objections. Many Conservatives also expressed disquiet - doubts which became an open mutiny against the government as the months passed. However, Mrs Thatcher probably was satisfied that her proposals were generally popular when the general election saw her dispose of Neil Kinnock's Labour challenge and return her to office with her largest ever majority.

In setting up the GLC, the Royal Commission on Local Government in Greater London had said: 'Local government means local self government. To surrender those powers [planning, traffic management, highways and housing] to central government would make administrative confusion worse. There are two fatal objections to any attempt to deal with London problems by the creation of further *ad hoc* bodies whether for traffic or for any other purpose. All these bodies are either creatures of central government or they are responsible to no-one. The second objection is that so many of London's problems are interlinked.'

'If only the lady in No. 10 had left the GLC alone it would have worked itself out,' said Sir Alan Greengross. 'If she had let the Livingstone administration run its course and be judged by the electorate of London on his four years....

'When I was made leader of the Conservative party, many senior politicians on the Labour side came up and said: "Congratulations. You will be the next leader of the council. Even at that stage, three years before the next election, very few members of the Labour party believed there was any possibility of Labour being returned to power. Livingstone was then extremely unpopular. Very senior Labour politicians were saying that there was no way they were going to win. Apart from anything else, the GLC had this long tradition of swinging back and forth.

'Instead of leaving it alone, the government played right into Ken Livingstone's hands and turned him into a folk hero. Incredibly the same thing is happening now with Tony Blair. It's quite spine-tingling to see another Prime Minister turning Ken into a folk hero that, not only London, but the country loves. Nobody has learned anything.'

As people began to realise that abolition of the GLC was no empty threat, the first of many public opinion polls took a sounding on the GLC's popularity. The Harris Research Centre had talked to a 1,500 sample of Londoners and found more than 50 per cent thought the GLC was doing a good job.

Then began a quite brilliant campaign to save the GLC, which saw Ken Livingstone increasingly transformed from villain to hero. Publicity director Tony Wilson bought up all the key advertising sites in central London and for the following two and a half years the government was embarrassed and angered as the weaknesses of its case were exposed and Ken Livingstone was personally promoted. The government was at a publicity disadvantage: it was prevented by law from spending on political propaganda.

Ironically, the council's slogan, 'GLC working for London' had been created by the council's design department for Conservative leader Sir Horace Cutler to anchor his ill-fated election campaign of 1981. Livingstone was persuaded that the slogan was too good to lose. Sue de Joodt, probably the most junior of the council's designers, adapted it by scripting the word 'Keep' above 'GLC working for London' and so was born the slogan which supported a £7 million a year advertising campaign - a buckshee, inspirational tinkering which would have cost a five figure sum if created by an advertising agency.

Elsewhere the GLC was telling the true facts of abolition via link teams, who were briefing editors and professional bodies, outreach workers whose task included organising public meetings and demonstrations, and through its newspaper *The Londoner* which carried the message directly into the homes of the capital's six million people. For the first time the true consequences of abolition were being spelt out; the government's claims of money savings were exposed for the sham they later proved.

If the government expected to be carried along on a tidal wave of anti-Livingstone popularity, they were soon disabused. A case in point was a highly successful pensioners' rally following which they were all invited to County Hall for a cup of tea.

As they filed by the score into the conference hall, one suddenly saw Ken Livingstone and asked him to pose for a picture with the man's group. Immediately tea was forgotten and the groups of pensioners lined the walls of the hall waiting for their turn to be similarly photographed. Ken's arrangements for the afternoon had to be cancelled.

The council proved to be more loved than they anticipated and the merits of the council's arguments were easy for the ordinary person to understand. In contrast, the government's case was ill-prepared and ministers, armed only with impressions and superficial data, found themselves out-gunned by an organisation which knew every detail of every fact because it spent its life dealing with them.

Gradually Conservatives began to break ranks publicly. One of the first was Bernard Brook-Partridge, a former Tory chairman of the GLC, who described the case for abolition as 'fraudulent, ignorant and deeply insulting.'

In a press statement he said: 'What could be more fraudulent than to propose the abolition of an elected tier of local government in the name of democracy? The proposal is ignorant in that it refers to a "return" from the GLC of "most of their functions to the boroughs and districts." The boroughs and districts did not exercise the functions in the first place. Thirdly the proposal is an insult to all those who have for many years given so freely of their time, money and talents to make the middle tier of local government work.

'However, the deepest insult is to the electorate which is apparently part of the "great British public" when it elects Members of the House of Commons but is judged to be unfit to elect representatives charged with the duty of taking less exalted but far more important-seeming decisions affecting their daily lives.'

Maurice Stonefrost, then the council's Comptroller of Finance, produced figures showing that the GLC's housekeeping record was far better than the government's. In the five years since 1977/78, government expenditure had increased by 101 pc and the GLC's by 88 pc. Accounts for 1982/3 showed the GLC was financially stronger, relative to any previous year of its existence.

But the government was already planning how to strip the GLC of its functions. First to go would be London Transport, snatched away and hived off to a quango, London Regional Transport. In the Commons, Transport Secretary Nicholas Ridley trumpeted that the transfer would reduce the level of ratepayers' and taxpayers' support to the buses and tubes £95m, compared with the £217m planned by the GLC.

Transport chair Dave Wetzel bemoaned the massive fares increases and service cuts this would entail and added: 'Just when we're getting it right they're taking it away from us.'

Fares were much in the news. No sooner had plans to wrench buses and tubes from GLC grasp been announced, than the results of the first year of 'Just the Ticket' became available - and with it came the promise that fares would remain frozen at that level.

The Standard commented: The freeze on bus and tube fares for another year from April is good news for passengers. Even better tidings for the future is that last year's cut in fares resulted in a 15 per cent rise in use and a deficit which is lower than expected by some £35/45 million. This is the type of transport policy we support and want to see continued. When Mr Ridley takes over London Transport he will have to do equally well, if not better.

Said *The Guardian:* The Society for the Abolition of Ken Livingstone has taken a bad knock with the latest report on London Transport. The well thought out 'Just the Ticket' fare restructuring introduced last year is handsomely living up to its name. A 15 per cent increase in passengers has ensued upon a 25 per cent reduction in fares... The Government, as it prepares to take over London's transport systems, should at least absorb the lesson.

Dave Wetzel announced that the success of 'Just the Ticket' had reversed a 30-year decline in the number of passengers using LT, and that its success was not limited to public transport. Road casualties showed a fall of 3,700 a year and the number of cars entering central London during the morning peak was down by more than ten per cent, the first reduction since 1965.

What became known as 'the GLC road show' took the anti-abolition message to the autumn party conferences and to the TUC. Ken Livingstone praised the unions for 'a marvellously encouraging response to the start of our campaign,' and there was more support at the SDP annual conference where one speaker, Roland Freeman, a former Tory GLC finance chairman and subsequently an SDP parliamentary candidate, demolished government arguments.

Predictable support followed from Labour at Brighton. Less expected was the reception at Blackpool where many Conservative MPs attended a fringe meeting where Ken Livingstone shared a platform with former GLC Tory housing chairman George Tremlett who said that he was horrified by his government's proposal to abolish the GLC and replace it with what he called 'a ragbag of unelected boards and quangos.'

He went on: ' I shall not be suggesting that the GLC be retained in its present form, but the government should change its present approach to ensure that whatever takes the place of the present Local

Government Act, the basic principle of elected London-wide city government should be preserved.'

Elsewhere, public support to retain the GLC was strong and growing. According to a Harris poll commissioned by Thames TV, 78 out of every 100 Londoners thought it either important or fairly important that London had a single body responsible for its services. Fifty-five of those thought it very important.

Adrian Slade, leader of the Lib-SDP Alliance on the GLC, described abolition as 'a move born of paranoia and prejudice and an insult to the intelligence of the people of London.' Liberals wanted the GLC to be the nucleus of an authority responsibility for all LT and surface rail transport inside the M25, and to become the regional health authority and, with the boroughs, a police authority, he said.

There was more embarrassment for the government when, in another opinion poll, over 90 per cent of interviewees thought that Londoners should have a direct say in services and fare levels on buses and tubes - a 6 per cent swing in favour of the GLC's transport policies in five months. Soon after, another Mori poll conducted in more than 20 constituencies showed that Londoners were now two-to-one in favour of keeping the GLC. Two months later this advanced to 3-1.

For the abolitionists, three London boroughs spoke up - Westminster, Bromley, and Kensington and Chelsea nailing their colours to the mast and claiming that abolition could save up to £369 million.

In an effort to justify its abolition decision, the government sought the opinions of organisations and professional bodies representing all aspects of London life. But the plan backfired. When 1,200 responses were in, the overall tenor was so unfavourable that the government refused to make them public.

In the Commons, Housing Minister Ian Gow admitted that submissions in support were 'not as many as we would like.' Many responses were severely critical of abolition, its implication, the loss of democracy, its likely cost - or all four.

The GLC acquired 700 copies of these responses and made them available to MPs at the County Hall research library. Those against abolition filled thirteen boxes, those in favour half of one box and all but two were from Conservative controlled London boroughs.

As opposition to government plans continued to swell, many prominent individuals voiced public support for the GLC. These included Cardinal Hume, Lord Soper, Eric Morcambe, Henry Cooper, Albert Finney, Bruce Forsyth, Sir John Gielgud, Lionel Blair, Susannah York and Duncan Goodhew. More than 130 of the most famous people in the arts signed an open letter protesting that the proposals constituted 'an unprecedented attack upon the arts.'

On LBC, 83 per cent of 12,745 people taking part in a 24-hour phone-in disagreed with plans to axe the council. A Mori poll revealed that 54 per cent of Londoners thought the proposals were motivated to silence a political opponent.

Twenty senior London clergy sponsored a statement which said: 'It is inconceivable that one of the world's major cities such as London should be deprived of the overall identity manifested by the GLC. We believe the existence of the GLC in whatever form, should continue and we give our support to those who oppose its dissolution.'

Among responses from prestigious bodies which the government sought to keep secret were the following:

Incorporated Association of Architects and Surveyors: The GLC has created a pattern of good building practice which brings the world to its doorstep for guidance and inspiration. This reputation persists in the fields of housing, planning, urban design, safety in public buildings and the promotion of good detailing and practice in the building industry.

Royal Institute of British Architects: There is an impressive array of schemes which have depended for their achievement on an authority that transcends borough boundaries and can think for London as a whole. Flood defences are so well designed that they are scarcely noticeable. The skyline owes much to the GLC and LCC: some 500 high blocks or masts have been refused permission or withdrawn because of the impact they would have on important views of London.

Urban Design Group: The Government's proposals are a recipe for confusion and procrastination. They are wrong in principle and ill-considered in detail. Unless the government is persuaded to change its mind   the cities will be 'strangled, not streamlined.'

The Civic Trust said that the history of voluntary co-operation between neighbouring local authorities hardly inspired confidence, and that the GLC historic buildings division had perhaps contributed more to the care of London's architectural heritage than any other body or institution.

There was more praise from the Arts Council which said that the GLC and metropolitan county councils as a group had been the unquestioned leaders in the field of local authority support for the arts and added: 'It is difficult to envisage alternative arrangements which, taken as a whole, would serve the arts as well as those which they are designed to replace.'

More praise was heaped on the GLC by the London Voluntary Service Council which pointed out that more than 1,000 organisations were now funded by the GLC and the sum distributed in grant aid during 1983/4 would be £34 million. Funding by the GLC, it said, offered hope to organisations which had been struggling to cope with inadequate resources.

A joint statement by 31 organisations representing disabled people said that the new policies would result in them being less able to influence relevant policies. The overall structure would be more complex and confusing, and existing provision would deteriorate, they feared.

And so the tributes continued.

The London branch of the Royal Town Planning Institute, said that government proposals that decisions be made by boroughs or the Secretary of State were 'disastrous for London and represented turning back the planning clock by 40 years.

More than 200 London-based anti-racist organisations put their names to a tribute praising the GLC for giving 'the kind of lead in London that no government of either party has given nationally and few other local authorities have given in their own areas.'

More embarrassment followed for the government when the influential Association of Chief Executives of the London Boroughs warned that the proposals could have the opposite effect of that intended and would result in less effective, less efficient and more costly local government. Two-thirds of London's 33 borough councils were against all or major parts of the proposals with most of the remainder expressing some reservations.

The cost factor was reinforced when respected accountants Coopers Lybrand estimated that far from there being savings, abolition would cost £167 million.

An even bigger outcry was to follow when the government, finding its abolition timetable too tight to be workable, announced a parliamentary Bill to cancel the GLC election due in May 1985. For the additional year required to complete abolition, the government proposed to substitute a council of representatives from borough councils to run GLC services. These appointments, it said, should reflect the balance of the parties in the constituent borough councils and should number 84 - one from each parliamentary seat.

At that time, 17 boroughs were Tory controlled, three joint Tory and Liberal, one Liberal and 12 Labour. The interim GLC therefore, would be composed of 56 Conservatives and 28 Labour and Alliance, so replacing an elected Labour administration with an appointed Tory one. At that time, the GLC had 48 Labour members, 41 Conservatives, two SDP and one Liberal.

These changes would be effected by what became known as 'the Paving Bill' because it paved the way for abolition.

Ken Livingstone called it 'a shabby attempt to trade democracy for political expediency.'

As so many august organisations and leading personalities were opposed to abolition and to the Paving Bill, what were the arguments in favour? I offered a page in *The Londoner* to Environment Secretary Patrick Jenkin to state the government's case. This is what he wrote:

> Only in 1979 Mr Livingstone was saying that the GLC *should* be abolished because it would be a major saving and would release massive resources which could be put into far more productive use. Just what game is he playing with Londoners and the £3 million of their money which he is spending on propaganda? Let's have a few basic facts.
>
> Fact One. The GLC does not run London. Most of the local services which are essential to our everyday life are not provided by the GLC. The GLC is not responsible

for education for most of London; for personal social services; the police; hospitals or the ambulance service; refuse collection; street cleansing and environmental health; water and sewerage; libraries; cemeteries and crematoria or even swimming baths! All these services are run by bodies other than the GLC.

Fact 2. The main providers of local services are the borough councils - smaller, closer to the people and run from the local town hall.

Fact 3. The only elections that are being abolished are elections to the GLC. Existing GLC councillors will complete their normal term of office next year and it makes no sense to go through the upheaval and expense of elections to a body which has only a few months' life left.

Fact 4. Elections to the boroughs will continue on exactly the same basis as at present - the next election will take place as planned in 1986 - and these are the councils that really count in London. And for the first time we are also introducing direct elections to the Inner London Education Authority. So it's just baloney to say that Londoners will have no say in who runs their local affair   I do not belittle for a moment the importance of the few services the GLC does provide, but they simply do not add up to a package of responsibilities which justifies the attention of 92 councillors, 35 committees and sub committees, and the 22,000 staff which try to keep the whole show on the road at a cost of £936 million this year alone. The abolition of the GLC will do away with this unnecessary and burdensome structure. But there is no threat to the services which can be provided perfectly well without it. Most of the GLC's functions will be devolved to the borough councils, so ending the present duplication, conflict and delay which result from having Big Brother GLC breathing down the boroughs' necks.

The fire service will be run on a London-wide basis by a board consisting of councillors from the boroughs. This will be the only statutory joint board for London. Mr Livingstone's extraordinary allegation that more Londoners will die in fire as a result of our proposals is without foundation and is no more than a callous exploitation of people's fears.

London Transport - as recommended by an all-party committee of the House of Commons - will be run by a new body with strategic control over buses and underground services in London. London Transport will no longer be the political football it has been under the GLC, and the new body will provide services which are attractive, reliable and offer better value for money. This is good news for Londoners.

One of the most offensive claims that the GLC has been making is that elderly people will suffer once the GLC goes - for example, that retired London tenants will lose the opportunity to move to seaside and country homes. This is nonsense. The Government has given a firm guarantee that the lion's share of seaside and country homes will continue to be available for London's elderly people. The GLC has also spread scare stories about concessionary fares for elderly and disabled people. More nonsense. Concessionary fares will continue to be available.

Leaving aside some well-publicised lunacies, the GLC has been funding a large number of voluntary organisations - for example in the field of housing, ethnic minorities and the elderly and disabled - which are doing a first-class job. They deserve to continue. But true to form, the GLC has been busy spreading scare stories about how these bodies will come to a sticky end after abolition. This is rubbish. There will be a special scheme for collective funding by the boroughs of the voluntary sector. This will do much to secure the future of the many worthwhile organisations serving a wider area.

I cannot stress too strongly that abolishing the GLC

and metropolitan counties does not mean abolishing the funds for the arts which those councils are currently responsible for distributing. The government will give an extra £34 million to the arts in England in 1986/87 and a similar sum in future years. Of this, £16 million will be made available to the Arts Council to look after the needs of major performing arts and other bodies receiving grants from the GLC and the metropolitan counties. £17 million will be provided to meet the costs of the major museums and art galleries.

There will have to be discussion about the allocation of funds to other organisations and institutions involving the Arts Council, and the Museums and Galleries Commission as appropriate, together with the various parties concerned. These arrangements should ensure that the many worthwhile cultural organisations, institutions and activities in our great cities will continue.

We are now firmly on course for cheaper, simpler and more effective local government in London. A vast bureaucracy with not enough to do but no shortage of ratepayers' money to squander on the whims and fancies of its eccentric politicians will be swept away. The cumbersome two-tier system of local government hasn't worked and has caused only delay and obstruction. The boroughs will in future become the focal point for decision-making in London and people will have a proper voice in local government as it affects their local area.

It's worth noting what another politician said less than two years ago. 'I believe that we should on principle have a system in which government is done at the lowest possible level, the level closest to people. To be really effective that means that we have to have unitary local government in this country and clearly people would be better served if it was provided by the borough councils in the metropolitan areas. I have always at heart been committed to the borough council rather than to regional government.' The politician who said that? None of other than Ken Livingstone. What price his commitment to the GLC?

Ken Livingstone replied:

The real story is that Mr Jenkin does not trust the people of London to use the ballot box to achieve the result he wants in getting rid of the Labour administration at County Hall. Instead he and his colleagues have decided to do away with the GLC and with the elections that were due to be held in May next year. Mr Jenkin plans to rob the voters of their rights by means of his Paving Bill.

This unconstitutional and anti-democratic measure will allow the government to cancel the elections to the GLC *before* Parliament has even had a chance to consider whether the GLC deserves to be abolished. The main abolition will not happen until 1986.

Nearly two-thirds of the responses from individuals and organisations to the Government white paper on abolition were totally opposed to the plan. There were few supporters of the government's belief that all the GLC's work could be more efficiently carried out by the London boroughs. Little wonder when you consider there were no facts and figures to support this claim, no examples of waste and delay to back their contention, no costings to show where and how money would be saved.

The facts are that the GLC is one of the most efficiently run local authorities in Britain with a staff cost (much of it firefighters' wages) which is just 16 per cent of total cost - the envy of many boroughs. GLC spending has risen by 80 per cent since 1979 compared with a central government rise of 100 per cent. There are a few other things that Mr Jenkin does

not mention either. Like the fact that only 16 per
cent of the GLC's current spending will go to the
boroughs. The rest, including the vast bulk of
repayments, which will still have to be paid no
matter who is in charge, will go to the jungle of
boards, commissions and other bodies that he wants
to set up in place of the GLC.

But even those services that will go to the
boroughs will not be free of Whitehall's
bureaucratic shackles. To Mr Jenkin, local control
means that boroughs will be saddled with
responsibility for waste disposal, recreation and
pollution control but will not get the money to pay
for them. Through rate-capping and manipulation of
grants, Whitehall will make the rules and tell the
boroughs what to do. So much for giving power
back to the people.

Among submissions to the Marshal Inquiry into
GLC powers was one from a senior Conservative
spokesman who said: I therefore believe we have
got progressively to return to the concept that the
GLC is a strategic authority." That senior
spokesman was none other than Patrick Jenkin.

When the Paving Bill reached the Commons, former
Conservative Prime Minister Ted Heath savaged the government in a
memorable speech during which he condemned it as 'a bad Bill
paving the way for a worse Bill.'

He went on: 'It is bad because it is the negation of democracy.
There is no point in talking as though indirectly elected
organisations are democratically elected. They are not. Worst of all
is the imposition by parliamentary diktat of a change of responsible
party in London government. There cannot be any justification for
that. It immediately lays the Conservative party open to the charge
of the greatest gerrymandering in the last 150 years of British
history. A vast number of Conservatives in London and in the

country care about what is happening and care deeply about it. It is no use just saying that there was a mandate. In my constituency [Bexley and Sidcup] I have always made it quite clear that I would not agree to the abolition of the GLC until I knew what would be put in its place. Nobody has yet told me that.

'There was no mandate for this sort of Paving Bill. The present path is extremely dangerous for local government, for the Conservative party and for the government because of the chaotic management that will result.'

Nineteen Conservatives joined Labour, Liberal and SDP MPs in voting against the Government when the Bill was given its second reading. About 20 other Tories abstained.

Introducing the Bill, Patrick Jenkin had said: 'The proposal in our manifesto was endorsed by the electorate. The main Bill will come before Parliament in our next session. This Paving Bill has been drafted carefully so as not in any way to pre-empt Parliament's decision on the main principle of abolition. However, it signals our firm determination to take decision-making closer to local people and to secure cheaper, simpler and more accountable local government in our major cities.'

John Cartwright (SDP Woolwich) said of the proposed change in political control: 'I cannot believe that can be right or justified. It is probable that the kind of people who will be serving on the shadow pass-out-of-existence GLC will be people with no experience of its functions. It would be rather like putting the crew of the Woolwich ferry in charge of the QE2. It is a recipe for chaos on a massive scale.'

Simon Hughes (Lib Southwark and Bermondsey) called the government's argument 'shallow, misleading, unprincipled and a sham.'

Subsequently, 11 GLC Tory members in a letter to *The Times* asked the House of Lords to exercise their constitutional right and throw the Bill out.

The shape of things to come seemed apparent when sweeping powers over another 300 miles of London's major roads were foreshadowed by the Department of Transport if abolition was agreed. Many borough high streets and highly sensitive roads which were largely residential were included. In theory, those roads were being transferred to the boroughs but the Secretary of State reserved the right to intervene if his 'guidelines for traffic movement' were disregarded, and to make changes to any proposal to alter traffic capacity.

In the face of Mrs Thatcher's enormous majority, the GLC realised it had little chance of getting the Bill overturned in the Commons. Nevertheless, it decided to appoint a parliamentary lobbyist to seek out waverers and feed them information for debate.

The choice of Roland Freeman did not immediately commend itself to the Labour Left wing, for Roland was formerly a prominent Conservative who had more recently joined the SDP for whom he was a parliamentary candidate - none of which bought him any favours. But Roland had other merits: he was a journalist, a former GLC finance chairman who knew his way round Parliament and who had a pedigree in politics and was respected by politicians.

The GLC's chances in the House of Lords, were seen very differently. Although, in theory, the Conservatives had a big majority, their attendance record left much to be desired, especially if debates clashed with important events on the social or sporting calendar. To farm this more fertile field, the GLC appointed Francis Sitwell to join Roland Freeman. Sitwell knew many of their lordships and was a master of the sensitive, subtle approach. He studied the views and voting record of each of their lordships, particularly the 200 crossbenchers. Together, the GLC lobbyists scented a chance of victory.

Most of the peers were elderly and several infirm, so when the Paving Bill came before them in the House of Lords for the second reading, the GLC laid on a fleet of cars to collect them and return them home afterwards. Rooms were booked, food and drink laid on.... everything possible was done to ensure they were in the chamber to vote.

Tension was high and the House was packed when the vote was called, the government winning by just 20 votes - 237 to 217.

The GLC kept up the not-so-discreet pressure on their lordships and in an amendment - that the elections could be cancelled only if the Abolition Bill became law - won by 191 votes to 143, thought to be the biggest defeat of a Conservative government for 60 years.

When the Abolition Bill reached the Commons, MPs arriving to vote were welcomed by an appropriate version of Nelson's famous Trafalgar message flying from the County Hall flagpole. However, insufficient Members did 'their duty' that day and the GLC was now just one step from being consigned to history.

The Abolition Bill was now more than 250 pages long and had 985 clauses. Some 1,116 amendments were tabled - 126 from the government, 701 from Labour, 86 from the Alliance and 203 from Conservative back-benchers. All the government amendments were accepted, one of the remainder.

Only 45 minutes were devoted to giving the Environment Secretary reserve powers described by Alan Greengross as 'terrifyingly wide.' Ken Livingstone called them 'the most wide-ranging ever conferred on a Secretary of State and a godsend for any radical Labour government.'

In the House of Lords, Lord Plummer, the former GLC leader, described the Bill as 'hastily assembled, badly thought out and unlikely to meet the needs of the huge population which it will affect.' In previous reorganisations there was a bringing together of staff, whereas abolition required fragmentation, which inevitably meant that there will be a serious loss of expertise.

The effect of the Bill was to destroy the London-wide authority and hand over its strategic responsibilities to 'a hotch-potch of hastily assembled groups of boroughs and remote unelected residuary bodies or commissions. This, he said, was a recipe for administrative chaos and conflict.

Major changes were forced by peers when the Bill was subjected to close scrutiny during the committee stage. Having been railroaded through the Commons by Mrs Thatcher's enormous Conservative majority, the Bill's glaring inadequacies were exposed by peers who inflicted a series of defeats on the Government.

When the Abolition Bill finally reached the Lords, an amendment in the names of Lord Plummer, Baroness Faithful and an independent peer, Lord Hayter, proposed the setting up of a new London-wide authority.

Once more the cars, the food and drink were laid on. Again the

House was packed, the gallery jammed and the atmosphere electric. Most of the speeches were against the government's Bill.

Viscount Hooson, the Liberals' spokesman, was to sum up but his speech was cut short by Lord Boothby telling him to shut up and sit down so they could get on with the vote.

'We were convinced that we could win,' said Lord Hooson. And so it proved. There was as near pandemonium as the House of Lords is ever likely to see when the vote was announced - 213 for the amendment, 209 against. The GLC had won!

Roland Freeman recalled: 'The atmosphere was quite astonishing. People were talking and shouting and cheering. They had never seen anything like this. Then we all poured into various rooms and celebrated. It was a most amazing experience. It was the first time, really the only time, we seriously defeated the government.'

That was almost the last time the GLC tasted success. It won minor amendments in the following weeks but almost every vote of importance was won by the government.

When the inevitable happened and the Bill was forced through, Lord McIntosh, the man who so nearly became GLC leader, remarked: 'What is in the Bill - I believe it is mentioned 132 times - are reserve powers for the Secretary of State.'

As the GLC's high profile campaign against the true facts of abolition continued, the district auditor reported on the many complaints that the council was wrongfully spending public money for party political purposes - and exonerated it. Leading counsel's opinion, he said, was that there was 'no overt evidence of any, let alone dominant, party political purpose in the campaign material, and the fact that it may be political in purpose and content does not make it unlawful,' he ruled.

Labour's extra year in power at County Hall was about to begin, when four members of the administration - including Ken Livingstone and his deputy John McDonnell - resigned to create by-elections to test public opinion on the abolition issue. The Conservative party saw this as a gimmick to turn the bogus by-elections into a referendum on abolition and took no part. All four Labour candidates were returned with handsome majorities.

Independent candidates who stood to support abolition all polled feebly. As a referendum, the voting was: For GLC abolition 1,726 votes, against 58,675.

Commenting on the extra year, Robert Mitchell, a GLC Tory member and former chairman of the council, revealed that only 91 of the organisations and persons who responded to the government's abolition consultation were for abolition, 882 were against and 512 had no overall view.

He went on: 'Public opinion polls in London are showing 65 per cent against abolition. It is insulting to assume that all Londoners are duped by Livingstone propaganda. The continuous references to Livingstone performances and sayings are a particularly depressing part of government propaganda. The discussion is (or at least should be) about the need for a directly elected assembly to deal with strategic London-wide issues. The success or failure of this or any previous administration is totally irrelevant. You don't chop a tree down because you don't like the bird singing in it.'

As the timetable for abolition neared its climax, the government, suspicious that money was being channelled out from County Hall, required the GLC to seek government approval for every new contract. Chaos ensued. The purchase of teabags, the erection of a pub sign and the letting of a fish and chip shop were among 2,000 applications a week that had to be submitted for approval to the Department of the Environment. It caused an administrative nightmare.

Applications from people wishing to exchange council homes now needed to be sent to Mr Jenkin's department. So did requests for concerts and exhibitions at the South Bank concert halls. His consent was needed to buy fried chicken for the County Hall restaurants, to let shops, to allow builders to cross GLC land.

Often civil servants handling what, to the GLC, were routine applications had little idea how to react and would be bogged down, asking time-consuming questions. Matters could only get worse as the DoE staff fell further and further behind with the work. To publicise the stupidity of the edict, Illtyd Harrington was pictured at the Environment department with a 100ft Telex of 200 items needing ministerial approval trailing from his hands and down the steps like a carpet. There was more humiliation for Mrs Thatcher's government when, suspicious that the council was trying to leave the County Hall kitty empty, it attempted to slash by half the GLC's proposed £80 million spending on new capital projects.

A parliamentary special committee of Conservative and Labour MPs took the unusual step of asking the Commons to think again. The committee found that the GLC case against the cuts was 'impressively established' and that 'very necessary, not merely desirable work would be stopped' if the cuts were enforced. The committee said the GLC's claim was restrained, diligent and careful and was less in real terms than ten years earlier.

With six months to go before the GLC died, Maurice Stonefrost resigned as director general - not in anger but because of the impossibility of the conflicting demands being made on him.

He was responsible for three major tasks: to arrange the transfer of functions to successor bodies, to establish transitional arrangements required by the government, and to continue to run the GLC according to the wishes of the elected body. Transferring functions involved massive changes but neither the government nor the boroughs had made any significant provision for them.

'Nobody was taking responsibility for steering the ship to another port and having the cargo unloaded in a proper manner,' he said.

The government line was: We are returning the functions to the boroughs. All the rest are unnecessary. But the GLC was created to handle those functions which could not be handled by the boroughs. Other bodies which would take them were not in existence.The main issue was: How, during the transition, to protect people's services.

Meantime, the council's Labour politicians were determined to carry on their policies to the end. That was their mandate. At the same time, whether to cause trouble or just let it happen, they would not allow staff to become involved with the government discussions about the future.

Maurice Stonefrost related: 'The GLC finally agreed to co-operate because we had to think about personnel. I don't think the politicians were too rabidly opposed to it but they knew that spending time on that would get in the way of running the authority.

'None of the boroughs or the receiving authorities were properly organised to manage change. All the government were seen to be doing was concentrating on the political aspects and attacking Labour and the leader. In management terms, all the things they did were destructive. Like the regulation that all contracts had to be approved by central government. It was laughable. They had no machinery for dealing with it. They didn't mean "every contract" but that was what they said. They didn't define it.

'We were told we had to provide information for successor bodies but, quite apart from the fact that we hadn't the staff to do it, a lot of bodies showed they had no idea what they were taking on. The information they asked for was not available in the form they expected.

When the Secretary of State instructed that the chief executive should be responsible for the management of this provision, I resigned the post of director general. It wasn't an angry thing. It imposed on me a statute of responsibilities that could not be done. Part of the reason for the resignation was to get a structure going that could manage the transfer of change.'

There was a desperation by some to dispose of the GLC's money to needy causes in the boroughs, known as tombstone funding. I was asked if I could spend another £1m on *The Londoner*. (It was an interesting contrast to earlier administrations when I was once required to write a lengthy explanation of why I had spent £1 on a taxi instead of going by bus).

In its final years 'a million' became a popular figure for the GLC, one which rolled easily off the tongue.

Thamesday, the council's highly successful South Bank festival, was estimated to have been attended by 'a million people.' Impartial observers listened in disbelief as attendances were wildly estimated and doubled and trebled for presumed afternoon and evening events. Police said the crowd was 50,000 at most.

` In its attempt to raise 'a million signatures' on a petition to save the GLC, the effort fell the way of so many petitions. It began with great integrity, the pages being scrutinised daily for Mickey Mouse or other hoax names. But, of course, there was no way of checking the genuineness of Jim Robinson or Jane Johnson. Estimates were that the millionth name would be signed at Thamesday, but with the hours ticking away it was clear it wasn't going to happen.

When the publicity tent was empty of visitors, the numbers were manipulated so a 'millionth' signature could be paraded. Later, other pages of signatures from the boroughs boosted the total, but many people admitted signing the petition more than once. One girl told me she had signed 13 times. Whatever the precise number of genuine signatures, there is no gainsaying that this was a stupendous effort which reflected the council's popular support.

When the dust of battle settled and the war had been lost, GLC staff began to count the cost. Most of the politicians came through with reputations enhanced. Not so the workforce. Although many went on to other jobs and early retirement terms were not ungenerous, there were still thousands whose careers would be destroyed or who would be robbed of their high-earning years and consequently their one chance to boost their pension.

One report claimed that on abolition day there were still 5,000 without jobs. The staff had been the cannon fodder in a battle between political titans. As they considered the personal implications, not all saw Mrs Thatcher as the only villain.

As the vocal guns fell silent, the great camaraderie began to dissipate and an atmosphere of gloom and despondency settled over County Hall. Somebody tried to set fire to the building but the blaze in the sub-basement was soon smothered.

Many of the political activists who had joined the GLC simply for the fight, wanted to go down with the ship. Some refused to acquiesce when told that the GLC must now co-operate with the government.

A handful of militants tried unsuccessfully to dragoon staff into joining a campaign of obstruction and disobedience. At least one meeting in County Hall with successor bodies was invaded by a banner-waving mob screaming 'Traitors! Traitors!'

Elsewhere the tail began to wag the dog. A press release in the name of Simon Turney was rejected by the relevant department who demanded: 'We want these words, not Simon Turney's. He's just a middle-aged, middle class, white man.'

It was an emotional afternoon when the council met for the last time on Thursday, March 27 1985. Two Prime Ministers, Lords Wilson and Callaghan, had notified their intention to attend.

Ken Livingstone has often said that he returned to his office and found himself in tears after his dissolution speech in which he said:

'Nothing could have have been greater than the pride of serving this city. I do not believe - I am sure I speak for my colleagues on all sides - nothing else that happens to us in our lives will be as rewarding and fulfiling as the years that we have spent in this building.'

Celebrations and a huge firework display were planned for the evening. Badges bearing the slogan 'We'll meet again' were distributed by the thousand and it was hoped that Dame Vera Lynn would be present at the wake to lead the crowds in the chorus of that moving wartime song she made so famous. Dame Vera had sung at a GLC concert some months earlier.

As darkness fell and fireworks lit up the sky, no one could say that the GLC didn't go out with a bang. Next day, All Fools' Day, would see the birth of a new London.

Next door at the Royal Festival Hall the last GLC concert was nearing its end, the orchestra playing that moving piece in which the house lights are extinguished and the orchestra plays by candlelight. All the violins have a candle which gradually dwindle until just one remains. The piece ends in total darkness. It was symbolic of the extinction of London's local democracy.

12. BIG BROTHER

Outside London, opinions after the demise of the GLC were mixed. In the annual round of rate support grant negotiations, the GLC had been the only individual local authority to have a seat at the table, a privilege much resented by some. All the counties, the rural and urban districts and the boroughs were represented by their associations. But London, being so large and its resources need so great, could not be ignored. The government had to include a London-wide representative body in the negotiations.

In planning, relations with south-eastern counties had been very amicable and productive. Maurice Stonefrost, the GLC's last director general said: 'It was amazing that we all worked so well together for the joint community interest. There were some tense issues - like the development and consequences of airports, industrial corridors, large commercial and housing developments, employment - yet the counties could always be persuaded that London wasn't trying to export its problems to them. A London that was balanced and had been looked after was for their protection and to their advantage.'

Although matters generally worked well at officer level, there were occasional political complications.

When Sir Reg Goodwin won County Hall on a Homes Before Roads ticket, his council looked askance at a plan to link the A3 in Esher with the M3 at Sunbury. Together with the government, Surrey County Council was investigating the possibility of a huge road and new river crossing, linking also with an ancient east-west road line in Sunbury, which had been blighting property for more than 50 years.

Traffic to Heathrow airport and the motorway network would have poured into west London, the council feared, and the proposed cross link could have created a traffic nightmare in Hampton. This pretty Thames-side village, a neighbour of Hampton Court, had only one narrow main street which was always badly congested.

Labour members of the GLC knew all about the tactics of anti-roads protesters, some were veterans of the fight and had personally been involved. They knew that the time to act against a road was before a provisional line was drawn. So they decided to discreetly leak the story.

The wealthy squires of Esher are not without influence, so it was decided to give the story to the *Esher News* whose worried editor Reg England telephoned to say: 'We've only been on the streets half an hour and already two people are threatening to sue us. They say this story has scuppered plans to sell their homes.'

Within hours Surrey was furiously back-tracking. They did not have the money for such a road which could only be built with government finance. Talks were at an early stage and they lamented that news of them had been made public. Views of Surrey councillors hardened against the road very quickly and it was later officially abandoned.

Within London, many boroughs regarded the GLC as an unwanted and very distant Big Brother, interfering in local matters which could and should have been for their consideration alone. There was a grudging acceptance that the strategic authority should, perhaps, have a say on high buildings and developments of great bulk; it was acknowledged that the GLC had special expertise in traffic management, was superb in the care and restoration of historic buildings and had an excellent track record in road safety. It was beyond dispute that it had the resources to provide major parks and multi-million pound facilities which were beyond the means of the average borough. But there the concessions ended.

It was not just dislike of the GLC. Some did not want a second tier of local government whatever its title - a situation which is unchanged today.

Pelican crossings were a major source of aggravation. If a borough wanted a crossing on a busy road, it had to ask the GLC's permission. Boroughs argued that it was they who best understood local conditions. If its own technical officers had examined pedestrian and traffic flows and the council had said 'yes' to the crossing, that should be sufficient. Why should they submit the application to the GLC whose highly qualified and highly paid officers would come down and re-check the statistics to make sure they fitted within its parameters for pelicans?

It was inconceivable that a strategic authority responsible for 620 square miles of one of the biggest cities in the world with a population of seven million should involve itself in such trivia.

Boroughs also complained that these and other applications would be lost in the huge bureaucracy which was County Hall and not emerge for a year.

Sir Alan Greengross has good reason to remember one visit to the office of Fred Pooley, head of Planning and Transportation at the GLC. Sir Alan, who was then chairman of the GLC transport and planning committee, recalled:

'To my horror I discovered that the planning department vetted every single borough planning decision. Thousands were going through the GLC, some in detail, others routinely. I said: "I thought we were supposed to be working with the boroughs and getting off their backs and just doing the strategic work." Fred replied that any planning action by a borough almost certainly had traffic implications, whether it concerned houses, offices, shops... Journeys would begin in a back street, then run on to a borough road and eventually finish up on a GLC road. The only way to plan effectively, he said, was to look at everything the boroughs did.'

There was enormous difficulty in dividing the planning roles between the two tiers of local government. This was a weakness dating from Day 1 when the GLC and the new GLC boroughs were created. Their respective roles were not sufficiently differentiated. There was too much overlap and therefore too much likelihood of friction. The conflict which this engendered was one reason for the call to abolish the GLC.

Relations could be further soured because, in a dispute, the sheer professionalism of GLC officers was generally so superior that they could run rings round their borough counterparts. In its search for the best, the GLC was prepared to pay more and top men in their profession tended to gravitate to what they saw as the peak of the local government hierarchy. Two GLC planning chairmen described the calibre of officers as 'world class, the cream of their profession.'

The council was famous for the excellence of its research and intelligence and scientific work, whilst in architecture, conservation of historic buildings and landscape design it was a world leader. There was one occasion when the chairman of the GLC gave a lunch to the presidents of three august bodies - the Royal Institute of British Architects, the Royal Institute of Town Planning, and the Royal Institute of Surveyors. The three presidents, men who had reached the peak of their professions, were all employed simultaneously at the GLC.

It was said that people joined the council to study for a PhD, and it's true that several gained their doctorate while in the GLC's employ.

Former planning chairman Norman Howard perhaps bears this out when he recalls: 'The GLC seemed to have detailed studies on everything. If you wanted to know how many left-handed people shopped at supermarkets on a Thursday, the facts were probably somewhere in a study at County Hall.'

Difficulties were exacerbated in the borough-GLC relationship if the two bodies were of different political persuasion. Tory boroughs were irritated when Labour GLCs would question the density of housing developments. Outer suburban boroughs wanted their homes to have sizeable gardens or landscaped grounds which was anathema to a strategic authority desperately trying to put roofs over the heads of the homeless.

Rents were also a bone of contention. The GLC was a good landlord and proud that, before the Cutler sell-off, it was Europe's biggest with more than 220,000 properties. Rents were generally lower than those the boroughs charged and when families were living on opposite sides of the same street this difference caused more resentment.

But the problem which outweighed all others for outer boroughs was that the GLC might one day descend with its overriding powers and huge resources and build massive council estates which, by accident or design, would alter the political balance of the borough. Not only outer boroughs had this fear, nor did it manifest itself only during the days of the GLC.

Some inner boroughs protested that the London County Council had 'destroyed' parts of their borough. Housing estates were usually a cause of disputes and bitterness. There were many examples of estates which, by accident or design, had changed the political complexion of an area. In Lewisham, London's strategic authority moved in and built the huge Downham estate, one of the biggest in Europe, with 25,000 homes. Like St Mary Cray (Bromley), the massive Roehampton development in Putney, and the LCC estate at St Helier in Merton, they all helped change the political complexion of the area.

It was this fear which galvanised some parts of the Home Counties to fight for exclusion from London when the GLC boundaries were drawn, and why Conservative administrations were so active in trying to sell council houses, believing that if occupiers had a stake in the property they would be more inclined to vote Tory.

The problem was compounded because many of the 20 outer boroughs did not - and still do not - regard themselves as part of London. Nor did they wish to be. To them, London ended with the 12 inner boroughs of the old LCC area of whom they were additionally suspicious.

Districts like Croydon, which had formerly been a county borough, did not take kindly to some far away bureaucracy based in Lambeth telling it what to do.

Problems were not simply between 'us' and 'them.' There was much sensitivity - even animosity - between some boroughs. And there is rivalry between the two cities, Westminster and the City of London.

Former *Evening News* reporter Len Vigars recalled: 'I broke the news to the City that Westminster was to have a lord mayor. It caused enormous consternation. The city has always been terribly sensitive about any rivalry or threat to its existence.'

Boroughs also watched warily whenever the GLC held a publicity event in their area, grumbling that the GLC personality was treading on the toes of the borough's mayor. They will be monitoring events closely when the new Mayor of London takes office.

As an example of the delicate relationship which existed between the GLC and the boroughs, Sir James Swaffield, director general (1972-84) tells a story of the Queen's silver jubilee in 1977, when the Labour regime of Sir Reg Goodwin found itself in a some political difficulty over how the event should be celebrated.

Sir James said: 'The London Labour party was not enthusiastic about celebrating the event and this was reflected in the GLC membership. Reg Goodwin was old Labour and a chap who knew his Londoners. He called me in and said: "My colleagues and the London Labour party don't want to do anything in particular to emphasise the silver jubilee. But I know that if we do nothing we will be in real trouble with the electorate. Would you see what you can do without any cost falling on the rates?"'

So was born the London Celebrations Committee, a group outside the GLC. Thanks to their efforts, a large cinder wasteland adjoining County Hall was transformed into Jubilee Gardens. It was funded by private enterprise. The committee was also responsible for what became known as the Royal Progress for which the Queen was taken down the river, landing at various points - which involved co-operation with the boroughs concerned.

Sir James continued: 'I found I could ring up the borough chief executives and they all co-operated splendidly because I claimed to be speaking on behalf of the lord lieutenant, who would, of course, accompany the Queen. The boroughs were prepared to co-operate with the lord lieutenant, they would do it on their own, but they wouldn't have done it for the GLC.'

So has London missed out by not having had a strategic authority to take an overview of its interests in the past 14 years?

Emphatically yes, says Maurice Stonefrost. 'Its lead has been missed on public transport and in planning. The GLC was set up to handle the things the boroughs couldn't manage. One such function was an overall role in planning - particularly continuing the attention the GLC paid to what should happen to the East End and how to avoid the worst scenario with the movement west of commerce and population as the airports took over from the seaports.

David Bayliss, the council's chief transport planner and later director of planning at London Transport, is more specific.

'The land use pattern suffered quite badly . The GLC tried to reorientate land use to fit better with the transport system, to have major town centres well served by public transport.

'The Greater London Development Plan identified major strategic centres throughout London. There were 26 for the 33 boroughs which, from a non-strategic viewpoint didn't quite fit. So when planning became essentially a borough responsibility, boroughs were vying with each other for major retail and other commercial development. So the coherence of the land use plan that the GLC developed was lost and nobody really bothered. The boroughs said they wanted to do their own thing.

'During the 1980s after abolition, planning was very *laissez faire* under Nicholas Ridley [Secretary of State for the Environment] whose view of planning was: If the developers want to do it why should we stand in their way? That was a period when a lot of horses bolted. Once you have development in the wrong place, you have to live with it.'

London's bus priority programme also came to a halt and stagnated for four years until London Transport took it on.

Bayliss adds: 'In Nicholas Ridley's day the bus lane programme was frowned on as being anti-motorist. Nobody was really interested between 1986 and 1990. We at London Transport agreed that, after a very difficult period in the eighties, we should take the lead and try to do something about bus priorities because there was no one else to do it.

'In the end LT set up a bus priority unit. Following that the number of bus lanes grew, the bus priority network grew and from that came the red route network, all now major features of transport management in London.

'Another thing which fell away and has now emerged was parking controls. Part of the GLC policy was that the amount of new private garage space and particularly private non residential parking space should be restricted - space in the basement of office blocks, etc. - to control commuting by car.

'Standards were enshrined in the Greater London Development Plan and subsequently, when the boroughs produced their own unitary development plans, they set their own standards. Almost without exception they were more permissive than the GLC's standards. More recently the government has given guidance to the boroughs for this kind of parking in new developments and they are almost exactly the same as those which the GLC adopted in 1974.

'In transport, the GLC developed a lot of good ideas which went into hibernation and are now beginning to re-emerge.'

John Howes, formerly deputy town clerk to the borough of Sutton, remarked: 'Since the demise of the GLC there has been no overall political will and London has been pushed down the government's agenda.'

The lack of just such an overview was certainly missed in Docklands, thinks Sir Alan Greengross. He recalled that Docklands was conceived basically as a seedbed for start-up enterprises which would then move on. The Docklands Light Railway was the transport system which would link it all.

'Then came the idea for Canary Wharf and suddenly the whole plan changed. Clearly the two-coach Mickey Mouse railway could not cope with the staff from even one floor at Canary Wharf. But no one did anything about it. The moment the government took over they charged ahead without giving a thought to the infrastructure and for years we suffered. No one thought about roads.

'Whenever the GLC planned a development, the first thing we thought of was the infrastructure. The Jubilee Line extension, the spine through Docklands, opened late last year - 20 years after we planned it. Twenty years after the government said it couldn't afford the money.

'The lesson of Docklands is the need for comprehensive planning in a world where comprehensive planning is so derided. However much you may laugh at planners, the simple fact is that unless you have an overall plan at the start of things you make a mess of it.'

At one stage workers were having to be brought to Canary Wharf by boat because of the inadequacy of access. The GLC had a planned road network which, if followed two decades earlier, could have avoided much heartache and the need for building the most expensive three-quarter mile road in the world, Limehouse Way.

David Bayliss says of Docklands: 'It has come out very well. Given the peculiar way it all happened it's remarkable it turned out so well in the end. We have a remarkably good system partly by accident, partly by late design initiative.'

Many thousands of people in West London opposing the current proposal for a fifth terminal at Heathrow, may have missed the GLC more than they will ever know. In November 1979, when a public inquiry was being held into building Terminal Four, this is what the council had to say:

'The GLC did not oppose in principle a fourth terminal subject to important conditions including that there is no fifth terminal. The additional road traffic would create chaos on the roads which are already congested, and the increase in aircraft noise would be totally unacceptable. The government has already said that a fifth terminal would over-saturate the area.'

13. AT YOUR SERVICE

From the wave of popular support for the Greater London Council in its fight against abolition and the flood of tears which marked its demise, clearly it was more loved in death than in life. So what went wrong? Was it simply destroyed by politicians or was it an unwitting party to its own downfall.

Perhaps a clue to the path the GLC should have taken appeared as early as its first year of operation when a survey showed that most Londoners had no idea what the initials GLC stood for. Others were convinced it meant Gas Light and Coke Company. On the other hand, that same survey showed that nearly a third of those interviewed did not know which of the new boroughs they lived in.

Was the problem that the people of London did not come into direct contact with the GLC? The council did not send out a rate demand. It did not collect the rubbish (that was done by the boroughs) though it did dispose of it. The GLC did not run schools as their predecessors, the LCC, had done. Although the GLC funded and dictated policy for London Transport, the ordinary person probably never realised - there was no GLC logo on the buses or tubes, only London Transport's. Tenants ceased to pay rent to the GLC when Sir Horace Cutler gave away the council's housing empire.

There was some personal contact with the GLC in London's parks, but many of those were ceded to the boroughs. It's doubtful if many of the thousands playing football on Hackney Marshes realised that the price of a pitch was low because the GLC kept it low as a matter of policy.

One of the only places where the GLC had a high profile was at the South Bank arts complex, though even here at the showpiece Royal Festival Hall, for years the council's ownership was marked by a discreet and fairly anonymous crest.

While the Conservative administration of Sir Desmond Plummer helped put the GLC on the map by providing a voice for London, little was done to advertise what the GLC was doing for London and for Londoners, often via their borough councils.

When Sir Reg Goodwin's Labour administration came to power in 1973, Evelyn Denington voiced her concern about this anonymity, suggesting a GLC livery for council cars and other transport. She was frightened off by the cost.

'GLC Working for London' was the slogan hatched for Sir Horace Cutler. It was a winner but too little money was spent on it until too late. Perhaps if the council had advertised itself more, it might have been that much more difficult to abolish.

Whether they knew it or not, the health and safety of every Londoner was the concern of the GLC's scientific branch. It checked the condition of the capital's water in rivers and streams and swimming baths; it monitored the quality of the air; took noise readings on busy streets and near airports; tested soil for harmful substances.

Rick Kelly, Head of Scientific Services, said that at any one time his staff of 130 had more than 3,700 jobs in hand. They were the watchdogs of public health and safety whose views were sought by public and commercial bodies alike and whose assent was the hallmark of approval.

Yet its beginnings were humble indeed. In 1869, the LCC's predecessor, the Metropolitan Board of Works, appointed a chemical supervisor and gas superintendent. Records show that he was called in when mould growing on damp wallpaper was suspected of leaking arsine gas into the office of Sir Joseph Bazalgette, father of the capital's sewage system. This unusual alarm proved false although in the 1950s, a similar situation led to the poisoning of Clare Boothe Luce, the US ambassador to Rome.

Among the inspector's other early tasks was checking alcohol at London's asylums where 'whisky' was almost 99 per cent proof.

In GLC days, scientific officers were more likely to be checking safety in school playgrounds (they produced a 'soft fall' surface which lessened injury), testing building materials and working alongside the fire brigade at incidents involving chemicals.

Hazchem, a life-saving system of orange-colour safety labels on tankers and some buildings, was a brainchild of a combined effort by the London Fire Brigade and GLC's scientific branch. From its coded symbols, firefighters and rescue workers can tell at a glance which type of chemical is involved, what to use to extinguish fire, the risk of explosion, what protective clothing to wear and how to dispose of spillage. Created in 1971, it is now used throughout Europe and further afield.

Between checking chalks, pencils and felt-tip pens used in schools, the staff of scientific branch found time to work as public analyst for some London boroughs. In one year they pursued 5,000 complaints by shoppers about everything from meatballs - finding them only 23 per cent meat - to baby foods and testing the fire resistance of furniture and lead pollution from petrol, toys and cosmetics.

They claimed some credit for the improved safety standards of plastic and foam-filled furniture and for revealing the danger of blue asbestos.

Their monitoring of the Thames proved its continuing cleanliness and in 1966 they reported that, for the first time in 50 years, every sample of Thames water contained dissolved oxygen.

On the roof of County Hall they sited equipment which detected fall-out from French and Chinese nuclear blasts in Asia, and tested domestic paint to see which brand weathered best.

London's air became markedly cleaner when the killer smog of 1952, which killed 4,000, led to the Clean Air Act of 1956 and the banning of open coal fires. Fifteen years on, the council's scientists studied the effects of motor vehicle fumes on traffic policemen and concluded that they were less harmful than the effects individuals would suffer from smoking. On the other hand, London's atmospheric gases were considered by the scientific branch, who cleaned it up, to have caused more damage to Cleopatra's Needle in its 80 years on the The Embankment than its previous 3,000 years in Egypt.

Scientists were able to measure the precise noise nuisance suffered by people living along new roads. In one spell they produced 100 noise maps leading to the payment of £23 million to families, compensation varying according to individual decibel readings at each home. They also conducted experiments into possible damage to people's hearing from helicopter noise, and worked on classroom acoustics to benefit children who were hard of hearing.

Ultimately, their work for London created so much public interest that their experts were given a course on television presentation.

Some curious problems exercised the minds of the scientific detectives. Mysterious clouds of dust which rose when grass was cut in a London park were identified as a rare fungus from New Zealand. The park was under the Heathrow flight path; the fungus was assumed to have been carried by an aircraft. Heathrow jets were blamed unjustly on another occasion, when enraged motorists in Chiswick asked the GLC to examine deposits on their parked cars. The marks were found to have come from bees.

For sheer drama, perhaps the branch's most memorable action was taken when a shop in West Hampstead was found to be radio-active and highly dangerous. Now empty, for decades it had been used for painting luminous faces on watches. The scientists' answer was to dismantle it brick by brick and bury the debris at a toxic waste dump.

On abolition, the scientific branch was privatised.

A more high profile GLC service was the London Fire Brigade, another organisation which, for years, showed its connection with the council simply by displaying its crest.

During a fruitful partnership, it enrolled the country's first woman firefighter - there were probably a dozen at abolition - and kick-started what became the nation's first fully computerised call-out system. This revolutionised the handling and processing of emergencies reducing them to a fraction of the time it took when handled manually. Instead of having to consult a wall map as in days of yore, an operator could see at the touch of a button where fire engines were available.

With the safety of its citizens a prime concern, the GLC was a willing listener to any good idea from the brigade. Council money enabled the brigade to replace wooden-wheel escape ladders with modern alloy ones and to increase its fleet of hydraulic platforms.

It was able to replace its ageing fireboat, the 50-year-old Massey

Shaw, with a steel and aluminium catamaran, London Phoenix, designed to navigate the shallowest reaches of the Thames.

Latest in a line of fireboats going back to 1760, its twin hulls gave stability for its hydraulic platform which could rise ten metres above water level. It could pump water at more than 8,000 litres a minute and carried 4,500 litres of foam for tackling oil fires, an ability undreamed of in the early days when London's fireboats had hand pumps and were rowed to the scene.

These were superseded by steam-driven vessels but they failed because their draught was too deep to permit them to get close to shore, a problem not solved until the Thames was artificially banked.

The famous Massey Shaw, which had an improved all-steel hull and could pass under all Thames bridges, hadn't long to wait to prove her worth. She was only four years old when war broke out. In addition to fighting ship fires, she proved invaluable during the blitz, pumping water inland when water mains were cut. She was one of the Little Ships at Dunkirk, making three trips and bringing home over 600 troops.

Later, the brigade benefitted by being part of a large GLC organisation, because of the advantage of being able to shuffle money around between various areas if an emergency arose, an ability not now available to them.

The London Ambulance Service, the biggest in the world, was another organisation to have felt the cold draft of leaving the comfort of the GLC family for more austere corridors, - in its case, of Whitehall and the health authority. London's ambulances and cars were carrying three million patients a year and covering 14,500,000 miles when reorganisation of the health service led to them being wrenched from GLC grasp.

Another service offered London-wide for the benefit of the capital as a whole was provided by the GLC's Supplies Department, a non-profit making buying organisation whose annual turnover topped £186 million in the final years before abolition. Its central warehouse at Tottenham Hale was as big as six supermarkets.

Before buying materials ranging from baked beans and hi-tech computers to furniture and bedsheets, all would be tested by the scientific branch for toxic substances, durability and fire resistance. So vast was the department's buying power that it could use the sheer volume of its purchases to negotiate large discounts from suppliers and pass on the savings to its customers. In any one year, the Supplies Department saved ratepayers about £15 million.

With a quarter of a million school meals to be provided every day, its annual shopping list included 3,400 tons of potatoes, 850 tons of sausages, 1,250 tons of baked beans, 80,000 boxes of fish fingers and nine million fresh eggs. All a far cry from the bowl of free soup for the needy which was how a school meals service began in 1898 under the auspices of the School Care Workers Association.

Seventy-five years ago,the supplies department's predecessor, the LCC stores department was buying 'best selected goose quill pens, hand cut,' at three shillings a hundred. In the last days of the GLC, Supplies were buying 15 million pencils and 12 million exercise books. One year's order book contained sales of 18,000 pairs of trousers, 43,000 sheets, three million books, 35,000 gallons of fuel, 26 miles of iron sewage pipe.

In another year it spent £24 million on milk and £38,000 on clearway signs. In preparation for severe winters, it purchased 46,000 tons of rock salt from Portugal and Sicily and, responding to the needs of the age, paid for a fleet of rent collection vehicles with bulletproof windows.

It continued to grow under the GLC and in its final years bought for every borough council in London, for 5,000 schools, homes for old people and for the county council of Buckinghamshire. Council requirements tended to be similar if not identical, so buying from the GLC Supplies Department enabled customers to buy more cheaply and they were not obliged to hold unnecessary stocks. Councils saved as much as 15 per cent using the supplies service.

Buying the right goods at the right price was not the end of the story. It experimented, testing the durability and noise insulation properties of various types of carpet for schools; sought the most comfortable uniform for firemen, and helped design new stacking chairs, contoured for comfort.

Spot checks were made to ensure quality. GLC testers smiled when one floor covering supplier wrote on its invoice an instruction for its own warehouse. It said: 'Must be special quality. Sample required for testing.'

In road safety, too, the GLC's initiatives led to London-wide benefits. In the last year of Sir Desmond Plummer's reign (1972) the council set up the Greater London Road Safety Committee, backed by a dedicated unit of traffic engineers and with members also from the Department of Environment, police, Royal Society for the Prevention of Accidents and the boroughs. Campaigns aimed at reducing various causes of death and injury became common - and successful.

But before these heady days, the GLC investigated various anti-skid surfaces at dangerous junctions - which halved accidents - and painted yellow triangles to prohibit stopping at other hazardous junctions. These strategically placed spots of paint cut accidents by a quarter.

In its first report, the Road Safety Unit revealed that motor-cyclists and their passengers were 27 times more likely to be killed or seriously hurt on London's roads than car drivers, and that nearly one-quarter of that number would be learners. In accidents between motor cyclists and car drivers, one-third of motorists said they did not see the motor-bike.

Conspicuity was clearly a problem, so the road safety unit launched a 'Ride Bright' campaign, aimed at persuading motor-cyclists to wear bright clothes and switch on their headlights during daylight. Responding to the slogan 'Be seen and not hurt,' the number of riders using headlights shot up 600 per cent, an improvement which remained evident four months later. One year on and there had been 570 fewer motor-cycle accidents than anticipated.

The campaign was repeated and casualties fell steeply for the next four years in spite of a 30 per cent increase in motor-bike use. At night, the trend continued to rise. Had daylight accidents risen at the same rate, another 1,400 riders would probably have been killed or injured during one year.

Is the colour of a car a factor in road safety?

Prolonged checks by the road safety unit produced the result one would probably expect: the more conspicuous the colour, the less the likelihood of an accident. Red was an exception. Despite its conspicuity, it did not have a good safety record, probably because red was the colour chosen by so many young, inexperienced drivers.

Statistics proved that November was the worst month for accidents.

In West London, a sophisticated computer system called Area Traffic Control was set up to bring order to the chaos of traffic around Earls Court. Traffic lights at 70 junctions were linked to a computer and the VDUs watched by GLC staff working at Scotland Yard. Besides co-ordinating the signals, the computers also measured and took into account variations in vehicle flow and adjusted the timing of traffic lights accordingly. In an emergency, lights over a wide area could be changed at the flick of a switch. In its first year of operation, accidents were down 18 per cent and traffic was speeded up.

Later ATC controlled 1,200 junctions in central and inner London, Croydon and Kingston before being replaced by a £2million system, called Scoot, which employed a new generation of more sophisticated computers and made even bigger savings.

Road safety solutions were not all hi-tech and expensive. In one year, some 1,778 low cost safety projects, such as redesigning junction layouts, improving visibility for drivers and pedestrians, averaged less than £200.

At the time the GLC was abolished, the road safety unit had details of 750,000 accidents and estimated that road safety work had saved 48,000 casualties. In addition, traffic was also moving 12 per cent faster.

Dave Wetzel, transport chair for the last GLC administration, said: 'Londoners continue to enjoy greater road safety than the rest of the country despite living in the busiest area.'

Among the good news was the bad. Although deaths and casualties on London's roads continued to drop, every year many hundreds were killed - 500 in the GLC's last year.

Too many people were being injured on or near pelican crossings. Pedestrians, particularly the elderly, handicapped and mothers with children, tended to be stranded on the centre island when crossing wide, busy roads. So serious had the problem become, that the council stopped introducing pelican crossings on high-speed roads.

While politicians warned that pedestrians were placing too much reliance on crossings and should be more aware of vehicles around them, the council's traffic detectives investigated.

They experimented by cutting one-third from the 30 seconds of vehicle-precedence time. To the council's surprise, while pedestrians enjoyed greater convenience, vehicle flows and queue lengths remained unchanged.

After studies with the Department of Transport, the GLC was convinced it had hit on the solution: To delay by two seconds the flashing amber allowing traffic to proceed if the road was clear until AFTER the commencement of the flashing green man warning pedestrians to hurry up and complete their crossing. They also sought to give crossings more prominence by introducing zig-zag markings on the carriageway and installing a sound device on the island.

The GLC pressed the Department of Transport for two years to release its grip on the pelican crossing regulations to allow it to pursue an experiment to test their theory. Four more years elapsed before it was allowed to put its evidence to the test at 37 sites. Results were conclusive. The GLC was right.

For the last word on pelicans, a comment from Callum Findlay, Surrey County Council's head of engineering: 'When we first saw the detailed GLC requirements for pelicans we fell about laughing. But the more we looked into them the more we appreciated their significance. Now we have adopted them as standard for all our crossings throughout the county.'

Some of the most valued expertise the GLC assembled for London's benefit concerned historic buildings. Its historic buildings board was the principal guardian of London's past. Such was the prestige of the professional team headed by planning surveyor Ashley Barker that the famous, including Osbert Lancaster and John Betjeman, became advisory members to the historic buildings board and gave their time without payment for many years.

The division was responsible for 30,000 listed buildings in London, from those of international renown to the humble prefab home and symbolic air raid shelter. In one year the division dealt with 3,500 applications for people wishing to alter them, its task to ensure that this was done in such a way as not to harm the building.

More than 1,000 listed buildings were owned by the GLC, from Queen Cleopatra's Needle to Marble Hill, the Market in Covent Garden and the ruins of Lesnes Abbey.

When the GLC was abolished and its historic buildings work passed to National Heritage, tributes to its expertise and sensitivity overflowed.

Among them, the Civic Trust said: 'It has perhaps contributed more to the care of London's architectural heritage than any other body or institution. Every one of the 62 local and voluntary amenity societies in London have made representations to the Civic Trust urging that the division should not be broken up.'

The average Londoner would most likely to be aware of the work of the Historic Buildings board through its conspicuous blue plaques, begun by the Royal Society and carried on by the LCC before being passed to the Greater London Council. More than 600 adorn buildings in London, recording the birth places and residences of the famous or the location of historic events.

Without them not many people would know that Mozart composed his first symphony in Ebury Street, Westminster, that Captain Bligh, of Mutiny on the Bounty fame, lived in Lambeth Road or that Marconi lived in Hereford Road, Westminster, and Karl Marx found sanctuary in Dean Street, Soho - from where he was summoned by the LCC for not paying his rates.

Events commemorated include: The first demonstration of television by John Logie Baird in 1926 (marked with a plaque at 22 Frith Street, Soho), and the world's first regular high definition television service, inaugurated by the BBC on November 2, 1936 and marked by a plaque at Alexandra Palace.

Before a plaque is awarded, the facts are researched until there is no doubt of its authenticity. It was, therefore, with much consternation that the appearance of an unauthorised plaque was reported, a copy of the GLC's to the last detail. This was no prankster having a quiet laugh at authority. It was a man whose home was a genuine gem and which did have a claim to fame, though not the one he advertised. He refused to back down and ultimately honour was satisfied through a good old British compromise. The GLC offered a blue plaque for the house's genuine claim to fame and agreed to site it on the front of the building, if he would agree to remove his to the back.

Yet one more service, a treasure trove for historians, was the council's maps and prints section which moved to the City Archives in Northampton Road, Clerkenwell. When in County Hall it was used by about 25,000 visitors each year, many researching their family tree.

Among treasures are some dating back to the 13th century, and the register of nurses who served with Florence Nightingale in the Crimea and a series of job descriptions for 1556 which says that a hospital matron should be 'a sad, grey, virtuous motherly woman.'

A number of parish registers, taken on deposit, contained little known facts and included the detailed account of an earthquake that hit London at 5.30am on March 8, 1749 when the top of a pier on the north side of Westminster Abbey fell down. So did two houses in Whitechapel.

A rare document is a nuncupative will. This is an oral will, now valid only when made on the battlefield. The one in the archives was dictated by a Mrs Joan Robinson from her bedroom window in 1609 shortly before she died of the plague in Uxbridge.

Although the staff were always willing to help, it was useful to be specific in your quest for research. There were more than a million prints and photographs, while documents and books filled shelving covering 13 miles!

14. TRIALS OF THE THAMES

It was perhaps an omen that when the GLC came into being in 1965, someone forgot to assign over the LCC's powers to run Thames piers and river services. Powers had to be reacquired some years later.

Although each GLC administration pointed to the Thames as being London's neglected asset and pledged to restore it to commercial life with commuter services, London is still waiting. Several attempts have been made. None has survived.

When one looks at the Rhine, or visits Bangkok where express and suburban river buses ply the Chao Phyra from one end of the city to the other, fast, frequent and cheap, it shows what can be achieved. Perhaps London needs to be 20 degrees further south to enjoy such a service.

The GLC began taking a special interest in the Thames in the late sixties when the Port of London Authority put Cadogan pier (by Albert bridge), up for sale. A working party recommended that the council ought to take over the piers to give public access to the river and with a view to subsequent use for passenger services for commuters. Pleasure boat operators were keen to acquire them and wanted to save money by opening them only during the hours of their own operations.

In 1973, the council paid the Port of London Authority £90,000 for six piers, though some were in very poor condition. Marine engineers insisted that Tower pier was taken away immediately to be made safer and some years later Westminster pier was filled with foam to ensure it wouldn't become waterlogged and sink under the weight of passengers. At that point Westminster was the only pier making money and was the centre of passenger boat operations. The foam-filling was to keep it going until a new pier was built.

Maurice Hudson, the GLC's aviation and marine transport planner, said: 'We spent about £1million a year running the piers. We were paying for the privilege of letting the people have access to the river. We took the view that it could be regarded as a parallel to spending on a public park.'

About half the cost was recouped from pleasure boat operators.

When the GLC was abolished, £500,000 was owing in tolls and two boats were seized and sold to recover debts.

The GLC's quest for commuter services on the river was answered when an Italian company brought over two hydrofoils to run between Greenwich and Tower piers in the early seventies. Their deep draught preventing them from going further upriver.

After six fairly successful months they were withdrawn - it was never intended they should continue for longer - by which time the Italians had achieved their objective of testing the effects of deep hydrofoils on a relatively shallow river. The craft hd been designed for inter-island service and were found to be unsuitable for Thames-type operations.

Passenger numbers suggested there was a market, encouraging an upbeat Sir Desmond Plummer to talk of looking forward to the day when Londoners could go aboard a hovercraft at Thamesmead and travel to Ramsgate or the continent.

Whilst this experiment was proceeding, the GLC agreed to join the government in sponsoring a service with British-built Sidewall hovercraft, leading the council to boast that it was now quicker to get from central London to Greenwich by hovercraft than by rail.

Financial aspects were inconclusive and when funding ran out, the government was disinclined to back it further. The GLC decided to go it alone, and the hovercraft became integrated into the London Transport system and Travelcards were accepted.

For the following year hovercraft became part of river life, though the nagging problem at Greenwich was that there was nowhere suitable for commuters to park.

Overcrowding on the trains led to pressure from the people of Thamesmead for a river bus. The council responded by getting London Transport's buses from Thamesmead to call at Greenwich pier pending Thamesmead getting a pier of its own. (Plans for this were in preparation when the GLC died).

Hovermarine services ran for about 18 months and were showing the first signs of success when another winter and another financial crisis loomed. Government cash to councils was cut, the GLC pulled out and Hovermarine's service went to the wall. The council had given a guarantee on the purchase of a third boat which remained in its ownership when the service folded. It was taken out of the water at Silvertown from where it disappeared, later turning up in Thailand.

As London looked for another entreprenuer to test the water, interest came from a surprising source - the Russian government. It wanted a shop window in the West for its hydrofoils and was prepared to run them without any hand-out from the GLC. The council's only contribution was to scale down pier charges to encourage what it regarded as a 'commuter service.' (This name is shorthand for a service which runs all day, it not being financially viable to run boats only during peak hours).

In due course two Raketa vessels arrived. Each carried 50 or 60 passengers and they ran up and down the Thames successfully for many months. Unlike the Italian foils, these were designed for river use, had a shallow draught and consequently could run upstream to more profitable Westminster.

Both hydrofoil and hovercraft services gave rise to inevitable complaints from the passenger boat operators that their livelihood was being threatened. There were also problems with wash from the craft, some real, some imagined.

The hovercraft caused a phenomenon known as 'low-water drag' where the wash went down and rebounded from the river bed and then spread out across the water. The PLA considered speed limits following complaints of danger to passengers caused by bobbing boats being loaded at piers and people working on barges fearing they were in danger of being thrown off.

In an attempt to boost the service and the popularity of the South Bank cultural activities, the GLC provided a new pier at the Royal Festival Hall. The first new pier for 30 years, it was based on a 100 ft. pontoon which had seen service at the Festival Hall before, having floated there during the Festival of Britain in 1951. During the intervening years it had lain unused and largely neglected at Battersea. Its second tour of duty on the South Bank began in an even more auspicous style than the first. Dredging its foundations, contractors brought up an unexploded bomb which brought central London to a halt for hours. After refurbishment, the new pier was opened in 1983.

Maurice Hudson said: 'The plan was a total disaster. Several companies tried to run services from it. They all failed. We managed to get the Queen to embark there on one or two occasions. It's much more suitable for the sovereign than overcrowded Westminster but it failed because it was in the wrong place. People couldn't get to it.'

Meanwhile, Westminster pier was at last to be replaced and leading engineers and architects submitted drawings to a GLC design competition. The winning entry planned a lavish double deck structure with private enterprise paying for restaurants and a museum on a top deck and giving the river level facilities to the council for nothing.

Politics got in the way when Ken Livingstone's administration came to power. Labour was pleased when the company backed out. It decreed that a new pier should be based on a Victorian theme. In due course plans for a £2.3m structure were in hand though work was overtaken by abolition.

Yet another river bus appeared on the scene in 1985. Costing £5m. to set up and £400,000 a year to operate, the experiment involved Thames Guided Tours providing two 156-seat vessels, sailing from central London to the Isle of Dogs and Greenwich. The council's aim was that it should cater for residents and workers and help economic regeneration of the Thames corridor.

A 30-minute service was planned, criss-crossing the river and calling at piers half a mile apart. Services were to operate between 8 am and 6.30 pm, stopping also at Tower pier and Festival pier during peak periods.

The GLC gave £93,000 to assist operations at which time Paul Moore, Labour's river spokesman, said the council anticipated 'an increase in this pleasant way of going to and from work, particularly in the summer.' By this time abolition was near and the government refused to ratify the council's contribution - and the latest river bus venture went the way of all the others.

Two constant problems emerged from the council's attempts to promote river buses - inclement weather deterring people from travelling by water and a lack of residents living near the waterside. Though the second point no longer applies and there are many more piers than formerly, river buses still have not been able to operate without subsidy. After abolition of the GLC, a river bus ran for five years, subsidised from a variety of sources including Canary Wharf, which agreed to give support until the Jubilee tube line was operational. When the line opened late in 1999, subsidies were withdrawn and the river bus failed.

Commuter services were not the GLC's only objective in reviving the Thames. More than 30 years ago 1,500,000 visitors to London were sailing on pleasure craft. Having seen some of them travelling in an open boat in a snowstorm, the council made the first of several attempts to encourage owners to improve standards. At least half the boat should be covered and heated, said the council. Owners replied that they could not afford such changes and would have to close. The GLC backed down.

Various action groups were set up to consider the growing demand for leisure use of the river and to improve amenity access over much of the river's 41 miles. More than £200,000 was spent on Cutty Sark Gardens and on rebuilding Greenwich pier; other work refurbished the river frontage at Greenwich and Richmond.

Before activity on the river became a major GLC objective it had worked ceaselessly to clean it up and improve the quality of the water, continuing the excellent work begun by the LCC. There was always a massive problem of driftwood - 7,000 tons every year collected by the PLA, different today only in the change of substance, plastic having superseded wood as the main nuisance.

If transforming the Thames into a commuter and freight highway had been a conspicuous failure, improving the quality of the water was a huge success.

Modernisation of the capital's sewage system was a long and expensive task which began bearing fruit in the late 1960s when fish began returning to the tidal Thames in the heart of London.

There was much excitement when a 15-inch carp was found stranded in river workings off the Embankment at Millbank, in 1968. The existence of fresh water fish so far downstream was unknown since before the infamous 'Big Stink' of the 1850s when the river was pronounced dead. Other fish had been similarly trapped in the water intake of Fulham power station.

There is no better way to monitor a river's ability to sustain life than by its fish so, full of hope, the GLC invited the Thames Angling Preservation Society to central London for a day's fishing. On a cold November day in 1958 was held the first of what was to become an annual fishing experiment. But that first day proved disappointing. They caught nothing.

Undeterred, the anglers returned a year later by which time GLC leader Sir Desmond Plummer had been made the society's president and had personally bought a silver cup to be presented to the angler with the biggest catch.

A year later, 36 anglers took up their stations between Wandsworth and Westminster bridges and landed 159 bleak and two roach. A year on, they tested the water between Chelsea and Blackfriars bridges and caught 48 fish.

In 1971 the council had proof of the landing of large numbers of roach, a 5lb bream and a 39-inch pike off Fulham. In the Blackwall tunnel area they caught a goldfish.

By January 1972 the GLC was proudly proclaiming 55 species living in the London Thames. Marine fish had been caught, apart from in the most polluted part of the river, and sprats, herring, plaice and sole had been landed near the Dartford tunnel. Even the fussy haddock, driven out by pollution from the southern area of the North Sea before 1966, had been seen at Barking.

In 20 years to 1971, sewage effluent and impurities had been halved leading to the council's sewage treatment works at Deephams, Edmonton, setting up a pioneering experiment. Six fish caught in the final effluent channel were kept at the works to see if they could be successfully reared under controlled conditions. Each week they were weighed and measured and checked for toxic materials and parasites while the water was monitored weekly for dissolved oxygen. They thrived.

Thames fish were making such news in 1972 that London's success in cleaning up the Thames was a feature of a GLC exhibition in Paris at which it was exploiting the industrial and commercial advantages of Docklands. On the flight to France with

Sir Desmond went Henri Jaume, a French Cockney from the GLC press office, whose prime duty was as interpreter and public relations adviser.

Among his luggage, however, was a tin of maggots and a fishing rod for Sir Desmond. During a pause in business, the GLC leader settled down near the Notre Dame Cathedral and cast his line into the Seine. He hoped to catch nothing and he was not disappointed. It hardly proved the metropolitan Seine was any less clean than the metropolitan Thames, but it helped attract attention to the GLC's cleaner Thames success.

By mid 1972 there were 63 species back in the tidal Thames. Two giant aquaria were set up in the foyer at County Hall to show off some of the captives. They proved a big attraction. The tanks replaced two large, ornate Italian marble fireplaces as a focal point in the imposing foyer.

The stories about the 'ones that got away' in this case, however, did not concern the fish. It was the marble fireplaces which had 'escaped.' When attempts were made to retrieve them from storage, they could not be found.

By now the annual fishing experiments were producing the biggest hauls ever both in numbers and types of fish and in 1971, Dr Basil Brown, the council's chief scientist, reported that the ammonia content was at its lowest and the nitrate content which helped cleanse the river and give it life was at its highest since collecting samples began in 1893. The battle against polution had been won.

Election pledges to restore life to the Thames had not been restricted to promoting commuter services and cleansing the river. Successive GLCs had been teased by the fact that water seemed an apparently unattainable means of transporting freight. It niggled that only 0.2 per cent of Britain's goods traffic was carried by water compared with 21 per cent in Germany and and a similar proportion in the U.S.

The administration of Sir Reg Goodwin investigated with the British Waterways Board the possibility of widening and deepening the Grand Union Canal between Brentford (where it joins the Thames) and Rickmansworth, Herts. Three seagoing barges, able to carry the equivalent of 70 juggernaut lorries, were used by the BWB in a six months marketing survey to see if companies would switch goods traffic from road to water.

Construction costs and other factors were found to make widening north of Uxbridge impracticable. Consideration was then given to modernising the eight-mile length from Brentford to a trans-shipment depot to be created near Heathrow, or to an alternative site near Slough. Costs were £1 million a mile, an expense which market potential could not justify and the idea was dropped.

If using the water to London's advantage was proving intractable, in downstream London the GLC was having more success in removing vast areas of water from development sites alongside the Thames - in Docklands and Thamesmead.

DOCKLANDS

Talk of London's Docklands and one thinks of the skyscrapers of Canary Wharf and the government's London Docklands Development Corporation. It could have been so very different.

When the GLC was in charge and preparing the area's future in consultation with the five riparian boroughs which each had a piece of Docklands, it had plans for thousands of homes with gardens, seedbed industries which would move on when established, and with no residential development higher than five storeys.

That was in the days when public consultation meant what it said. Countless local families consider themselves sold down the river by the Canary Wharf project which has changed the face of their 'town' and, they say, does not offer the type of jobs they need. It is perhaps true that the jobs are not for them but for their children.

The task of redeveloping Docklands was daunting. The site was enormous - eight and a half square miles, 1.4 per cent of Greater London's total area - and much of it obsolescent. Land was becoming disused, though not necessarily available for redevelop-ment, within an unusually short time-span, much of it a developer's nightmare needing to be cleared, drained and de-polluted. Contours of the river and the barriers of the dock basins divided the area into isolated communities, all very badly served by public transport.

Sir Horace Cutler, GLC leader 1977-81, summed it up: 'It has a problem of obsolescence. It is inaccessible and deficient in amenities and those it has are old.'

Accepting that you can never please all of the people all of the time, the success of Canary Wharf and the LDDC was built quite literally on a sound foundation, thanks to the GLC.

While planning proceeded, the GLC and its borough council allies spent years draining the Beckton marshes, filling and consolidating dock basins and detoxifying vast areas of contaminated land - all crucial before development could begin. Most spectacular of the pollution discoveries was a borehole drilled in Surrey Docks to check the characteristics of the sub-soil which burst into flame when it reached a pocket of methane gas.

Vital infrastructure, too, was advanced before Docklands was snatched away. The GLC planned and began boring the Jubilee tube line extension from Fenchurch Street to Docklands in 1977 - almost 23 years before it was opened!

In the late 1960s the docks had entered an era of irreversible decline. Containerisation had arrived. The introduction of sealed metal boxes of standard sizes which could be transported by ships, trains or lorries and could be handled mechanically, meant that docks could be located at the mouth of the Thames, saving the expense and time of an extended journey up-river to London. New technology enabled larger ships to be used and these required deeper water. The case for keeping the docks in London was not helped by a poor record in industrial relations, so when the opportunity came to relocate at Tilbury, every consideration was favourable.

When it came, the container revolution was swift. First the smaller upper docks ceased to be viable and were shut down in the late sixties. By 1970, the writing was on the wall for the rest. Dockers whose lives had revolved around ships for generations hoped that something might be saved and were comforted by the continued use of the West India and Millwall docks and the Royal group. But early in 1980 only the Royals were still functioning and on a much reduced scale.

The need for massive redevelopment was seen by GLC leader

Sir Desmond Plummer as the type of opportunity for which the council was created. It offered the biggest redevelopment site of any capital city in Europe, and London's biggest since the Great Fire in 1666. He went to see Peter Walker, then Secretary of State for the Environment, and returned rather despondent because Walker had decided that, before anything could be done, there must be a major study by consultants. Travers Morgan were commissioned and they reported nearly two years later with five options for redevelopment. Their report, in the spring of 1973, coincided with the GLC elections.

Brian Buckle, PA to Sir Desmond and later director of development co-ordination for the Docklands Development Organisation, said: 'The consultants' report became something of a political football. Because of this and the long delay caused by the study, the whole thing became diluted. With a Labour victory, all five of the consultants' scenarios were rejected and everything was thrown back into the melting pot. It was a lost opportunity. Under the Plummer administration the opportunity was recognised and there was a will to do something.'

Docklands' population at that time was about 55,000. Half the area was in the borough of Newham, one quarter in Tower Hamlets, about one eighth each in Greenwich and Southwark and a slither in Lewisham. Housing in the area was generally poor and a mismatch to people's needs. There were too few shops, open spaces, places of entertainment. Above all, employment was declining alarmingly.

After the election, which Labour won, a Docklands Joint Committee of the GLC and the five riparian boroughs was set up to prepare a strategic plan and co-ordinate its implementation. Later a Docklands Forum, a kind of built-in opposition, representing the interests of the many action groups and other interests, was created.

During the preparation of the strategic plan there was wide public consultation, so by the time it was published it reflected most of the wishes and aspirations of the local community.

The committee had adopted as its objective: 'To use the opportunity provided to redress the housing, social, environmental, employment/economic and communications deficiencies of the Docklands area and the parent boroughs, and thereby to provide the freedom for similar improvement throughout east and inner London.'

Brian Buckle commented: 'Although stories that the Docklands authorities were constantly at loggerheads were a myth, various third parties were involved and the joint committee had to proceed by consensus. We usually achieved consensus but there are costs involved and maybe, if the GLC had been left to proceed on its own, it might have made some harder decisions earlier.'

As some of the docks were still in use and much of the other land was in public ownership, the essence of the plan was to allocate land assuming when it would become available. It was considered that a major switch from industrial employment to offices and services would be irrelevant to the needs of the East End, whose workforce was predominantly industrial, and futile in view of the proximity of central London. Therefore the plan relied on the regeneration and the attraction to the area of industrial enterprises, especially manufacturing industry.

An American entrepreneur unveiled proposals for a vast trade mart complex in Surrey docks, a shop window for Britain's goods. Politicians hoped it would go ahead and prove a catalyst for development though, after dragging on for years, it failed to find sufficient financial backing. The possibility of establishing a free port was raised at various times without ever reaching the planning stage.

Two years on and the £3.5bn strategic plan (£2bn of public money) entered its second phase. DJC chairman Sir Hugh Wilson announced that the 'dull but vital' planning stage was now complete and they would be mounting a major offensive to attract industrialists, businessmen and investors. Only overseas investment could be targeted: advertising London's advantages at home had been banned by governments desperate for firms to locate in the industrial wastelands of the north.

Elections, both at County Hall and Westminster, bedevilled progress over the years and another election saw the GLC change hands once more.

Four years after the strategic plan was announced, it had achieved about 85 per cent of its industrial target: more than a million square feet of factory and warehouse space had been built and a further three and a half million were programmed. Housing was a year behind with its scheduled 6,600 completions, but the Phase Two target of 13,800 dwellings by 1986 was still considered attainable.

Nearly 100 acres of open space were acquired and laid out and a further 180 acres was programmed for development. The plan envisaged 350 acres of new parks, connected to each other and to the river frontage to open up the banks of the Thames as a public walkway.

There was bad news on the Jubilee Line: the Minister of Transport and leader of the GLC agreed that there should be a pause in preparatory work while low cost options were examined. Construction of the vital Northern Relief Route was guaranteed when the government and the GLC announced that £100m was to be made available over 15 years for transport, but it was not enough for Docklands' needs.

Brian Buckle explained: 'With Sir Horace Cutler at the helm in County Hall, it was decided that Docklands should now be reorganised on more commercial lines and they appointed Air Commodore Alan Mawer, formerly general manager of Basildon new town, to run it.

'This new organisation had barely got underway when there was a change of government. Michael Heseltine flew over Docklands in a helicopter, didn't see much happening on the ground - although a lot was going on under the ground - and decided that what was needed was a development corporation. And the DJC was wound up.'

Heseltine claimed that the present arrangements and the existing machinery of local government and the private sector could not meet the particular demands and opportunities of the area. He went on to list as 'things they were unable to do' - planning, land assembly and disposal for industry, commerce and housing, provision of infrastructure - precisely tasks the DJC had been performing since its inception.

It was argued by the borough councils that what was needed to maintain momentum was not a new organisation but the release of land held by various public authorities including the Port of London Authority, British Gas and British Rail, and a commitment of government financial assistance for a medium to long term programme of works.

When the DJC was finally wound up in 1981, its chairman Sir Hugh Wilson said: 'In a few short years a new infrastructure has been provided on a major scale. The Surrey Docks scheme now under construction will provide a new community - and 8,000 new jobs - new industry has been brought into Greenwich and Lewisham. North of the Thames there has been great industrial development - the News International project, the new Billingsgate market and the West India dock conversion in Tower Hamlets and the London Industrial Park in Newham. There, too, new housing is well on the way and Newham have completed an ambitious programme of new parks and playing fields.'

Labour was now in power at County Hall and planning chairman Ed Gouge was quick to express fears that the strategic plan, agreed by all the boroughs after much public participation, would be disregarded. The main reason things had not happened as speedily as one would wish, he said, was because the government had not provided the funds. He warned Michael Heseltine to abandon any ideas of by-passing the normal planning procedures and ignoring local democracy. The development corporation must be made more responsive to the feelings of local people, he said.

One feature of the LDDC's involvement which worked successfully was the creation of an 'enterprise zone' in the Isle of Dogs. A brainchild of Geoffrey Howe, its basis was that development was encouraged by the relaxing of planning constraints which might normally apply and giving developers a rates holiday for several years.

But more GLC-government animosity was not long delayed. Plans were announced to build nearly 2.5 million square feet of offices at Hays Wharf, an area previously earmarked for homes, industrial space and recreation.

Ed Gouge called it 'a disaster that would leave a permanent scar on the face of the capital.' There had to be a better way of developing the entire south side of the Pool of London, he said, than with the equivalent of 52 acres of offices which was 13 times the size of Wembley Stadium. The scheme was later abandoned. Then came Canary Wharf with 7-10 million square feet of offices and towers up to 40 storeys high - all approved, claimed the GLC, without any consultation with local councils or the GLC. George Nicholson, the council's Docklands planning chairman, described the development as 'sheer madness.' The challenge of Docklands was to use the existing fabric of what was once the world's greatest port and what had been inherited rather than knock it all down and start again, he said.

The £77 million Docklands Light Railway, serving 18 stations with what critics called a two-coach Mickey Mouse train, came into service. Later, because of its inadequacy, Canary Wharf was obliged to contribute towards river bus services for five years as part of an agreement with tenants to get their staff to work until the Jubilee line opened.

The GLC sought to take the Environment Secretary and the LDDC to court over their failure to consult or hold a public inquiry into Canary Wharf, challenging the speed and manner with which it had been 'rubber stamped.' George Nicholson claimed that every level of elected representation in Docklands - MPs, GLC members, local councillors and community representatives - were united in their protest at the 'cowboy tactics' of the corporation.

When the GLC was finally abolished, Canary Wharf was being built.

THAMESMEAD

Another huge riverside development which raised enormous problems of site preparation was Thamesmead, the GLC's virtually new town at Greenwich.

In its constant search for land to provide the homes London desperately needed, Sir William Fiske's first GLC, in March 1966, produced a master plan for a massive housing development for 60,000 people.

On the south bank of the Thames at Greenwich lay the site of the former Woolwich Arsenal - 1,300 acres described at the time as 'the last remaining big opportunity site for development in London.' So was born what became known as Thamesmead, the nearest thing to a New Town the GLC attempted. Promoted as a 'town of the 21st century,' it was regarded as a blueprint for developments of the future. Because the water table was so near the surface the town would have no human habitation at ground level. Dwellings began on first floors like town houses, with garages and store rooms underneath. Walkways were at first floor level and there was an elaborate emergency plan in the event of flooding. It never needed to be used and subsequently Thamesmead became protected by the Thames Barrier.

Pedestrians were segregated from traffic, but plans for the entire development to be one-way were abandoned when studies showed that this would cause unacceptable problems for public transport. Thamesmead would have a three-mile river walkway, yachting marina and two substantial lakes and be linked to a system of canals to give it 'cohesion.' Six hundred acres were earmarked for housing, 200 for open space and 100 for industry with an optional increase ultimately to 284 acres.

Built in partnership with the adjoining boroughs of Greenwich and Bexley, Thamesmead was frequently referred to as a New Town though this, said the councils, was not technically accurate because, when completed in 15 years, its boundary would come within a few hundred yards of Woolwich town centre.

It cost what seemed a bargain £6.8 million, including part demolition, but there were problems from the start. The site was a catchment area both for rain and high tides and was largely marshland which entailed most homes having piled foundations to a depth of 30-40ft.

So unusual was Thamesmead that it attracted architects and planners from all over the world. The Queen and Prince Philip once spent an entire day there, visiting people in their homes, visiting the schools and enjoying the town's unique design.

After the initial rush, it became less desirable and some of the accommodation ultimately found its way on to the 'hard to let' register.

Over the years plans changed with the political complexion of the GLC and twice work was delayed for a substantial re-think about the way ahead. When Thamesmead was devised, the desperate need for housing of any type, resulted in plans to cram it with council housing, as much as could reasonably, cheaply and quickly be built.

Early enthusiasm saw a construction workforce of 600 on the site within a year and the first residents moved in during June 1968, housed in the first of a dozen 13-storey blocks of 48 flats. By now the Conservatives had won County Hall and Sir Desmond Plummer's administration winced at what they regarded as the creation of a huge council estate.

Land preparation was so expensive it became essential to sell some land to finance the public sector. Refinancing had become a problem and would continue to be throughout Thamesmead's lifetime.

Private homes were substituted for many of the municipal ones, but providing houses with gardens for sale at a lesser density led to the target population being scaled down by a quarter to 45,000-plus. The homes ratio was now 8,800 municipal to 5,120 private. Completion date for the town had also slipped - from an over optimistic 1981 to 1988.

Six months into its life, Thamesmead was the setting for high drama. It was Boxing Day and gunshots had been heard. The duty staff across the river at Beckton sewage treatment works dialled 999. Was this to be Thamesmead's first armed robbery? Police at Woolwich were on high alert as investigating crews sped to the scene. There they were confronted not by armed villains, but by a red-faced Seton Forbes Cockell, chairman of the GLC's Thamesmead committee, who had invited some friends along for a duck shoot.

Forbes Cockell died and was succeeded by David Harris, a *Daily Telegraph* journalist later to become an MP. He stated that the new housing and population targets were no cut-back, just a realisation that the original figures were unrealistic. After five years practical experience, forecasts were being revised to attainable targets rather than improbable estimates. Growing pains were inevitable, he said, but there were real achievements, too. By now Thamesmead was home to 4,000 people and shops and employment had arrived.

Under the Labour administration of Sir Reg Goodwin, emphasis shifted once more towards municipal homes and this lack of social mix led to what the Tories called 'a council estate philosophy. This had a generally depressing effect and was a deterrent to business moving there, a mood not helped by housing areas still lacking names and continuing to be identified by numbers given them by planners and builders.

Thamesmead became home to Vietnamese refugees while the council wrestled with ideas to make the area more attractive. It was vital to broaden the town's appeal and widen the social mix of the population. The town was not flourishing as its planners had anticipated. It was reputed to have the worst rent arrears of any GLC estate in London and one-third of the population was on income support. The brutalistic environment, typical of other new estates, was noted by film makers who shot scenes for 'A Clockwork Orange' there.

Labour's Thamesmead chairman was Bill Simpson, a popular man who was blind. Colleagues recall a day when Thamesmead was being promoted vigorously, part of the promotion being production of T-shirts bearing the Thamesmead logo. Two attractive girls from the GLC staff agreed to model them at a photo-call.

Press photographers are an earthy bunch who can tell at a glance which pictures sell newspapers and which are not worth the film they're taken on. They looked askance at the pretty models in their bright T-shirts and jeans and said: 'Can we see a bit of leg?'

Both girls agreed to remove their jeans to male approval, not least from chairman Simpson.

The press were still not satisfied. They could see lines under the shirts, they grumbled and then suggesting: 'Can we get rid of the bras, girls?'

Again the girls obliged, their action greeted even more enthusiastically by Bill Simpson.

'Hey!' said one of his party. 'I thought you said you were blind.'

'Only when it suits me,' Bill replied.

Sadly, Bill Simpson's sight lived only in his memory. At one time he nursed high hopes that it was returning but it was not to be.

The housing mix changed yet again when Sir Horace Cutler's Conservatives won the GLC. His chairman at Thamesmead, Victor

Rae Langton, forecast that they would breathe new life into the town and make it more desirable. Thamesmead had moved away from its original concept of a riverside town with low level housing around the town centre. All housing currently at the design stage would be re-examined to ensure it would be attractive to potential purchasers and tenants alike.

Thamesmead's marshy sub-soil continued to cause problems. A novel £1m pumping station was built, based on what was thought to be a 2,000-year-old invention of Archimedes. It consisted of four giant screws, each weighing 20 tons, as wide as a double-deck bus and twice as long. Their sensors would detect excess water and the turning screws would draw it up and pass it through a channel and into the Thames. Such systems were said to be in use on the Nile. Manufacturers claimed that the power of the screws was such that, if all four were used, they could empty an Olympic size swimming pool in five minutes.

Thamesmead's sub-soil also interested scientists who suspected it could harbour an underground hot water lake. They drilled a 400-metre bore hole, one of the deepest in London, but their search for geothermal energy ended in disappointment.

Parks, two lakes and a swimming pool now added to Thamesmead's amenities, and firms at last began to consider it as a base for operations. Additional land was released for industry as the town advertised its desirable amenities, though there was still an occasional demand for a rodeo to round up stray horses which continued to damage gardens and fences.

After two years of difficult construction on waterlogged ground, a spine road, the main artery into Thamesmead, was completed. The road needed embankments along most of its two-mile length, which led to 100,000 cubic metres of in-fill material being imported.

By December 1983, Labour was in power again and the Livingstone administration announced that agreement had been reached for another 1,000 homes - half for sale - on five sites and that Thamesmead was now half way towards its target population of 40,000 plus.

By its 18th birthday in 1985, the complexion of Thamesmead had changed considerably, as had Labour's attitude towards it. By now £200 million in private sector money had been channelled to the town to provide, among other things, a long delayed town centre. Another £200m would be needed to complete Thamesmead over the next few years, the council said.

With coming abolition, the GLC, made its final decision for Thamesmead, a gift for the town hall - a clock and cupola, a relic from Nelson's day, 30ft high, made in 1783 and rescued from the defunct Royal Dockyard at Deptford.

Inevitably the question then arose: Who looks after Thamesmead when the GLC is no more? The council supported a suggestion that it should be run by an elected committee of tenants - tenants had been politically active throughout the town's life. Labour's housing chairman Tony McBrearty said this option would 'guarantee a high level of services, no privatisation and no quick profits at the expense of the long term future.'

Put to a vote of tenants, that solution got the thumbs down. A majority of 600 decided they would rather be looked after by a private trust.

Why wasn't this blueprint for a 21st century town handed over to either of the participating boroughs, Labour Greenwich and Tory Bexley?

It was offered, but neither was willing to accept responsibility.

15. THE GLC LEGACY

Which was the GLC's greatest legacy to London, the single project for which it will most be remembered? Thousands of elderly people will point to free travel for over-sixties; others may opt for the classical charm of renovated Covent Garden, or the engineering wonder of the Thames barrier. For some, it may be the seaside and country homes scheme which enabled retired couples to realise an otherwise impossible dream of a flat by the sea or a bungalow in the country. The GLC left a bountiful legacy, all assembled without a suspicion of corruption by members or officers.

But history may ignore all these claims and say that the GLC's greatest gift to society was its New and Expanding Towns programme. Former GLC director general Maurice Stonefrost considers that the map of southern England was re-created by that 1965-75 era when London's population was growing too fast and was being encouraged to move to other parts of the country.

There were plans to move a million Londoners under the scheme. Although it fell short of that figure, nearly a quarter of all Londoners rehoused in that ten-year span were moved to new and expanding towns in an organised, planned exodus, taking jobs with them. When the scheme was halted in 1975 because the situation was then so changed that London needed to import, not export industry, 52,500 homes had been built for London tenants in 32 towns, among them Basingstoke, King's Lynn, Swindon, Thetford and Milton Keynes.

Maurice Stonefrost emphasised: 'Many of those people don't realise that they are living in towns and cities which, in a sense, resulted from an administrative initiative to decentralise the mass of population in London. Families, many living in poor conditions, were given a new lease of life; towns were put on the map. Everyone benefited. Now it is all just taken for granted.

'And when it came to an end because the population of London stopped growing, there were no jagged edges. It came to an end so smoothly that hardly anybody remarked about it. Everything was so well organised, looked after sensibly and handled with great sensitivity and expertise by my predecessors. I think that was a huge success story. The lives of a lot of people and the economy in the south-east have been much improved by the way it went.'

His sentiments are echoed by Norman Howard, for 13 years a GLC member and Labour's planning chairman in the Goodwin years.

He said: 'New and expanding towns were a huge success. Families were not dumped, it was planned growth. Jobs went with them. Big developments like King's Lynn, Basingstoke and Swindon eventually had a momentum of their own and the GLC just faded away. But we got them started. It helped put many new towns on their feet.On the personal side, I used to meet people who had lived in grotty old flats in Islington and Hackney and who suddenly found themselves starting a new life in greenfield locations.'

GLC politicians also went out to give the development corporations the benefit of their experience. Sir Reg Goodwin served on Basildon new town corporation; Evelyn Denington was on the board of Stevenage new town; Sir Horace Cutler chaired Milton Keynes development corporation.

Political expertise went hand in hand with planning know-how and development.

Seaside and country homes brought a new, leisurely lifestyle to many of London's retired. Families who had lived all their working days in inner London were given the chance to realise a dream and move out to the coast or the country, often to be near their children.

Here, too, couples were not dumped. There was no mass immigration which could have caused local animosity and overloaded the local health and welfare services, though this was an initial fear in some towns. Occasionally there were demonstrations when the pensioners arrived for the customary preview of their new home before the move became final, but any hostility soon faded.

The GLC built 3,200 flats and bungalows, always deliberately small numbers, in 19 counties from the Wash to Weston-super-Mare. Half the couples were taken from borough council lists and the remainder form the GLC. Despite moving far away, they remained tenants of the GLC which often gave them an advantage compared with rents charged by the host town. They were kept in touch with London and with each other by a nominated representative on each estate and a small team working at County Hall.

Tenants moving out were not the only ones to benefit. For the most part they left behind large family homes, too big for them but ideal for younger families on the capital's waiting lists.

In London, the GLC introduced another winning scheme for council tenants - inter borough transfers. Previously tenants had been trapped in one borough, limiting their job opportunities and their lifestyle. Under the new system, they were able to switch their home for another in a different borough.

Millions of Londoners benefited and continue to benefit from the GLC's free travel for over-sixties. Originally it was a 'Cinderella' pass which required holders to be home by 4.30 and could be used only on London Transport's red buses. Gradually the hours of use were extended and its validity widened to encompass other types of bus and trains.

Its cost is astronomical but woe betide any politician who tries to curtail it. When borough council representatives of various parties meet to discuss matters of mutual interest, they joke: 'We are going to stop pensioners' free travel - but you do it first! '

COVENT GARDEN

For local, national and even international prestige, the GLC may wish to point to Covent Garden, particularly the speciality shopping market, as one of the gems in its crown. Today it is a premier attraction to Londoners and tourists and has a turnover exceeding *£100,000 a day*. Such success seemed beyond its wildest hopes during the ten years of arguing and bickering when plans and dreams were shredded, when the residents of Covent Garden fought for their environment and refused to allow it to be changed. It might have been so different.

For 300 years, the market of Nell Gwyn and Eliza Doolittle had been London's principal supplier of fruit and veg. By the 1960s it was falling victim to progress. New-age juggernauts could no longer negotiate the market's confined spaces or find the easy access they needed along the surrounding narrow streets. The market authority decided to move out of central London to a purpose-built site at Nine Elms, Battersea, where there was the added bonus of a railhead nearby.

This move was the catalyst for action. As early as 1968, six years before the market's departure, the GLC began buying up property in Covent Garden, a policy which would pay rich dividends in the years to come.

Finally, in 1974, the market was gone and the GLC, together with Westminster and Camden councils across whose boroughs the land lay, produced a grandiose £140 million plan to redevelop the whole Covent Garden area - 96 acres bounded by the Strand, Charing Cross Road, Shaftesbury Avenue and Kingsway. This was the Covent Garden of Charles Dickens and Samuel Johnson. Oliver Cromwell lived there. So did philosopher Voltaire, artist Joseph Turner and actor David Garrick, some of whom are remembered by streets names in the area.

Dominant feature of the councils' plan was to be a 4,000-seat international conference centre, with 'several' hotels, offices, shops and a doubling of the resident population to 7,000. Planners envisaged a parallel four-lane road to take traffic off the Strand, and another driven north from the Strand, through the Coutts Bank triangle and on to a widened Charing Cross Road - a first step to providing a traffic-free setting for the National Gallery and St Martin's-in-the-Fields.

Elevated walkways would leave ground level to motor traffic and eventually link with similar aerial pavements to Piccadilly, Trafalgar Square and Whitehall.

Those were the days when it was fashionable to plough massive roads through the urban fabric, to sweep away the old and replace it with the latest architectural fad, the bigger the better. But to 3,500 people, Covent Garden was home and they were not prepared to stand aside and become spectators at the rape of their environment. The councils themselves were also split. The GLC, paying the lion's share of the expense, expected to chair the Covent Garden committee, but the boroughs and opposition members banded together and chose Alan Greengross from Camden council. Not long afterwards the GLC decreed that Covent Garden was a strategic project and seized all the powers for itself.

Views of Covent Garden's future were fiercely divided even among residents. Some felt all the housing should be council-owned, others put business interests first. Independently, developers were rubbing their hands and considering potentially fat profits from flooding the area with offices.

Raine Dartmouth, daughter of author Barbara Cartland, was a stalwart fighter but an early casualty in this conflict. An astute politician from the top of her immaculately coiffured head to her elegant fingertips, she was the new chairman of the GLC's Covent Garden Committee. But Lady Dartmouth did not react kindly to having her luxurious Mayfair home besieged by Covent Garden protesters who feared their patch was about to become a concrete jungle. In a resignation letter to Sir Desmond Plummer, the Conservative leader of the time, she said that she felt the councils' plans were 'out of date and out of tune with public opinion.'

Robert Mitchell, one of three England international swimmers on the GLC, succeeded her in time for a public inquiry into the GLC's request to make Covent Garden a Comprehensive Development Area. It was the only way to save it from piecemeal development, he argued. Turning it into a CDA meant creating a working framework, not razing it to the ground.

Since publication of the three councils' plan, the property market had collapsed, burning many fingers, and the initial grandiose schemes were dead and buried. All that was certain, said Mitchell, was that there would be twice as much housing, scarcely more offices and more public open space. Strategic buying of substantial holdings in key locations made certain that the GLC could exercise a major influence over the design of buildings.

The public inquiry granted the GLC its CDA - enabling it to stamp on any rogue development - but it also threw out the road plans, which had been quietly dropped anyway, and the proposed increase in hotel space. Most important of all, Environment

Secretary Geoffrey Rippon, himself a former GLC member, listed a further 250 properties as being of special historic or architectural merit. They were scattered all over the area and concentrated in the middle. This surprise action totally stymied any chance of major redevelopment. Instead, refurbishment became the objective. In this way, the attractive character of Covent Garden would be retained.

At last the warring factions were working to the same end. A unique forum was born, elected by people who lived, worked, or had an interest in Covent Garden. They were chosen to speak for the community and would ultimately work alongside the council and jointly plan for their own future

Another GLC election - which returned Labour to power at County Hall - saw the forum idea blossom. Under a new chairman, the Honourable Tom Ponsonby, later to become chairman of the London Tourist Board and known to all as 'Hon Tom Pon,' the unique forum began making progress. It was slow, but for the first time everyone was pulling the same way. Probably for the first time in local government history, residents, politicians and professionals sat side by side and planned their environment. In this way, a new Covent Garden was gradually stitched together piece by piece.

Antagonists-turned-allies held their breath when, after four years, the Conservatives were returned to County Hall and a familiar figure returned to the Covent Garden helm - Camden's Alan Greengross, the first chairman and now a front bench spokesman for the GLC. The new hybrid plan included elements of socialist policy and now required Tory approval. To everyone's relief and delight Alan Greengross said that no changes were needed.

After ten years of debate and public participation, the blueprint for the future of Covent Garden had been adopted.

In a press statement, Alan Greengross said: 'This whole exercise probably represents a greater involvement in public participation and in media interest than any other major inner city development project in the history of town planning.'

Work was already advanced on a painstaking £2 million refurbishment of the classical 19th Century Central Market building with its two halls flanking a central avenue. Built by Charles Fowler in 1830 for the Duke of Bedford, this would become the focal point for the whole redevelopment, the centrepiece of Inigo Jones' 300-year-old piazza. There was some wartime bomb damage and much of the market's great architectural value had been hidden for more than a hundred years by additions and alterations. As a market building, it had been exempted from normal building and fire regulations, and traders had installed their own partitions and staircases.

It had been decided to return the building to its original state, masterminded by the GLC's Historic Buildings division, though one element caused much controversy. As designed by Fowler, it had been open to the elements. Only after years of complaining by market porters was it finally roofed over. Traditionalists argued that the roof should be omitted, even though it would give desirable cover to shoppers. Finally, only the casting vote of the then chairman, Hon Tom Pon, led to the present glass roof being added.

Following the original design was not easy. Cast iron columns supporting the roofs had been fractured and a few derelict remains were all that survived of the original 19th century shopfronts. By a stroke of luck, some of Fowler's original drawings were found and shopfronts which could not be restored were based on these.

The elegant pendant lanterns in the North and South Halls were designed by the Historic Buildings division. Additional lights along the colonnade needed new iron brackets and were copied from the only one to survive unbroken.

Gas lighting was considered but maintenance problems outweighed the loss in elegance. This was one of a number of changes dictated by present-day demands.

Excavation, partly required as a fire precaution, offered the chance of more shops fronting on to the lower pedestrian level. Other facilities, not considered 300 years ago, included staff cloakrooms, loading bays, modern services to each retail unit and gas supplies to the restaurants.

Victorian cast iron trading stands in the North Hall were re-assembled and tenants asked to co-operate in harmonising colour to the original, basically pale blue and brown.

One Christmas when restoration was nearly complete, part of the market was decorated and a large Christmas tree positioned on the piazza. The search for a celebrity to place a star on the top led to a plea to the opera house for a young singer from the current production of Die Fledermus. A singer obliged and when he returned to ground level he joined a small knot of people singing carols. It was doubtless the smallest Covent Garden audience ever to hear Placido Domingo.

After five years the Market had been magnificently restored, using skills officially recognised when it won the prestigious Europa Nostra medal for work to improve cultural and national heritage and the environment. Now units were ready for letting. It was to be a speciality shopping and eating-out district, so would-be traders were all vetted to set high standards and to keep out the multiples.

The Market was opened in June 1980 with 47 shops, galleries, wine bars and restaurants. Its popularity was immediate and soon it became a tourist landmark. At its opening, GLC leader Sir Horace Cutler forecast that it would become as famous throughout the world as the Tower of London and the Houses of Parliament. The GLC had bought it in 1974 for £388,000, an outlay more than recovered by rents in the first year.

Inigo Jones' famous piazza, which surrounds the market building and is similar in size to Trafalgar Square, was set out in the 1680s when it was hailed as England's first example of classical town planning. In an attempt to re-create its previous state, it was again cobbled with granite setts and surrounding it, the post and rail wooden fencing were copies of that which enclosed the area 300 years before.

Street theatre returned to the portico of St Paul's church, with buskers sometimes playing to audiences of several hundred. All were auditioned by Alternative Arts. Today, having played at Covent Garden is the busker's equivalent of a singer having sung at the opera house.

Street entertainers the world over fly to London and head straight for Covent Garden to try to book a spot. Overseas visitors who have watched the shows ring up to ask if entertainers they saw on a particular day on the piazza would take part in festivals in their country.

Other attractions were completed by the GLC during the

following years after the Market was reopened. London Transport museum was sited there - leading to a near catastrophe when a Tube train exhibit almost ended up in the sewers of nearby Wellington Street as the weight of the train and the strength of the road surface showed an incompatibility not anticipated.

After years of indecision, the National Theatre Collection (a branch of the Victoria and Albert Museum) leased part of the old flower market in Russell Street, becoming the first major museum in the country devoted entirely to theatre and opera. For the first time costumes and memorabilia going back hundreds of years could be displayed.

Still there was one more river to cross. Jubilee Hall, a £5 million two-year project aiming to retain its use as a sports hall whilst providing 200 homes and 300 market stalls, was the subject of much debate. When drawings were released, the Royal Fine Art Commission announced itself 'dismayed' at the hall's size and bulk.

Dr Mark Patterson, then Covent Garden committee chairman, replied regretting that the commission had not noticed that it was the same size and bulk as the other buildings which surrounded the piazza and which were so admired. He noted that the Commission's last positive contribution on Covent Garden was to suggest removing the roof from the Market building 'which the GLC wisely rejected to the benefit of all.'

Patterson's three years as chairman - the longest apart from Tom Ponsonby - was remembered for his humour and much appreciated by the Covent Garden team. The good doctor would arrive on Mondays with boxes of eggs from his farm - he had one in the Isle of Wight and another in New Zealand.

Most of the graft had been completed before Mark Patterson's arrival, though as current chairman he held the reins as the GLC basked in glory. Other prizes came Covent Garden's way, including one for the residential development of Odhams Walk which won the 7th International Prize for Architecture from 422 contenders.

Today, Covent Garden is on the itinerary of most visitors to London.

It was the dogged determination of the people of Covent Garden to fight for their neighbourhood which set it on the path to its international prestige. Once converted, the GLC put its resources and expertise to excellent use and can look back with pride on its part in the achievement and on its business acumen.

It ended up owning about 10 per cent of the property in the area, spending £24 million on acquisition and development. Its value at abolition was many times that sum and today's annual income tops £3 million.

For the fruit and veg traders, memories of the old Covent Garden soon faded among the modern facilities of Nine Elms. Two pictures which would have jogged memories are no more. On the first day of the Nine Elms operation, Sir Horace Cutler attended for a champagne breakfast and handed over two pictures, a gift from the GLC, which hung in the authority's smart new offices. By breakfast time next day, they had been stolen.

With envious eyes on Covent Garden, the freeholders of Billingsgate fish market sought to emulate this success when its business moved to Docklands. There was, however, one impediment which proved insurmountable. They couldn't get rid of the smell of fish!

GLC members used to look with envy across the Channel at the speed with which redevelopment took place on the continent where the motto seemed to be: Build it first and consult the public afterwards. When Sir Horace Cutler was council leader, he once complained that the planning and consultation processes meant that it took ten years to build a major road.

Yet there was a credit side to this delay. In addition to the greater likelihood of getting it right, it allowed time for opinions to change and for the latest planning whim or architectural fad to work its way through the system.

PICCADILLY CIRCUS

Just such a delay may have saved Piccadilly Circus from what traditionalists may call 'sheer Philistinism.' Yet in its day modernists hailed plans to redevelop the circus as 'brilliant... innovative...

creating a pedestrians' world.' They were certainly different from anything London had seen before and they were certainly contoversial.

Instructed by the GLC and Westminster City Council to prepare a study for the re-creation of Piccadilly Circus and its setting as 'a place of public resort,' Lord Holford (then Sir William Holford), produced an innovative scheme with traffic at ground level and pedestrians on a raised deck. This was to be a basis for detailed engineering and design and economic assessment.

It was the government which started the ball rolling by pressing for redevelopment and requiring accommodation for vehicles to be increased 50 p.c. Traffic in the circus was fairly constant throughout the day, being generated by its own activities. It was not commuter traffic. When Holford's plan emerged, his proposal for a 20 p.c. traffic increase had already been overtaken by events and he was sent back to the drawing board to provide for another 30 p.c. In time, his second, more detailed plan emerged.

Still pedestrians were on a raised platform, bigger now and with Eros removed from street level and placed on the platform as its focal point. The deck, 200 ft. by 140 ft. would be 25 ft. up, the maximum structurally possible by the technology of the day. From underneath - there would be no pavement at ground level - it would look like a giant umbrella, with steel ribs radiating from a central column. Access would be by broad steps and also by escalators, some enclosed.

The pedestrian platform linked the four main sites on three sides of the circus and went on to connect with other aerial walkways planned for the entire length of Regent Street, over a new Shaftesbury Avenue and in Covent Garden. The circus deck would be on two levels, a central oval space 2 ft. lower, ringed by steps, to be used for exhibitions or filled with water and used as a skating rink in winter.

A separate study being produced by the Regent Street Committee for the Crown Estates, considered that the famous Nash colonnades of Regent Street were old fashioned. The way ahead, they thought, was for Nash's concept to be 're-expressed in modern terms' with traffic below and people above on a walkway covered by a transparent roof. On three sides of the circus, Holford envisaged spectacular, futuristic developments.

A 435 ft slim tower of bronze glass, containing offices, conference suites, shops and restaurants would soar up from the site where the Criterion theatre stands. This would be regarded as the centre of London.

Opposite, on the Monico site, was proposed a 195 ft square building with offices, shops and restaurants grouped around an interior covered courtyard which would be sprung with arches, heated in winter to encourage sitting out, forming a covered extension to the circus.

On the site of the London Pavilion was a spectacular pyramid, a building of receding terraces giving a covered grandstand view of the circus. It would be lit at night and was seen as one of the sights of the new London. Its design would also act as a foil to a 500-bedroom hotel on the adjoining Trocadero site, present location of the London Experience. This would include offices and shops built round a courtyard with each floor tiered outwards to take up minimum space at pedestrian deck level.

Architects heralded Holford's 'new and exciting proposals' as creating 'a pedestrian's world, free from hazards of traffic.' It was not long in scooping a major architectural prize.

At the unveiling of the plan, Duncan Sandys, then president of Civic Trust, summed up the mood for change when he said: 'Unlike other famous areas, the problem here is not to preserve what exists. It is to create something entirely new and exciting.'

He described the circus as 'a small, shapeless area surrounded by buildings of no great architectural merit,' and went on: 'Piccadilly Circus was never a thing of beauty though it used to possess a certain informal charm. But this has been progressively destroyed by the roar of traffic, the stench of petrol fumes and the maze of road signs, and islands of safety railings. To strangers who come with high expectations, it is a fearful anti-climax.' He hoped that the 'adoption of the two-level system in Piccadilly Circus and Regent Street would set a new pattern and encourage 'bolder thinking' in other great cities.

GLC leader Sir Desmond Plummer said that Piccadilly Circus,

in spite of its emotional appeal and superficial glamour, was 'a tatty mess' of old buildings on which adverts had been superimposed haphazardly and where pedestrians and traffic got in each other's way.

He added: 'Let us show future generations that we have the will and the energy and the design skill to do justice to something which has so great and warm a place in the hearts and minds of Londoners and people the world over.'

The general euphoria was echoed by Westminster city council for whom Ald. David Cobbold praised the proposals as 'extremely imaginative,' and a vital key to a radical planning of the West End from Oxford Circus down Regent Street, through Leicester Square into Covent Garden, and into Soho, Trafalgar Square and Whitehall.

When the plans went on public exhibition, 9,270 people visited in the first six days. Of the 1,000 who commented, 300 were in favour, 500 suggested change. The other 200 gave it the thumbs down.

At that time, a start on bringing the first phase to fruition was three years away and it depended on site owners stumping up the millions required.

Any chance of early progress was foiled because property owners wanted to include far more money-spinning offices than the GLC or Westminster were prepared to allow. Four years on and still there was no progress. Labour's planning chairman, Norman Howard, remembers that plans for the circus stood 3ft high and were dusted down from time to time but the days of grandiose developments was past.

Hugh Cubitt, chairman of Westminster planning committee, referred to years of 'frustration and apparent inaction' and explained that the difficulty was to produce the right architectural and planning solution which was also financially viable. Meanwhile the property bubble had burst and planning ideas were changing yet again.

Not until the late seventies did redevelopment begin and then, on a far smaller scale. Sir Horace Cutler's man in the driving seat with a brief to lift Piccadilly out of the doldrums was Sandy Sandford, a former Westminster City alderman and then chairman of the GLC's central area planning committee.

A good ambassador who made friends easily, he announced yet another plan, 'Piccadilly for the People.' Holford's proposed redevelopment of well known and much loved landmarks were confined to the waste bin. Suggestions for towering office blocks and hotels were swept away; demands for more traffic space were banished in the new anti-car mood; gone were the elevated walkways.

Said Sandy: 'Until recently it was felt that the solution of separating people from traffic was to put walkways in the sky. But now we know that was just pie in the sky. Planners and developers have come back down to earth and brought Piccadilly's pedestrians with them.'

Later proposals were announced to build the London Experience entertainments complex, pavements were widened, some surrounding streets were part pedestrianised, and traffic heading east and south was diverted around the circus instead of across it. Eros overlooked the area from a pedestrian piazza instead of being marooned on an island in the middle of the road.

In December 1980, Sandy Sandford announced the end of the 'hundred years war.' After 100 years of argument, the shape of the modern Piccadilly Circus had been finally decided. The old eyesores would soon be gone and the shabby traffic whirlpool which was once Piccadilly Circus would be transformed.

Past grandiose plans all bit the dust, he said, because they were too big, too expensive, too radical and because they did not have the support of Londoners who loved their Piccadilly and basically they wanted it to remain as it was. All the familiar landmarks would be retained. It was only when one looked behind the facade that the new and exciting 21st century circus became apparent.

Slowly, very slowly, the new Piccadilly circus began to emerge. Almost the final touch was a £200,000 refurbishment of Eros, the statue designed by Sir Alfred Gilbert as a tribute to the life and work of Lord Shaftesbury. Appropriately, after repair in Scotland, the Roman God of Love returned to London in 1985, on St Valentine's Day.

WASTE GOLDMINE

Collection of London's domestic and commercial waste has come a long way since the days when Shakespeare's father was fined for 'depositing filth in a public street.' Household rubbish thrown into London's roads and rivers was such a problem in those days that residents were encouraged to spy on their neighbours and were paid by results. Not until dustbins were legally recognised in 1875 did the problem begin to fade.

Today, with our consciences stirred to separate and recycle, it seems incredible that only 20 years ago families dumped everything into their dustbins. Ten years earlier, before the disposal of rubbish became more scientific, it was collected and dumped in the same raw state, usually in holes in the ground.

Not far from Heathrow, Stockley science and technology park looks an ideal example of a 21st century commercial estate, neat buildings surrounded by neatly manicured lawns with an adjoining golf course. It all looks green and serene. But beneath its tranquil surface lie untold hundreds of thousands of bottles, tincans, newspapers, ashes and scrapings from dinner plates. For this was once a huge 350-acre rubbish pit, one of the biggest in Europe.

When the GLC was formed in 1965, there were 90 separate authorities concerned with collecting and disposing of the capital's rubbish. The London Government Act reduced the number of collecting agencies to the 32 boroughs and the City of London. Gradually all the other disposal authorities were absorbed, leaving the GLC to get rid of the lot - three million tonnes of household waste each year.

As time went on, the council's innovations were to make it a world leader in this Cinderella service. At first, 90 pc was tipped in the same state as it was collected and used mostly to reclaim marshland and fill worked out gravel pits. Spread in a layer six feet deep and covered with soil, many of the dumping grounds were soon producing crops. But suitable locations were becoming fewer. Burning it would reduce its bulk to one-tenth.

With this in mind, and following studies of systems on the continent, the GLC planned a ring of state-of-the-art incinerators.

Each would burn 1,330 tons of rubbish a day and in doing so would create electricity - enough to supply the daily needs of 25,000 families. This would be sold to the national grid. There would also be a sale for the clinker and ash.

First of the incinerators, hailed as a £10 million step into the future, was built at Edmonton, on a 27-acre site of a disused sewage works. It was the biggest in Britain and one of the largest in the world. Excavation began on what the press called 'London's biggest hole,' 560ft by 320ft, and 45 ft deep. The site was difficult: there were rivers on two sides and the water level in the gravel strata was only 3ft from the surface. Boffins devised a plan to keep the water out, digging a 700-yard ditch and filling it with Bentonite slurry and then back-filling with sand and cement.

It opened in August 1970 amid a blaze of publicity and attracted the interest of local authorities and engineers all over the world. Described as looking 'more like an ice cream factory', it was a far cry from those grim Victorian incinerators of the past, belching smoke and charred paper.

The plant worked silently without smoke or dust, automatically handling refuse from eight boroughs. Staff worked in white coats and nothing was touched by hand from the moment of delivery by collection vehicles. Working round the clock it boasted that it could consume anything Londoners discarded from a cigarette packet to a piano.

Electricity - made when heat from the incinerator process was converted to steam used to drive turbo alternators - would be sold to the National Grid for £650,000 in the first year, reclaimed metal would fetch an additional £250,000 and clinker ash would be used for building and drainage. As the publicity blurb stressed: Switched-on Londoners are being plugged in to last year's rubbish.

The early euphoria quickly evaporated. Edmonton had long and difficult teething problems. There were recurring failures of the boiler and the project was initially regarded as such a failure that plans for other incinerators were scrapped. But persistence paid off. Finally Edmonton was seen as such a success story that other incinerators were planned by the following administration.

Four years after its opening, electricity sales from Edmonton topped £1 million and were exceeding £4 million when the GLC was abolished. Rubbish consumed went up to 400,000 tonnes annually. It was handling 12 pc of London's refuse and sales now recouped nearly three-quarters of the incinerator's operating costs.

It won the prestigious LAMSAC (Local Authorities Management Services and Computer) award for exemplary energy saving and, in 1986, a new hi-tech incinerator was added to solve the troublesome problem of clinical waste from hospitals and nursing homes.

The incinerator received the ultimate accolade that same year when it was given a clean bill of health after exhaustive studies showed that emissions, when checked against other plants in Europe, the US, Canada and Japan, showed it to be one of the world's cleanest. Subsequently, it was upgraded with a new £9.2 million incinerator-boiler to increase handling capacity 25 pc. This represented an annual saving of £360,000 over landfill costs.

Burning the capital's rubbish may be seen as somewhat short of peak viewing material, but when the incinerator held its first-ever open day more than 2,000 people visited.

Electricity was not the only by-product of London's refuse disposal. Investigating complaints of smells from its 70-acre landfill site at Aveley, Essex, GLC scientists found a field of methane gas worth millions, created naturally from decomposing rubbish dumped there over 12 years.

In what was thought to be the first time a British local authority had exploited such a situation on a commercial basis, the GLC linked up with the National Coal Board to supply a factory nearby. A plant and pipeline were built at a cost of £2.3 million, which soon paid for itself. Then followed an initial contract to supply five million therms a year for five years. It was thought there would be sufficient methane to extract a similar quantity for another ten years, thus turning an unpleasant odour into a very sweet smell of success.

Traditional collection and disposal of rubbish continued but with a difference. Work began on creating Cringle Dock, a £2.5 million state-of-the-art refuse transfer station on the Thames close to Battersea power station. The plant contained 20 of the biggest pulverisers in Britain, each with forty 140lb rotating hammers which reduced to fragments the refuse from five boroughs. When finished after two years, it received up to 800 tonnes of refuse daily which was transferred to barges for shipment down the Thames to a land reclamation project in Essex.

Yet even this paled to insignificance when a vast, fully automated transfer station, the most modern in Europe, was built on eight acres of the old Wandsworth gas works. Costing a hefty £18 million, it handled 4,000 tonnes of refuse a week under the cleanest and most hygienic conditions, replacing the primitive eyesore of Feather's Wharf which had been vacant and derelict for years because of contamination. Feather's Wharf, a relic of Victorian times, was infamous for its antiquated barges which, loosely covered with tarpaulin, could be seen daily on their way to the mouth of the Thames, rubbish working loose and flying off in the wind to pollute the river.

Named Western Riverside, the new station was built on 500 pre-cast concrete piles driven deep into the contaminated soil. In a totally enclosed building, dustcarts unloaded their contents into steel containers which were sealed and loaded, 30 a time, by massive cranes into 400-tonne superbarges for shipment to Essex. The new system eliminated the smells, spillage and pollution so linked to the infamous operation of Feather's Wharf.

Additional refuse was transported by rail. An ultra modern transfer station in Ruislip shifted a million tonnes of compacted rubbish in five years to the London Brick Company's worked-out clay pits in Bucks. Night trains of 60 containers ran to the site, were emptied during the day and sent back to Ruislip next evening. From this depot alone, the rail alternative kept off local roads each week 600 juggernaut journeys, the crucial measurement of the time.

Earlier the GLC had played a pioneering role in the transfer of waste by rail when it opened its first rail depot at Brentford in 1977. A second, fully automated station was built off the North Circular Road at Hendon, and together the three railheads saved Londoners from 2,100 juggernaut journeys every week.

When the GLC was being put to the sword, this was the accolade offered by the Institute of Waste Management:

'There is no informed impartial opinion known to this institute and its members that is other than complimentary about the improvement in the control and disposal of waste since this function became the responsibility in London of the GLC.The improvements have been dramatic.'

After an uncertain beginning when just fridges, pianos and prams were collected, the age of recycling dawned in 1984. Income from early recycling was donated to charity with Friends of the Earth the recipients of the first £1,000 cheque. Collections and income soared and, as abolition of the council loomed, Ken Livingstone gleefully announced that the GLC had acted to recycle the six dustbin loads of wine and spirit bottles generated each day from the bars and restaurants at the Houses of Parliament.

RAILWAYS BOOST

Millions of pounds were ploughed into the Tube by the GLC after it was given control of London Transport on New Year's Day 1970. The council was always in the vanguard of providing new lines and extensions to existing ones, often dragging the government along on its coat-tails. Twice Sir Horace Cutler threatened to go it alone and pay the entire cost (traditionally the government paid half, the GLC and London Transport one-quarter each), when government lethargy threatened delay.

The tube may have its critics, but some think that one of the GLC's greatest bequests to London was the care it took of the Underground in its years of stewardship.

One who shares this view is Maurice Stonefrost who said: 'Public transport in London, apart possibly from some aspects of modern systems which serve some parts of other cities like Hong Kong, is still vastly superior relatively to public transport in any equivalent large city in the world. The fact that you can point to other better looking bits of system in other countries doesn't mean that, taking it in total, it is as good as it is in London. That's a hell of a statement but I would put that as one of the great pluses for the GLC. Within the limits of what it was allowed to do it maintained the system very well, as best it could. Both parties were good on that. Without that support there is no doubt what would have happened.'

Stations were spruced up and, in some cases, virtually rebuilt and more millions were spent on rollingstock, as both Labour and Tory administrations acted to get motorists off the streets and into public transport.

In its role as London's strategic authority, the GLC's largess also encompassed British Rail

Thameslink, London's only north-south railway is very much on the line of the GLC's plan for what was called 'B.R.Through Running,' a project using the Snowhill tunnel between Blackfriars and Farringdon, thrown up by the council's 1974 London Rail Study.

British Rail liked the idea but couldn't afford it. A seminar was held at County Hall, addressed by Sir Peter Parker and other members of the BR board and tea had been served Just as Sir Peter was about to ask the council for £13million, a waitress walked in and plonked the bill for the tea in front of him. She was hustled out by an embarrassed GLC officer only to return ten minutes later and do the same thing.

Sir Peter called over to one his men and said: 'Write a cheque will you, Bob.'

Over many years, British Rail had been given money to buy off service cuts, modernise stations and build new ones. This extra cash possibly saved two of British Rail's Cinderella lines from oblivion as income and viability were shrunk by a vicious circle of fares increases, reduced services and fewer passengers.

First to benefit was the antiquated North London Line which ran from Richmond to Broad Street; the other, the nine-mile rundown link between North Woolwich and Stratford/Tottenham Hale, later to become the Crosstown Link.

During the administration of Sir Reg Goodwin, his transport chairman Jim Daly persuaded the Labour group to take the unique step of giving British Rail £180,000 to buy off cuts proposed on the North London line. This ran in an arc on a similar route to that followed by the North Circular Road, stopping at 19 tumbledown stations which saw few passengers.

A year later, the council staged a similar rescue for the North

Woolwich line. Both subsidies were continued when Sir Horace Cutler's Conservatives came to power and foresaw the potential for linking the two lines via three and a half miles of freight track through Hackney. This would also provide improved rail access into Docklands and connect it with central, north and west London.

Soon plans were laid for a £3 million first stage to include three new stations along the old freight line. In 18 months and ahead of schedule, the stations of Hackney Central and Hackney Wick were born, financed by the GLC, built by British Rail. The third, Dalston Kingsland, followed on time two years later.

Meanwhile the vision for electrification of the entire line moved nearer when the GLC approved a £10 million grant for the last eight and a half miles of what was now called the Crosstown Link from Dalston to North Woolwich, with interchanges with the tube at West Ham and Stratford.

When Labour recaptured County Hall, Ken Livingstone pressed on with the programme which, soon after completion, announced a doubling of passenger usage to 6,500 a day since more frequent and reliable electric trains had replaced diesels on the Woolwich leg. Work was completed ahead of schedule and cost £7.7 million. In addition to providing a route to Docklands, the intention also was to unlock Hackney which had no tube.

Transport chair Dave Wetzel praised the new through line as 'an outstanding success and a model for what should happen to all under-used railway systems throughout the capital.'

As good as its word, Labour had already found another: the West London service from Clapham Junction to Willesden Junction. The council set aside £500,000 for running costs and £3.5 million for new track and five new stations around Shepherds Bush, Chelsea and Battersea. When completed - after abolition - up to 10,000 passengers a day were expected to use it.

THOSE FUN DAYS

When Londoners settle in their armchairs to talk of the old days and the outings they enjoyed in the time of the GLC London, events organised by the council's parks department could figure prominently. Well over 1,250,000 would attend annually.

Its annual two-mile Easter Parade at Battersea Park and the Horse of the Year show at Clapham Common drew tens of thousands. Musical concerts featured strongly among the 1,500 events staged in the parks every year, including children's entertainment for the long summer holidays. Newer events like Thamesday drew crowds by the hundreds of thousands.

Motor racing at Crystal Palace and athletics at Hurlingham were also star GLC attractions before redevelopment of those venues.

For the more energetic, the annual cross-country championships had been staged over Hampstead Heath since the early fifties, involving upwards of 700 runners. Sportsmen and women who wanted to compete were offered the opportunity in championships for swimming, table tennis, golf and many others.

The guiding hand behind many of these events was James Kennedy, chief parks officer and a veteran of 32 years with the GLC and its predecessor. He also played a key role in developing more than 500 acres of new open space plus 750 acres of country parks. Among them, Burgess Park, Southwark, created when the GLC bought up bomb sites, slums and old factories in a mile long wedge to create, piece by piece, an 88-acre open space, the first major park in the world to be carved from the urban landscape.

MUSIC FOR THE MASSES

The Livingstone administration took the council's culture one step further by taking music to the people. The Royal Philharmonic Orchestra played for shoppers at Wood Green centre and for car workers at Ford's Dagenham plant.

Tony Banks, chair of the GLC's arts committee, contended: 'We want to take arts to the people. We don't want it to be elitist and available only in central London for the relatively well off.'

Popularising the Royal Festival Hall, begun under earlier GLC administrations, continued under Livingstone whose council set up the free Friday lunchtime jazz concerts which continue to this day.

It is not generally known that the name 'Royal Festival Hall' was suggested by King George VI. The LCC wrote to Buckingham Palace for permission to use the word 'royal' in the title and invited the king to choose between 'Royal London Hall' and 'Royal Thames Hall.' The king didn't like either.

Through his private secretary, Sir Alan Lascelles, the king wrote back and said: 'Could not the hall be called the Royal Festival Hall, which would perpetuate the conditions of its origin [it was built for the Festival of Britain] and would be quite appropriate because every musical gathering is a festival.'

It took two years to construct the £2 million first stage of the hall in time for the Festival of Britain, opening on May 3, 1951, the first luxury public building since the war.

When the roof was put on, a piano was brought in for a 'wetting the roof' ceremony. As the beer flowed, the first tune to be heard in the hall was 'Put another nickel in,' a hit-chart song of the fifties.

Bernard Bligh, the council's assistant ceremonial officer at that time, recalled: 'Everybody wanted to visit the building while it was being finished, and I took a number of parties of visitors to see it. One of a group of members of parliament from Finland stood on the conductor's rostrum and sang a Finnish folk song. All the workers stopped to listen, and gave him a cheer when he finished. Perhaps he was the hall's first performer.'

When the hall was nearly ready, it was filled with volunteers so that the acoustics could be adjusted. Admission tickets said 'bring a cushion,' and everyone sat on the floor. The programme was chosen to test the sound - one piece was played three times and a revolver was fired to test the reverberations.

The hall's acoustics have been highly praised by many performers and it is perhaps a sign of the times that when they were being fine-tuned and the hall's soundproofing re-examined in 1999, they were planning to use a helicopter.

It took four months to 'tune' the hall by altering the finish of the ceilings and orchestra reflector. A series of test concerts were attended by famous musicians and acoustics experts from Britain and 18 overseas countries. Adjustments were made when musicians, including Myra Hess and Leopold Stokowski, complained about over-clarity of sound which prevented the fusing of the individual instruments.

At the time it was probably the most acoustically perfect hall in Britain. It broke new ground in other ways too.

Stewards and programme sellers were all music lovers who worked one night a week for six shillings expenses and provided their own black suit or dress. When their duties ended they could listen to the concert from an empty seat.

Another innovation was the signal for the audience to take their places. Instead of a bell, there was an A note which the orchestra could use to tune their instruments.

Members of the royal family were concerned about the chairs in the ceremonial box. There had to be room under the chair arms for crinolines, and sitting up straight had to be comfortable. The LCC architects borrowed a music room chair from Buckingham Palace and designed a replica in a style matching the rest of the building.

It did not find royal favour, so whenever there were to be royal guests at the Festival Hall, Bernard Bligh used to borrow whatever vehicle he could, take it to the side door of Buckingham Palace and collect music room chairs.

He recalled: 'On my last visit, just before King George VI died, the only vehicle I could get was a butcher's van from the school meals service. I did not feel welcome. Next time I phoned to arrange to collect chairs, the answer was: We have stopped all that.'

Bligh, who was present on opening night, recalled: 'This was a great occasion. The Lord Mayor of London went up in a lift which stuck between floors. He missed the first part of the programme, a service of dedication. After the second part - Boult and Sargeant alternately conducting British music - there was a small party for people who had been involved in planning and building the hall. Two waiters tipsily handed out gin glasses of water, probably having drunk the gin during the performance.'

THE THAMES BARRIER

It was hailed as the Eighth Wonder of the World, took eight years to construct and cost an incredible £435 million -   nine times its original estimate. But was the Thames barrier really that necessary? London is not generally regarded as a city subject to flooding.

The catalyst for its construction was the East Coast floods of 1953 which cost 307 lives and made 23,000 homeless. Although London was not much affected, had the river walls downstream and at Rotherhithe not broken, London could have had a disaster then.

As it was, no one drowned in London though millions of pounds' worth of damage was done. Well over a million people live in 45 square miles of London on ground below the highest point reached by the 1953 floods.

Scientists warned that a combination of factors was making a catastrophic flood more likely. For 140 years Thames tides had been rising - high water at London Bridge rose about three feet every hundred years; the south-east of England was sinking 1ft every century and the Polar ice cap was slowly melting, causing potentially enormous surges of water down the North Sea and into the Thames.

In justification of the barrier, Sir Horace Cutler said that a combination of certain tides and weather conditions was increasingly putting London in danger of a natural disaster on the scale of the Great Fire of London. In addition to the million people who would be at risk, damage could cost between £2bn and £3bn, a quarter of a million homes and factories could be threatened, parts of the Underground put out of action for a year and many main line stations paralysed.

Research showed that traditional bank raising could give London lasting protection only if they were raised six or seven feet, which would destroy the character of the river.

In London's last serious flood (January 1928), four sisters aged between two and 18 died together in a basement bedroom in Westminster. Ten others drowned, six more in Westminster, two in Hammersmith and two in Fulham. The tide rose 6ft 1in above the predicted height, surging into basement flats through windows and making it impossible to open interior doors. Windows were often barred as was the case with the sisters and a youth who was similarly trapped in Horseferry Road.

In Putney, people trapped in basement flats were rescued by those above letting down sheets and pulling them up, while in the Tate Gallery, a night porter was knocked off his feet and swept across a basement room as he tried to telephone a warning when 165ft of the river wall gave way.

Hundreds of basement rooms were made uninhabitable and people were given refuge in churches and schools. Many acres on both sides of the river were flooded and at Battersea police station a fish was claimed to have been caught in the flooded kitchen. Two barges laden with timber sank at Limehouse and Lots Road power station was flooded, restricting service on the Underground.

After the 1928 flood, the LCC raised river walls and there was no further flooding in central London until the East Coast disaster.

But warnings of the planet's geophysical changes left no room for complacency and in 1969 the GLC of Sir Desmond Plummer considered how to barricade the Thames and keep London safe until well into the 21st century.

In an early experiment, dozens of boats were stationed at key points between Kew and the the estuary near Southend to test silt and tidal conditions for the construction of a dam or a movable barrier.

After engineers had visited the Netherlands and examined a dam project near The Hague, the idea of an immovable 'barrage' was dropped and a barrier decided upon. Woolwich Reach was considered the most advantageous site and construction began in November 1972, preceded by a £2 million clearance of 37 acres of land.

The cost was then an estimated £75 million and the barrier was expected to be in operation by the winter of 1978. It was another five years and an extra £360 million before it was opened. The government paid 75 per cent.

Spanning 570 yards from bank to bank, the barrier consists of a series of enormous steel gates set between concrete piers which house the hydraulic machinery powering the gates. When not in use, the gates lie horizontally on the river bed in concrete cills - the four largest each half the size of a football pitch - so allowing shipping to navigate the Thames normally. When raised to close the barrier, each of the four main gates stands as high as a five-storey building above the water, as wide as the opening of Tower Bridge and weighing over 3,200 tonnes - about as much as 260 double-deck buses.

Together, the foundations for the main central piers contain half a million tonnes of concrete - enough to build nine miles of a six-lane motorway. Conspicuous steel shells cover the tops of the piers, the top of the tallest 112 feet above the river bed.

Closing the barrier takes 30 minutes, the gates turning through 90 degrees to a vertical position, leaving underneath a gap of eight inches which may be increased to a metre by tipping the gates further, to prevent a reflected wave.

Rising costs, technical problems and industrial disputes bedevilled construction and had put back completion by two years when Sir Horace Cutler's Tories came to power in 1977, determined to make up the loss. He hailed the barrier as 'an ingenious concept to save London from drowning.' Engineers, VIPs, journalists and students came from all over the world to chart its progress.

Ray Horner, the chief of the GLC's public heath engineering division, is credited with being the father of the barrier. A man of immense technical ability he was also a good ambassador for the barrier, always willing to give his time to explain the intricacies of its construction and operation.

Early drawings of the barrier show its observation tower on the south bank of the river, from where the gates could be seen with the naked eye as they opened and closed. Work was always behind schedule, costs were constantly rising and, particularly under Sir Horace Cutler, the pressure was always on to complete the barrier quickly.

East London was - and still is - short of river crossings and one politician suggested that a road bridge should be routed on top of the barrier. After all, he reasoned, the foundations were already there. Ray Horner was not pleased. He could imagine the enormous delay while engineers tested load bearings and stresses for putting a road over the top and held consultations about roads linking it on either bank. So he acted. The observation tower was moved. From its position on the south bank it was shifted to the end of the barrier, so road-building over the top would be impossible.

London's barrier received the ultimate stamp of approval when the Post Office used it for the royal mail, at that time one of the first occasions a picture other than of royals had been used.

On November 7, 1982 the barrier was closed for a test trial and Old Father Thames stopped rolling along for the first time in its history. It remained shut for nine hours with unpremeditated results: It affected a fishing competition at Richmond which enjoyed the biggest catch of dace in memory, the winner landing 33lb in seven and a half hours. An angling expert suggested that reducing the river flow caused the fish to feed.

The closure also affected oarsmen. Those who rowed downstream expecting to coast back on the flood tide found that the tide never came and it was a hard slog all the way home.

As the official opening neared, Ken Livingstone's Left-wing administration was getting into all sorts of bother deciding who should perform the opening. The Queen was the natural choice but some left-wing diehards considered the honour should go to a worker who had been on the site longest, or to the GLC chairman. This view was not shared by the barrier workforce which threatened to picket the opening if anyone other than the Queen did the honours. Television held a viewers poll in which the Queen inched home by 14,000 votes to seventeen.

Buckingham Palace was not pleased. Knowing that the decision had been made by the trade unions and supported by the public but against the wishes of London Labour party members, they were concerned lest there be an incident.

Some members of the GLC did not want to be associated with a royal opening, so it was arranged to put them out of harm's way on activities for which they would be sympathetic - like accompanying disadvantaged children, disabled people or the elderly.

Said Maurice Stonefrost: 'I didn't think there would be a problem but there was some failsafe planning and little manoeuvrings to help ensure everything ran smoothly.'

Opening day, May 8, 1984, arrived and the Palace held its breath. The GLC had chartered 18 boats and packed them with 2,000 schoolchildren, senior citizens and disabled people. More children and other spectators linked the banks.

When the Queen's launch, the Royal Nore, arrived it was greeted by historic craft from the Maritime Trust, a water display by the London Fire Brigade, a Royal Navy minesweeper and scores of private vessels. Her Majesty sailed through the open barrier to the Barrier Gardens where Ken Livingstone waited with other GLC members, civic dignitaries and senior officers involved in the barrier's construction. Later she was to press the button which would activate the mighty barrier gates and stop the Thames.

Hordes of news cameramen waited, all wanting the same picture and asking the same question: 'Would Ken Livingstone bow to the Queen?'

In the event, he did. 'From the ankles,' said Beryl Evans, who was handling media arrangements for the council.

Another of the guests on the royal launch received not a bow from Ken but a hug and a kiss. His mum. Ken Livingstone's queen for the day.

In the loft at Maurice Stonefrost's home lies an old box containing a small white candle. It is a souvenir from the GLC's farewell concert at the Royal Festival Hall. On that final night, the orchestra played the final piece by candlelight, extinguishing candles one at a time until the concert ended in darkness. It was symbolic of the ending of local democracy in London, and Stonefrost took the last candle.

'I hoped I would live long enough to see democracy returned to London,' he said. 'Very soon now I shall be getting it out, mounting it on a candlestick and I hope to present it to the Mayor of London.'

THE BEGINNING

Please refer to...